MW00698444

ALSO BY FALL RIVER HISTORICAL SOCIETY PRESS

Anti-Slavery Days in Fall River and the Underground Railroad
by Edward Stowe Adams (2017)
(Discourses in History Series, Number 1)

Women at Work: an Oral History of Working Class Women in
Fall River, Massachusetts, 1920-1970 (2017)

Parallel Lives: A Social History of Lizzie A. Borden and Her Fall
River (2011)

The Commonwealth of Massachusetts vs. Lizzie A. Borden: The
Knowlton Papers, 1892-1893 (1994)

GRANITE, GRIT, AND GRACE

AN EXPLORATION OF THE FASCINATING SIDE STREETS OF FALL RIVER'S HISTORY

WILLIAM A. MONIZ

FALL RIVER
HISTORICAL SOCIETY
PRESS

Fall River Historical Society Press
451 Rock Street
Fall River, MA 02720
fallriverhistorical.org
(508) 679-1071

For information, write us at Fall River Historical Society, 451 Rock Street, Fall River, MA 02720.

ISBN-10: 0-9641248-6-6
ISBN-13: 978-0-96-412486-8

Printed in the United States of America on acid-free paper.

Book and cover design by Stefani Koorey, PearTree Press, Fall River, MA

Printed in the United States of America

GRANITE, GRIT, AND GRACE

CONTENTS

LIST OF ILLUSTRATIONS

Unless otherwise noted, all images are from the collection of the Fall River Historical Society.

INTRODUCTION

Bill Moniz

First came the decision to become a roving reporter. There would be no idle retirement for this talented writer, driven by an insatiable spirit of inquiry. And so Bill Moniz proceeded, on occasion, to provide newspaper columns intended to capture the spirit of our times. But Bill's forte was in writing abundant "The Spirit of Past Times" articles about the city that he has had a strong attachment to over seven decades.

Fall River's former uniqueness as a textile colossus, along with its garment industry prominence, has been well chronicled by a plethora of popular writers and scholars. Then there is a subset focus and seemingly eternal in scrutinizing Lizzie and all aspects of the Borden case. "Old Yankee" high culture, so beautifully and lovingly preserved and displayed at the Fall River Historical Society, cultivates an appreciation of tasteful lifestyles once enjoyed and promoted by the elite families.

Through this combination of ample resources, our political, social, and economic history is available to anyone curious about the Spindle City heritage. There is, in fact, an atypical amount written about our city, compared with most similar sized communities. But this book serves to remind us that we have but a skeletal rather than full-bodied understanding of the dynamic lifeblood through which our history flows.

Urban life is complicated, and lives are intertwined in thousands of minute details. Church, neighborhood, ethnicity, business, building construction, transportation, workplace experience, leisure activities, social organizations, food and drink, banking and environment serve as the connective tissue whereby the populace is brought together, usually for the better though sometimes for the worst.

Bill, as a student of the city experience, has done many things well. He instills a sense of optimism by exploring how knowledgeable and talented forebears created a better society in their time and how, in some cases, we still reap the blessings today. Perhaps better still, he has a special sense that fascinating information can be extracted from what at first blush would be dismissed as mundane matter. What was pink granite? Where can you locate a granite tree? Why was it wise to select a white bronze burial marker if you did not want your name obliterated by the ravages of time?

Our author's great wit shines through in clever headlines, snappy punch lines and perfectly crafted introductory and concluding essay sentences. And like the Uneeda Biscuits that are mentioned for their unique protective sealing package, Bill's writing style "seals in the freshness."

333

Bill learned how to properly locate, investigate, and utilize essential information from primary sources and, whenever necessary, to consult with local historians. He has also sought out contemporary residents from all walks of life who have special memories of events great and small, and his superb interpersonal skills and deft questioning result in meaningful interviews.

Readers will delight in colorful vignettes about why someone went bananas over a truck sale, how Fall River provided enhanced mobility opportunities for Brazilians, how it came to be that a nun preferred boating to flying, and how a monsignor helped to rescue an abused hooker (trust me, this last one has innocuous content).

These light touch moments should by no means obscure the substantive material throughout this monograph that is abetted by Bill's ability to transcend myopia that sometimes afflicts local historians. Bill has intensely researched national topics and connected the outside world to Fall River's historical development, as when he discusses how Thomas Edison helped to light our way.

All this will become obvious to readers as they sample a wide variety of topics, some of which would have been lost to history if not for the diligent commitment of the author.

Philip T. Silvia Jr., PhD.

FOREWORD

Granite, Grit, and Grace: An Exploration of the Fascinating Side Streets of Fall River's History as a title is perfectly apropos for the articles contained in this volume: they are as solid as the city's native bedrock; as resolute as the multicultural people who made up the fabric that is Fall River; and they are quintessentially graceful, in the genuine form once seen in the careworn faces of the shop girl, or waitress, or the immigrant laborer, or anonymous pedestrians going about their business on a busy Main Street.

These stories are stoic, and proud, and enduring, much like the city itself.

Bill Moniz possesses the rare ability to write just as he speaks, in a conversational tone and seemingly effortlessly; the voice of this Fall River boy, born and bred, is present in every one of these articles. He knows Fall River because he has lived it.

Having been immersed in various aspects of city life since birth, Bill's saturation in local culture is reflected in a writing style peppered with various high and low notes—sometimes sweet, and sometimes pungent—that satiates the reader with the flavor of Fall River.

The city Bill was born into was one that still possessed traces of its glorious past; though the gilt had long tarnished it still glowed mellow with that lovely hue that only comes with age—downtown still bustled, businesses still employed thousands of workers, civility was commonplace, and postwar life, for many, though by no means extravagant, was good. But economic hardship and evisceration by the Federal highway system was fast approaching on the horizon, and Fall River would be changed forever.

This is the city captured in *Granite, Grit, and Grace.*

I cannot remember exactly when I first met Bill Moniz, but it was likely sometime in 2010, when he had begun his second career, as a stringer, writing local history and human interest articles for the now defunct *Fall River Spirit*, a weekly newspaper published by Hathaway Publishing Company under the auspices of SouthCoast Media Group. On occasion, Bill would visit the Fall River Historical Society when conducting research, or when searching for photographs to accompany his articles, always irked by the fact that newspaper space, being at a premium, limited his selection of images. The initial visit was customarily followed-up by a second call, to deliver a copy of the published article for inclusion in the society's archival collection.

It was apparent that Bill thoroughly enjoyed his avocation as a writer, and that he was extremely knowledgeable—indeed passionate—about the history of his native city. Over ensuing years, Bill's visits to the Historical Society increased; he became a member of the organization, a more familiar face, and, perhaps most importantly, his collection of archived articles, fascinating and diverse in subject, grew in number.

But I do remember, exactly, the day that the idea of this book came to fruition. Bill and I were standing on the driveway of the FRHS, and in the course of conversation he asked if I thought there would be a market for a compilation of his articles, published in book form. He further mentioned that he was willing to give the FRHS the rights to publish the articles—providing that his former publisher agreed—and that any proceeds generated would directly benefit the museum.

That I eagerly answered his question in the affirmative is evidenced by this book.

Thus, the editing and design phase commenced, sans being hindered, as Bill previously was, by having to limit the use of photographs. Indeed, in this volume, each article is fully illustrated with myriad photographs and images pertinent to the text, enhancing the stories and visually creating a sense of time and place.

I always hoped that when his schedule permitted, Bill would become more involved with the Fall River Historical Society, and so it fortuitously came to pass that he was, eventually, asked by the Nominating Committee to accept a position on the Board of Directors, to which he readily agreed. He now represents the board as the head of Fall River Historical Society Press, our fledgling venture dedicated to publishing works pertaining to the history of the city.

The society is indebted to Bill for his generosity in allowing the organization to publish this work and, for that, he has my sincere thanks. For his largess in donating all the proceeds generated from the sale of this volume to the society, what more can one say than a heartfelt "Thank you."

So, too, is the society grateful to SouthCoast Media Group, for their part in bringing this project to fruition.

With the publication of this volume, Bill has earned for himself a place among the most noted authors of Fall River history, though I doubt this was his goal at the onset of his writing career. I think, perhaps, that he has underestimated the importance of his work as a chronicler of local history.

Michael Martins
Fall River, Massachusetts
October 2017

CHAPTER ONE

EARLY DAYS

THE BATTLE OF FALL RIVER

The Redcoats, 150 strong carrying 60 pound knapsacks, marched up the steep hill expecting little resistance … they got plenty.

Warned by sentry Samuel Read that British boats were landing troops at the foot of what would become Anawan and Pocasset Streets, Colonel Joseph Durfee and his sixteen volunteer militiamen were waiting. Establishing a defensive position behind a stone wall on the high ground of the ridge, they rained down withering musket fire on the advancing infantry. The Battle of Fall River had begun.

On its 231st anniversary, historian David Jennings vividly recounted the 1778 skirmish at a May 20th, 2009, Fall River History Club presentation.

As true "Minutemen," Colonel Durfee's irregulars had formed on a moment's notice. "Unlike today," said Jennings, "everyone had to own a weapon, it was expected. These men were courageous," added Jennings, "they were greatly outnumbered but they were defending *their* village."

In 1778, operating from an established naval base at Newport, Rhode Island, the British were regularly raiding the nearby coastal villages and towns expropriating food and provisions and generally harassing the population. Only a few days earlier, on May 25th, a force of five hundred British and Hessian troops had marched on Warren, Rhode Island, burning the town's grist mill and many boats, and taking several townspeople prisoner.

Under the Command of a Major Robert Ayres, the company attacking Fall River had come up the bay on three ships; *Juneau, Kingfisher,* and *Pigot,* a fourteen-gun galley. The *Pigot* had the misfortune of running aground in the Bristol Passage and took a pounding from the town's shore batteries. Before the Royal Navy managed to kedge and tow the *Pigot* free, two of its sailors had been killed.

Ayres' regulars, approaching in formation two ranks deep, were towing a small three-pounder artillery piece. The gun began firing grapeshot at the rebels causing Colonel Durfee to order a withdrawal across the Quequechan River taking up the plank bridge as they went. According to *A History of the Town of Freetown, Massachusetts,* published in 1902: "Here he made a determined stand, and so valiantly was he supported by the loyal volunteers of old Freetown and Tiverton, who had rallied around him, that the enemy soon sounded the retreat."

"The British felt it was uncivilized to shoot at a single enemy," said Jennings, "instead, they fired general volleys from their two rank formations." The rebels had no such compunction. "The militia routinely used flanking tactics. They would attack the enemy's rear using bayonets to stab individual soldiers."

In his hasty retreat to the boats, Major Ayres would leave one dead and one dying on the battlefield. Redcoats Charles Brigham and William Danks were buried by Colonel Durfee's men at a spot near what is now South Main and Anawan Streets. In the early-nineteenth century, they were reburied in the North Burial Ground. The exact location of their unmarked graves is unknown.

Although the colonial forces suffered no casualties in the battle, upon landing the British burned 1,500 running feet of whaleboat lumber, put the torch to a sawmill and a grist mill, and set fire to the home of Thomas Borden. According the 1902 history of Freetown: "On their retreat they set fire to the house and other buildings of Richard Borden, an aged man, and took him away prisoner. Colonel Durfee followed closely with his men, who kept up an annoying musketry fire upon the retreating troops. He also saved the latter burning buildings from destruction."

As the British rowed down the bay to their troop ships with Richard Borden as captive, another of their men was hit by musket fire. A few days later in Newport, Mr. Borden was released and he returned to the village. The Battle of Fall River was over.

David Jennings, along with Herb Tracy the program's coordinator, teaches an afternoon session for transitional children at the Doran and Greene schools. Jennings tells of a young immigrant girl who after listening to an account of the battle exclaimed, "Those men were heroes." "She's right," says Jennings, "unless we keep teaching these things we'll lose our sense of history."

Note: Although called the Battle of Fall River, the encounter actually took place in what was then known as Freetown. In 1803 Freetown became Troy and would not become incorporated under the name Fall River until 1834. British military history still refers to the action as the Battle of Freetown.

May 24, 2009
Fall River, Massachusetts

1.1.1 Detail of an idealized version of the Battle of Fall River, painted by Fall River artist John Mann (1903-1970) as part of a Works Progress Administration mural project. The mural, dedicated in 1940, remains in situ in the auditorium of the Resiliency Preparatory School, formerly the Durfee Technical High School, for which structure the paintings were commissioned.

1.1.2 Purported portrait of Col. Joseph Durfee (1750-1841) that appeared in an unidentified Fall River newspaper at the time of the Cotton Centennial celebration in 1911. According to the original caption: "This is said to be a picture of the man who built the first cotton mill in Fall River 100 years ago." The present whereabouts of the portrait, and its provenance, are unknown.

REMINISCENCES

OF

COL. JOSEPH DURFEE,

RELATING TO THE EARLY HISTORY OF

FALL RIVER AND OF REVOLUTIONARY SCENES.

JOSEPH DURFEE is the eldest son of the late Hon. Thomas Durfee. He was born in April, in the year 1750, in what is now the village of Fall River—and is now 84 years of age. At that time, and until within a few years, the Fall River stream was owned by the Bordens. Much of what now is the village, where are elegant buildings and a dense population, was then a wilderness, where the goats lodged in the winter seasons. The Bordens and the Durfees were then the principal proprietors of the Pocasset Purchase, and owners of the land on the South side of what is now Main-street, for more than a mile in length. Thomas and Joseph Borden owned the South side of the stream, and Stephen Borden owned the North side. Thomas Borden owned a saw-mill and a grist-mill at that time, standing where the old saw and grist-mills now stand, near the Iron-Works establishment. Thomas Borden left a widow and four children, viz: Richard, Christopher, Rebecca and Mary. Joseph Borden, brother of Thomas, owned a falling-mill which stood near where the Pocasset Factory now stands. He was killed by the machinery in his falling-mill. He left four children, viz: Abraham, Samuel, Patience and Peace. Patience was my mother. Stephen Borden, who owned the North side of the stream, had a grist-mill and a saw-mill, standing near where the Woollen establishment has since been erected. He left six children, viz: Stephen, George, Mary, Hannah, Penelope and Lusannah.

1.1.3 A rare, original copy of *Reminiscences of Col. Joseph Durfee,* published privately in pamphlet form, circa 1834; the author vividly recounts his recollections of "Revolutionary Scenes."

1.1.4 Detail of a bronze tablet marking the scene of the Battle of Fall River that was originally mounted on the southwest corner of the old City Hall building, placed there through the auspices of the Daughters of the American Revolution on May 29, 1899, the 121st anniversary of the battle. It is currently on display in the southwest corner of the lobby of the Fall River Government Center.

1.1.5 "Reenacting the Battle of Fall River," 1936.

THE LAFAYETTE-DURFEE HOUSE

If you ask the average Fall Riverite about the Marquis de Lafayette, chances are you'll be directed to his namesake park presided over by the gallant general himself. Although the most visible, the park with the dashing figure on horseback is far from the city's most intimate connection to the Revolutionary War hero.

Nestled among the two and three-deckers on lower Cherry Street sits the Lafayette-Durfee House. The restored colonial farmhouse, dating from 1750, was built by Judge Thomas Durfee and was once homestead to a vast plantation-style estate stretching from the Taunton River to North Watuppa Pond.

Originally located on North Main Street, just south of what is now the Fall River Children's Museum, the house has twice been moved. In 1838, when North Main was straightened to accommodate horse cars, the house was shuttled across the street to make way for the tracks. In 1875, then under the ownership of Charles Lewin, it was again moved to its present Cherry Street location.

Judge Durfee's eldest son, Joseph (1750-1842), was a Colonel in the Continental Army. In the spring of 1778, Colonel Durfee and sixteen local militiamen used the high ground of the ridge to successfully repel a force of 150 British regulars in the Battle of Fall River.

Later in 1778, the Durfees hosted a close friend of Joseph – another soldier fighting for American liberty—the twenty-year-old Marquis de Lafayette. Colonel Durfee served with the tall, red-haired, French general in battles in New York and across Rhode Island. Becoming a way station between Boston and Newport, the Durfee house was visited by Lafayette many times and he was given his own bedroom in the southwest corner.

By the mid-twentieth century, the historic house had suffered the ignominy of being converted into a warren of apartments by new owners. In 1973, as the country's Bicentennial approached, another Durfee rode to the rescue. The late Miss Caroline Durfee, a direct descendent of Squire Thomas Durfee, purchased the house.

Keenly aware of the significance of the house and its direct connection to the nation's birth, Miss Durfee was determined to see it preserved. Hiring historic buildings contractor Vaughn Baasch of Westport, Massachusetts, Miss Durfee oversaw the beginnings of the structure's restoration to its original 1750 state.

This year the Lafayette-Durfee Historical Foundation Inc. marks its fortieth anniversary as caretaker of the historic house and its educational outreach. Foundation Secretary Patricia "Pat" Taylor, a retired postal clerk, explains why she became involved with the house almost thirty years ago: "I'm partial to the underdog, and this house was the underdog to the more well-known historical attractions in the city. It's remarkable that a 250-year-old house is still standing," added Taylor, "it's the only colonial era house open to the public in Fall River."

Foundation president Dave Jennings, a retired Fall River District Fire Chief and self-described history buff, was recruited by Taylor after appearing as guest speaker at the organization's 2008 annual meeting. "Too often all one hears about Fall River is negativity," said Jennings, "If we don't take pride in our own historic heritage, who will?"

Jennings, a reenactor with Southcoast History Associates, was cast as an extra in the made-for-television *American Experience* film, *John & Abigail Adams*, and has made in-costume presentations for the Fall River History Club. He strongly believes that the city needs a tourism director: "There's a lot of history in Fall River," he said, "We need to coordinate and market ourselves just as Salem has done with the witch trials."

Herb Tracy, Foundation board member and retired educator in the Fall River school system, works with Jennings in the twenty-first-century After School Program. The Community Service Learning Project, based at the Doran and Greene schools, includes field trips and explorations of the city. The Lafayette-Durfee House is used as a focal point in teaching transitional children local history. "Many of these children are here for only a short time," said Tracy. "They have no sense of place."

According to Tracy, the House has proved an invaluable setting for conveying to students what life was like in eighteenth-century Fall River. "The kids are hands-on while they're here," said Tracy, "We card wool, cook on the hearth, and even play the same games popular in colonial times."

December 1, 2013
Fall River, Massachusetts

1.2.1 Marie-Joseph Paul Yves Roch Gilbert du Motier, Marquis de Lafayette (1757-1834) depicted in an early-nineteenth century engraving by an unidentified artist.

1.2.2 94 Cherry Street as it appeared in the 1920s, with period clapboard intact; the residence was built circa 1750 by Judge Thomas Durfee (1721-1796). The Durfee family entertained the Marquis de Lafayette as a houseguest in the summer of 1778, and on other occasions.

1.2.3 94 Cherry Street as it appeared in 1955; the addition of asphalt siding drastically altered the appearance of the structure. At the time this photograph was taken, the house had been subdivided into apartments and was home to four families.

1.2.4 The Lafayette-Durfee House, home to the Lafayette-Durfee Historical Foundation as it appeared in 2013 at the time this article was written.

THE EULOGY OF CAPTAIN HENRY BRIGHTMAN

Fall River sea captain Henry Brightman was twice buried, fittingly; two of his pirate murderers were twice hanged.

This past Sunday, the Fall River Country Club was the setting for the Friends of Oak Grove Cemetery's presentation of *The Eulogy of Captain Henry Brightman.* The riveting historical account of deceit, treachery, and seagoing murder, was vividly brought to life by actors portraying Brightman's family and his surviving crewmembers.

Brightman's brig, the *Crawford*, bearing a cargo of rum, sugar, and tobacco, set out from the Cuban port of Mantazas on May 28, 1827, bound for New York. Unbeknownst to the captain, four of the fifteen passengers and crew were brigands led by the notorious pirate chief Alexander Tardy of Hispaniola.

Often posing as a physician to gain ships' passage, Tardy would gradually poison passengers and crew during a voyage by mixing arsenic into the daily rations. As his unsuspecting victims became ill or died, Tardy, under the pretense of ministering to them, would steal their valuables and ultimately the ship itself.

Phebe Brightman, the captain's widow, played by Gale Powers, told of her husband's "frequent attacks of asthma" and how during one such attack while in Cuba he had consulted the poser Tardy for treatment. "Thus Tardy was able to gain my husband's confidence," declared the widow sadly.

Actress Gail Leferriere Caprio, as Sally Bicknell Brightman, the captain's mother, told of her childhood in Ashford, Connecticut, "during the reign of King George," and of moving to Freetown in 1804 after marrying Benjamin Brightman of the Massachusetts Bay Colony. Lamenting their murdered son, she remembered him as "sickly, with frequent spasms of coughing and laborious breathing." "But my Henry excelled in navigation and the family was always captivated by his sea stories," she added wistfully.

Early in the fateful voyage, the Crawford's black cook, Stephen Gibbs, thwarted Tardy's first poisoning attempt by secretly removing his added seasoning which the pirate innocuously called "native pepper." The cook intuitively mistrusted Tardy; "I could just feel it," said Gibbs in the person of actor José Fernandes.

On the morning of June 1, 1827, Tardy volunteered to cook at a breakfast for the ship's company hosted by the unsuspecting Captain Brightman. Following a hearty meal of bacon, eggs, and chocolate, many of the passengers and crew began to exhibit symptoms mimicking severe seasickness. "I experienced the most severe headache and gut-wrenching pain," said First Mate Edmund Dobson, voiced by actor David Mello.

Tardy's band of buccaneers consisted of Felix Barbeito, José "Pepe" Cesares, and José "Couro" Morando. Lugging a heavy sea-chest ostensibly filled with gold, the three had gained passage on the *Crawford* under the guise of businessmen bound for New York to purchase a ship of their own. The chest would later be found to contain only lead.

Five days into the voyage, having grown impatient waiting for the poison to take full effect, the Spaniards entreated Tardy to employ more immediate measures. Tardy agreed, and during the early morning hours of June 2nd, the carnage began.

From First Mate Dobson's eyewitness account: "At about 1:40 a.m., I heard shouts and screams coming from the deck. I rushed above and was confronted by a figure emerging from the shadows who stabbed me repeatedly in the shoulder. I could see that there was a massacre taking place. Passengers and crew were being hacked at and I saw the helmsman die at the hands of Tardy as he came up behind him and slit his throat from ear to ear."

"I saw Felix stab the captain over and over again and Deane [*Seaman Nathaniel Deane, a cousin of Captain Brightman*] threw himself into the sea to escape," Dobson continued.

"I climbed the mainmast and found crewmen Potter, Gibbs, and Dolliver already there. Potter was severely wounded and his blood dripped down on me as I climbed."

Soon, Tardy commanded that the four crewmen come down from their refuge. Only Tolliver did so and, according to Dobson, "he was immediately stabbed and thrown over the rail." Tardy then gave his word to Dobson that he would not be harmed if he surrendered and cooperated. Seeing little choice, the first mate complied and was taken prisoner as was Gibbs, the cook. Potter later fell from the mast, dead of his wounds.

By dawn, only three shipmates survived: Dobson, Gibbs, and a French passenger by the name of Ferdinand Ginoulhiac, whom Tardy spared as a countryman. While the rum-soaked pirates celebrated their conquest, the three were forced to swab the bloody decks and whitewash the blood spattered sails.

Almost certain to be recognized in most Caribbean ports as well as the Carolinas, the notorious "Tardy the poisoner" decided to take on provisions in Norfolk, Virginia. While Gibbs cooked "stew meat, rice and beans" for the pirates, the hapless Dobson was presented with a choice—death, or continue to navigate the *Crawford* to its final destination, of all places, Hamburg, Germany.

As dusk fell on June 12th, the *Crawford* approached the Virginia coast at Old Point Comfort Light near the mouth of the James River. Here, Dobson made his move. While pretending to ready an away boat for Tardy, he quickly pushed off, set his oars, and desperately pulled for shore.

Reaching the military detachment overseeing the construction of nearby Fort Monroe, Dobson related his tale of piracy and murder to Army Captain Nathaniel G. Dana of the 1st United States Artillery. Dana immediately dispatched a nine-man boarding party to the *Crawford*.

Realizing that Dobson had escaped, the Spaniards pilfered a boat from a ship anchored nearby, made their way to shore and fled on foot across country. They were later captured by authorities as they slogged through the swamps of Virginia's Isle of Wight County. Tardy, when hailed by the approaching soldiers, vowed never to be taken alive and was later found below decks with his throat slit, an apparent suicide.

On July 16, 1827, the three captured pirates were put on trial at the Old Hall of the House of Delegates in Virginia's capital of Richmond, United States Supreme Court Chief Justice John Marshall presiding. Prominent Richmond attorney and future United States Senator Benjamin W. Leigh stood for the defense, State's Attorney Robert Stanard was appointed to the prosecution.

"Scared and jittery," the black cook, Gibbs, did not appear as a witness, but First Mate Dobson and the Frenchman Ginoulhiac both took the stand. His arm in a sling, Dobson's grisly testimony of treachery and murder held the three separate juries' rapt attention during the four day trial.

The Spaniards were convicted and sentenced to death by hanging. While awaiting their execution date in Virginia's Henrico County jail, the three pirates confessed to their crimes. Tardy's corpse was decapitated, his head sent to Baltimore for scientific examination in hopes of learning what caused his life of crime.

On August 17th, bound hand and foot and cloaked in hooded robes, the condemned Spaniards made their final journey to a date with the hangman. Resigned to their fate and sitting forlornly on their wagon borne wooden coffins, the trio was paraded past thousands of curious onlookers lining the streets of Richmond. Hundreds more thronged around the triple gallows as a Catholic priest solemnly intoned the Church's last rites.

The trap doors sprang, three men dropped, but only one continued to swing. The ropes intended to hold Cesares and Morando had snapped and the pair tumbled to the ground. As the crowd cried out in fear and shock, the men were unceremoniously carried back to the gallows platform, fitted with sturdier ropes, and dropped again. This time, three bodies slowly twisted in the air.

The pirates were quickly buried, but later that same day they were exhumed when authorities had the idea that they might be of some experimental use. Removed to a nearby armory, the corpses were charged with galvanic ally generated electric current to see if they might be revived. It was to no avail, the men had apparently decided to remain reunited with their chieftain, the late Alexander Tardy.

According to Michael Keane, president of the Friends of Oak Grove Cemetery, Captain Henry Brightman was also buried twice, the first time probably in a family burial ground near what is now Willow Street in Fall River. Brightman's headstone at his current Oak Grove resting place bears his 1827 date of death. Since Oak Grove was not officially opened until 1855, it is likely that the Captain was re-interred there in a new family plot sometime after that.

"The story of Captain Brightman and the *Crawford* is a tale noticeably missing from our local history books," said Keane, "but after nearly 200 years we were able to reference enough bits and pieces to finally put it together."

November 15, 2010
Fall River, Massachusetts

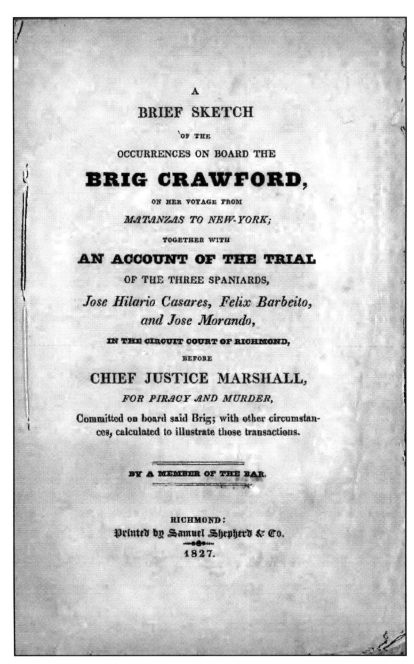

1.3.1 An original copy of "A Brief Sketch of the Occurrences on Board the BRIG CRAWFORD," published in Richmond, Virginia, in 1827.

1.3.2 Headstone of Captain Henry Brightman (1797-1827) in Oak Grove Cemetery; originally buried in a private cemetery, his remains were later reinterred in their present location. The carving on the stone vividly details the manner of his demise:

Capt. HENRY BRIGHTMAN
Was massacred by the Pirates
on board the brig Crawford
June 1, 1827 in the 30th year of
his age.
May this sudden call awake us all,
And make us think of death.
By this we see how frail we be,
And how uncertain is our breath.

MURDER ON MOUNT HOPE BAY

Mention murder and nineteenth-century Fall River in the same sentence, and the name Borden immediately springs to mind. But sixty years before Lizzie allegedly "took an axe and gave her mother forty whacks," another sensational slaying horrified the citizens of the growing mill town and neighboring Tiverton, Rhode Island.

Wicked Conduct, published by The History Press, is a lively examination of the 1832 murder of Fall River "Mill Girl" Sarah M. Cornell, allegedly at the hands of her lover, a respected Methodist minister. "Nobody has written about this case in a long time," says author Rory Raven, "but at the time it was front page news as far away as New York and Philadelphia."

Cornell was born in Rupert, Vermont, in 1802. Although her mother, Lucretia Leffingwell, was from a wealthy family of Connecticut paper merchants, Sarah's father, James, was a ne'er-do-well who abandoned the family and disappeared when Lucretia's father declined to continue financial support.

Under the care of an aunt, Sarah had a checkered early adulthood, including failure to make payments on credit purchases and a charge of shoplifting. As did many young women of that era, she eventually gravitated toward work in the cotton mills with stops in Dorchester and Taunton, before settling in Lowell, Massachusetts, in 1828.

There, twenty-six-year-old Sarah applied for membership in the Methodist congregation. Arriving in Lowell two years later, the thirty-two-year-old Reverend Ephraim Kingsbury Avery entered her life. "At 6 feet tall, and as an elder in the church, Avery was an authoritarian, even coercive figure toward Sarah," says Raven. Becoming her spiritual advisor and confessor, the married Avery would begin a relationship with Sarah that would later be called into question.

Although regularly attending services, as well as the outdoor "camp meetings" then peculiar to Methodist societies, Sarah continued to behave badly including "a tendency toward colorful profanity," writes Raven. Soon, this would be the least of her transgressions as she eventually confesses to Avery that she's had illicit intercourse with young men that she's met in the mills.

Tried before the church on charges of fornication and expelled from the congregation, Sarah moved to Dover, New Hampshire where she joined another Methodist congregation. Her reputation soon followed her, however, when Avery wrote her new minister warning of Sarah's bad character. "She was in an awful situation," says author Raven, "having confessed her sins to Avery both verbally and later in writing, he held tremendous power over her."

After a brief attempt at a new start in Great Falls, New Hampshire, in 1832 Sarah moved to Fall River and easily found work in the mills; she roomed at the boardinghouse of a Mrs. Harriet Hathaway, the location of which is thought to have been near Columbia Street and the corner of what is now Milliken Boulevard. Between her expulsion at Dover and her arrival in Fall River, Sarah continued in contact with Avery who had been reassigned to a congregation in nearby Bristol, Rhode Island, that same year. Included were frequent exchanges of correspondence as well as encounters at his home, camp meetings, and the church itself.

On the cold morning of December 21, 1832, Tiverton farmer John Durfee rousted his cattle from the barn to the sloping pasture overlooking Mount Hope Bay. Spotting a peculiar object among distant haystacks, Durfee decided to investigate. As Raven writes: "There among the haystacks, hanging from a fence post, was the frozen body of a petite young woman, her disheveled dark hair hiding her face." Then a part of Tiverton, the body was found in what is now the northwest corner of Kennedy Park near the intersection of present day Bay Street and Bradford Avenue.

After cutting her down with the help of his father, Richard, Durfee sent for the town's elderly coroner, Elihu Hicks. Following a brief examination Hicks pronounced the obvious and selected six of the gathered townspeople for a jury of inquest. Richard Durfee was elected foreman.

Her body was identified by Methodist minister Ira Bidwell, and Sarah Cornell's death was initially ruled a suicide. But after secretive and incriminating letters between she and Reverend Avery were found among Sarah's belongings, her hastily buried corpse was exhumed and an autopsy performed. In addition to originally overlooked bruises and signs of manual strangulation, Sarah was found to have been four-and-one-half months pregnant.

"Even before the hanging," says Raven "there was talk of Sarah and Avery's intimate involvement, and of attempted abortion." But this note, found in a small box in her room, put the Methodist minister squarely in the crosshairs of the newly formed Fall River Committee of Investigation:

> *If I should be missing enquire of the Rev. Mr. Avery of Bristol he will know where I am.*
>
> *Dec 20th*
> *S. M. Cornell*

Wicked Conduct completes the story by skillfully guiding its readers through the investigation, indictment, and trial of Reverend Avery. The minister's surprising ultimate acquittal places the case alongside the equally infamous Borden killings as another of Fall River's "unsolved" murders.

"I've always wondered why the Borden murders so eclipsed this case," says author Raven. "It was national news at the time."

Note: Rory Raven is also the author of *Haunted Providence*. He is the creator and guide of the Providence Ghost Walk, the original ghosts and graveyards walking tour that runs through the haunted history of the city. He lives in Providence with his wife, Judith.

December 27, 2009
Fall River, Massachusetts

1.4.1 *View of Fall River Looking South Down Main Street,* 1839.

1.4.2 Rev. Ephraim Kingsbury Avery (1799-1869) depicted in an 1833 engraving. The unidentified artist considered this portrait a good likeness of the subject, however, Rev. Avery's supporters thought it a harsh misrepresentation done to impress upon the public that he was a "savage and libidinous monster."

1.4.3 Sarah Maria Cornell (1802-1832) meets her death at the hands of Rev. Ephraim Kingsbury Avery (1799-1869) in a dramatic 1870 engraving captioned: "The unsuspecting girl was strangled by the scoundrel ere she became aware of his cruel intention."

1.4.4 The Durfee farm, Tiverton, Rhode Island, in an 1833 woodcut. The body of Sarah Maria Cornell was discovered among the haystacks in the stockyard, hanging from a fence post.

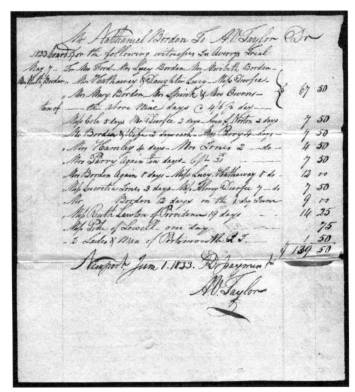

1.4.5 Invoice from Nathaniel Briggs Borden (1801-1865) to Anthony V. Taylor of Newport, Rhode Island, for "Board for ... witnesses in Avery Trial," June 1, 1833.

1.4.6 "LINES Written on the death of Sarah Maria Cornell," 1833.

1.4.7 Headstone of Sarah M. Cornell in Oak Grove Cemetery; originally buried in the private family cemetery of John Durfee, owner of the farm where she was murdered, her remains were later reinterred in their present location.

IN
memory of
SARAH M. CORNELL
daughter of
James & Lucretia
Cornell.
Who died Dec. 20, 1832
in the 31st year
of her age.

THE CRONE OF THE QUEQUECHAN

She lived in a rickety log cabin on a precipice high above the great falls of the river; she was the Crone of the Quequechan.

New Bedford Whaling Museum docent and Fall River native John O'Brien told the tale of the Crone at a June 1st, 2009, presentation at the museum. "Some say it's legend, some say it's true, either way it captures your imagination," said O'Brien.

Although its origins are lost in the mists of time, according to O'Brien the tale first appeared in print in the April 3, 1845, issue of the *Fall River Weekly News.* "The hut was on the southern bank of the river near where the Massasoit mill stands today," said O'Brien. "According to legend, it always appeared as though it were about to fall in."

O'Brien recounted excerpts of the tale from the 1845 newspaper article:

> By whom it was created, and why in that uninviting if not dangerous spot, nobody could tell. It had long been deserted except by bats and reptiles, and was fast going to decay under the alternate action of the sun and rain.

> Like most deserted houses it had a bad name. Lights, it was said, had been seen on dark and stormy nights, through the crevices in the walls, sometimes emitting red or blue flames; and strange noises had more than once been heard by passers-by, issuing from this dilapidated structure.

According to O'Brien, the legend tells us that one particularly bleak December night a column of sparks and flame was seen escaping from the hut's small chimney. Their curiosity aroused, the villagers gathered at the store of Peter Leonard, on the east side of what is now North Main Street.

According to the 1845 report: "Great was the excitement among the neighbors when assembled. Women and children were crying; strong men looked grave and doubtingly at one another."

The gathering considered several courses of action; Leonard himself said, "I propose that we take the Bible and move in a body on the spot." Welcome Brownell suggested taking guns and other weapons and attacking the hut. Stephen Davis, "the noisiest braggart of the settlement," proposed taking six men and plunging the hut into the Quequechan. "I propose," said Joel Wilson, "that we stay where we are."

The newspaper account goes on: "the door of the shop flew open, and exhibited standing within the entrance a hideous old crone, bent half double with age, her face disfigured with irregular streaks of smut and her blood-shot eyes flashing fire as she gazed on the motley group within. Her large boney hands, foul with sore and accumulated filth, were thrust forward, and her long hooked fingers, incessantly in motion, seemed eager to seize whoever or whatever might come in her way.

"Who talks of throwing me or mine into the Quequechan?" said the crone, looking round the room and scowling horribly as her eyes fell on each individual of the group in turn. She made four or five turns, each time approaching near and nearer the place occupied by Welcome Brownell in front of the great fireplace. At length she came closer to his side and cast at him a quick, fiery look of defiance and determination. With the quickness of thought Brownell drew back, raised his arm and planted a deadly blow, with his heavy iron fist, directly between the eyes on the lower edge of her forehead."

"The crone fell to the floor as still as death," said O'Brien; "Brownell thought he'd killed her." But, as the story goes, a few moments later, to the relief of Brownell and the entire assemblage, she sprung to her feet very much alive. A religious man, Brownell laughed with joy that he had not committed murder.

"Laugh imp of the fiery world! But know that my revenge is certain and speedy," shouted the crone as she bounded toward the door snatching as she went an infant from the arms of Mrs. Brownell. With surprising speed she raced across the small bridge over the river, up the opposite bank, and stood on the edge of the precipice overhanging the falls near her still illuminated hut.

"Not another foot nearer!" shouted the infuriated hag, holding the shrieking child at arm's length over the dashing current below—one step and the heir of Brownell never breathes again."

Standing paralyzed with fear, the assembly expected the hag to carry out her threat at any moment. As the villagers stood watching helplessly, an athletic young man named Lot Lee was stealthily making his way over the open ground toward the rear of the hut. With her back towards him the crone did not detect his approach and he was able to conceal himself around the corner of the cabin.

The nineteenth-century newspaper account continues: "Lee made a single bound forward and, seizing the crone with one hand, and the child with the other, hurled her with the strength of a giant several feet from the edge of the chasm. As she fell he leaped toward the spot and placing one foot upon the breast of the prostrate hag, held up the exhausted child freed from the iron grasp of the raging crone!"

They bound the crone with rope and quickly turned their attention to the hut. After several tries a heavy rock finally succeeded in bashing in the door and Lee dragged the crone into the single room followed by the entire gathering. A solitary stool sat by the hearth with nothing else in sight except a bed of straw in one corner.

Satisfied that nothing valuable was in the hut, the men prepared to set the torch to it but stopped when the hag cried out in anguished protest. As this was going on, Stephen Davis found a small box hidden in the crone's bed of straw. Seeing this the crone sprang forward, loosening her bond in the process, and fell prostrate at the feet of Davis.

"Though finding herself thus relieved, she made no effort to escape, but deliberately seated herself upon the rickety stool, which still remained undisturbed in the center of the room, and took from the box a small package, which she handed without uttering a word to Lot Lee.

He opened it and read as follows:

> *Boston, June ye 10, 1700*
>
> *Mary... ...*
>
> *I am in the iron grasp of the king's bloodhounds! Take care of thyself.*
>
> *KIDD*

Every eye was instantly turned on the old crone, who still sat on the stool, intent on the effect which the reading of this note might produce.

'And you are,' said Lee.

'The last mistress of Kidd the pirate!' shouted the hag, snatching the note from the hands of Lee and walking deliberately out of the hut.

No effort was made to detain her; each individual stood riveted to the spot, as if chained by a spell more potent than human will. She mounted the riding ground on the south of her cabin, paused a moment, as if to take a last look at her strange habitation, then dashed off into the high road leading to Newport. This was the last ever heard or seen of the Crone of the Quequechan!"

"Some say she still lives in Newport," said storyteller O'Brien with a twinkle in his eye.

Note: No one knows for sure whether the tale is fact, fiction, or a combination of both. But history shows that the notorious pirate Captain William Kidd, was captured in Boston in 1699, taken to London in 1700, and hanged for his crimes on May 23, 1701.

June 5, 2009
Fall River, Massachusetts

1.5.1 A section of falls on the Quequechan River, Fall River, 1948.

"She lived in a rickety log cabin on a precipice high above the great falls of the river; she was the Croan of the Quequechan."

1.5.2 A portrait of Captain William Kidd (1654-1701) by the British artist, Sir James Thornhill (1675-1734). A notorious privateer, and the legendary lover of the Croan of the Quequechan, Captain Kidd was charged with murder and sentenced to death; he was executed by hanging, in London, England, on May 23, 1701.

Across the Bay

Beginning with its colonial past as part of Plymouth Colony's Freetown, Fall River has a long history. In 1778, during the Revolutionary War, the Battle of Freetown [*Fall River*] was fought here with Colonel Joseph Durfee and his militia putting up a spirited defense against a British raid.

Separating from Freetown in 1803, Fall River was incorporated and officially became a town. The town would become a city in 1854. That's old. But there are nearby communities with ties to Fall River that are even older and were the site of even earlier wars.

In 1667, Baptist minister John Myles, founder of the first Baptist Church in Swansea, petitioned Plymouth Colony to allow formation of a new town. Until 1700, the original Swansea extended from the Taunton River to Narragansett Bay, encompassing present day Somerset as well as much of eastern Rhode Island including East Providence and the current towns of Barrington, Bristol, and Warren.

In 1675, Swansea would see the first skirmish igniting a conflict that what would become known as King Philip's War, the first of America's Indian wars. (Although the Chief Sachem of the native Wampanoags was named Metacomet, the colonists honored him by dubbing him Philip, after Philip of Macedon.)

In January of that year, John Sassamon, a Wampanoag and so-called "praying Indian" (Christian convert), and an intermediary and translator between the colonists and the Indians, was murdered. Another praying Indian claimed to have secretly witnessed the murder carried out by three Wampanoags.

The accused, all of whom were members Metacomet's inner circle, were tried by a jury consisting of both Indians and colonists. Although it was later learned that the eyewitness owed a gambling debt to one of the accused, all three were convicted based on his testimony; they were hanged at Plymouth on June 8, 1675.

On June 20, a war party of Pokanoket Wampanoags attacked the settlement of Swansea, beginning a five-day siege that killed several settlers and razed the village. King Philip's War had begun and would engulf much of eastern New England until April 1678, when colonist Sir Edmund Andros negotiated a treaty with holdout Indian bands in Maine.

As stated on the website historybits.com, "Over half of New England's towns were attacked during the war. Over 1,200 homes were burned and destroyed and over 8,000 precious food cattle killed. Countless amounts of food, supplies, and personal belongings were totally destroyed. Approximately 800 English died in the war and, measured against the small total population of New England at the time, the death rate was nearly twice the death rate of America's most costly war, the American Civil War. Moreover, this proportional death rate was seven times the death rate of Americans killed in World War II."

In 1693, settlers led by Samuel Gardner bought the small peninsula called Mattapoisett Neck for 1,700 pounds. All of the houses having been burned by the Indians during King Philip's War, the families set out to rebuild dwellings and establish farms.

According to information contained in the Swansea Historical Society archives, "Samuel's son, Samuel, would later have ten children, nine of whom would live to grow up on the farm and eventually raise their own families on the Neck. One of these children is named Peleg who marries Hannah, and they produce sixteen children. Mattapoisett Neck is now known as Gardner's Neck."

Later, in the nineteenth century, Swansea, known simply as "over the river" to Fall Riverites, was a popular summer recreation destination for city dwellers. In 1871, Andrew Jackson Borden purchased land in Swansea and had extensive farming interests there right up to the time of his 1892 murder.

Michael Martins and Dennis A. Binette, in their comprehensive volume, *Parallel Lives: A Social History of Lizzie A. Borden and Her Fall River*, state: "The Borden family apparently spent a good amount of time at the Swansea farm, residing in their one-and-one-half-story double house, painted white with dark shutters in typical New England fashion."

In addition to summering at her own Swansea house after her acquittal in her father's murder, Lizzie Borden was a guest of the Gardner family in the summer of 1896, (probably while her house was being renovated) and was even once erroneously rumored to be engaged to Orrin Gardner. By 1918, Lizzie and her sister, Emma Borden, had disposed of their inherited and jointly owned Swansea property.

Like Gardner's Neck, another historical section of Swansea associated with a prominent Swansea family is Barneyville. The Barney family traces their Swansea roots to Jonathan Barney a Baptist minister who moved to the town from Salem in 1673. One of the first seven landowners in Swansea, in 1690 Barney built a house that still stands on Old Providence Road.

Beginning near the southern end of Mason Street, Barneyville extends westward along Old Providence Road, crossing the Palmer River at the John Myles Bridge where it intersects with Barneyville Road itself. The bridge, refurbished and rededicated in 2007, and commonly known as the Bungtown Bridge by locals, is named for the preacher from Swansea, Wales, acknowledged by historians as the town's founder.

Barneyville has a colorful history. The land along the tidal Palmer River was the ancient site of the Wampanoag Indians summer encampment where they fished, hunted waterfowl, and planted crops of corn and beans. By the late 1600s, Jonathan

Barney had developed it into over a thousand acres devoted to cattle, pigs, and corn.

During the late-eighteenth century, Jonathan Barney, grandson of the original, began a shipyard on the Palmer River, building small vessels. Jonathan moved to New York in 1801 and the following year his nineteen-year-old son, Mason, decided to revitalize the business by contracting to build a full-size ship.

> Although young Barney was acquainted with the nature of ship building, through his father carrying it on, he himself did not know the use of tools. His courage and self-reliance in taking such a contract, when so young and inexperienced, foreshadowed the character of the future man. By his zeal, enthusiasm and determined will he overcame the great difficulties which to most men would have been insurmountable. From this beginning sprung up the ship building business at Barneyville, and Mr. Barney's subsequent great prominence in business circles. He sometimes employed two hundred and fifty men, annually disbursing large sums of money. The sails of the good substantial vessels, which in the course of half a century he built, whitened almost every sea.

> (*History of Swansea Massachusetts*, Otis Olney Wright, 1917)

During his career, Mason Barney built some 150 vessels from small fishing boats to a ship of 1,060 tons, the largest vessel that had then been launched in this section of New England.

Through the years, Barney's estate evolved into a self-sustaining empire, including a brick making kiln using native clay from the banks of the Palmer River, and a cooperage manufacturing so many hundreds of barrels that the immediate area became known colloquially as "Bungtown." In a commune-like setting, Barney provided housing for scores of workers, and even established a company store. Not surprisingly, the store accepted only Barney tokens.

Mason Barney amassed great wealth and lived in style. He was especially fond of rum parties, and his ship christenings were great social events drawing businessmen and dignitaries from New York to Boston. With the advent of steam powered ships and the clouds of Civil War on the horizon, the Barney Shipyard ceased operations in 1860.

Twenty-first century Barneyville is now a quiet residential area. But part of the land once ruled by the Barney dynasty has been preserved by yet another descendant of the clan. In 1931, Algernon Barney designed and built what many consider to be the hidden gem of Bristol County golf courses.

A nine-hole, links-style track, Wampanoag Golf Course's classically small but undulating greens, aided by the prevailing southwesterly winds, provide a strong defense to the par of 36. The pastoral layout serves up scenic vistas of the Palmer River and its abundant population of waterfowl. And as a fitting legacy to the family

who developed the land, the historic Jonathan Barney House overlooks Wampanoag's
ninth green.

January 3, 2016
Fall River, MA

1.6.1 Idealized portrait engraving of "POMETACOM [sic] alias KING PHILIP."

1.6.2 The Myles Garrison House Monument stands at the junction of Old Providence and Barneyville roads.

Near this spot stood the John Myles Garrison house, the first place of the meeting of the troops of Massachusetts Bay and Plymouth Colonies commanded by Majors Thomas Savage (1608-1682) and James Cudworth (c.1612-c.1682), who marched to the relief of Swansea at the opening of King Philip's War, A.D. 1675. There fell in Swansea, slain by the Native Americans, Nehemiah Allin, William Cahoone, Gershom Cobb, John Druce, John Fall, William Hammond, John Jones, Robert Jones, Joseph Lewis, John Salisbury and William Salisbury. To mark this historic site, this monument was erected by the Commonwealth of Massachusetts A.D. 1912.

1.6.3 The historic Jonathan Barney house, begun in 1690, overlooks the ninth hole at Wampanoag Golf Course in Barneyville.

1.6.4 Portrait of Mason Barney (1782-1868).

1.6.5 The Swansea farm of Andrew Jackson Borden (1822-1892) on Gardner Neck Road, circa 1895.

1.6.6 A monument marks the site of the former Mason Barney Shipyard, which operated on the Palmer River from the late-eighteenth century until 1860.

1.6.7 The former Mason Barney School stood on Old Providence Road in Swansea, near Mason Street, in the Barneyville section of town. The structure was built in 1935 and closed in 1992; the building was demolished in 2007 and the town's water desalination tanks occupy the site. The cupola was saved and was incorporated into a monument on Swansea's Veteran's Memorial Green.

CHAPTER TWO

WAR AND SLAVERY

THE UNDERGROUND RAILROAD

The Underground Railroad was neither underground, nor was it an actual railroad, but Fall River was one of its stations.

During a February 19, 2013, walking tour of the lower highlands with a group of history buffs, historian Alfred J. Lima revealed how the city became an important stop in the loosely organized network helping southern slaves escape northward to New England and Canada during the nineteenth century.

In the 1830s, a group of New England Quakers began advocating for the end of slavery. One of the most passionate of these was Arnold Buffum, who along with his wife and five daughters moved to Fall River in 1824 from Smithfield, Rhode Island. From Lima's book, *A River and its City,* "Arnold Buffum had learned to despise slavery by the stories told him by his family's old escaped slave, who related the horrors of being captured in Africa and being brought to America on a slave ship."

Buffum, along with William Lloyd Garrison and others, would found the New England Anti-Slavery Society in Boston in 1832, becoming its first president. In 1835, two of Buffum's daughters, Elizabeth and Sarah, and a score of other local women, founded the Female Anti-Slavery Society in Fall River. Sarah Buffum went on to marry Nathaniel B. Borden, manufacturer and third mayor of Fall River.

According to Lima, ships leaving southern ports bound for the north would frequently harbor stowaway slaves seeking freedom. Sometimes, the fugitive slaves would come aboard with the captain's consent. "Captains took chances," said Lima, "if caught harboring runaways they could be imprisoned or even hanged."

Many of these ships carrying what was euphemistically called "freight" in Underground Railroad terms, unloaded in New England ports, including Boston, New Bedford, and Fall River. The usual route for a runaway landing in New Bedford was, next to Fall River, and then on to Central Falls, Rhode Island, where sympathetic "conductors" would arrange passage to Canada. "Slaves coming to Fall River would be fed and kept overnight before moving on," said Lima.

Although many local sympathizers were involved in the Underground Railroad, a Fall River man named Isaiah Borden kept three horses in his stable, two of which were on alert to take slaves to Central Falls if "slave catchers" were suspected in the area. "Unfortunately, we don't know where Isaiah Borden's stable was," said Lima. "We really should find that out."

Lima pointed out several homes in the area of Rock and Pine Streets where abolitionists temporarily sheltered fugitives from southern slave catchers. Two well-known safe houses were the Slade Double House at 286-292 Pine, and the 1833 Wright-Fiske-Dean House at 263 Pine, where Dr. Isaac Fiske hid runaway slaves in his attic.

Further up Rock Street is the Fall River Historical Society whose building is probably the best known safe house in the city. Originally built by Quaker Andrew Robeson on the once fashionable corner of Columbia and Fountain Streets, the mansion's still operable movable bookcase lead to a secret underground hiding place once used by escaping slaves.

"Although we know that there were probably many more safe houses in Fall River," said Lima, "we're only certain of these few."

February 24, 2013
Fall River, Massachusetts

2.1.1 Arnold Buffum (1782-1859), depicted in a miniature portrait painted in 1826. During his residency in Fall River, he became the first president of the Massachusetts Anti-Slavery Society.

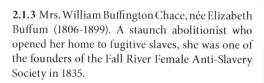

LIST OF OFFICERS.

PRESIDENT.
ARNOLD BUFFUM.

VICE PRESIDENTS.
JAMES C. ODIORNE,
ALONZO LEWIS.

CORRESPONDING SECRETARY.
WILLIAM LLOYD GARRISON.

RECORDING SECRETARY.
JOSHUA COFFIN.

TREASURER.
MICHAEL H. SIMPSON.

COUNSELLORS.
MOSES THACHER,
JOHN E. FULLER,
OLIVER JOHNSON,
ROBERT B. HALL,
BENJAMIN C. BACON,
JOHN STIMPSON.

At the regular monthly meeting of the New-England Anti-Slavery Society, held on the evening of Feb. 27, 1832,

Voted, That a copy of the Constitution and Address of the Society be sent to all the editors of newspapers in New-England, respectfully requesting them to insert in their columns a notice of the formation of the Society, with the Constitution, and such portions of the Address as they may find room to extract.

Voted, That a copy of the same also be presented to every clergyman in New-England, earnestly soliciting his co-operation in promoting the objects of the Society.

Voted, That the friends of the people of color, and the people of color themselves, in the various towns in New-England, be invited to form auxiliaries to this Society, and to notify the Corresponding Secretary of their organization as soon as may be practicable.

2.1.2 List of Officers of the New England Anti-Slavery Society, February 27, 1832.

2.1.3 Mrs. William Buffington Chace, née Elizabeth Buffum (1806-1899). A staunch abolitionist who opened her home to fugitive slaves, she was one of the founders of the Fall River Female Anti-Slavery Society in 1835.

2.1.4 Nathaniel Briggs Borden (1801-1865). A wealthy Fall River businessman, politician, and abolitionist, he served as Fall River's third mayor. In 1834, he founded an anti-slavery society in Fall River.

2.1.5 Nathaniel Briggs Borden residence, 40 Second Street, Fall River, as it appeared in the early-twentieth century. An active and important station on the Underground Railroad, the structure was razed in the 1930s.

2.1.6 Double house at 335-337 Pine Street (190 Rock Street), Fall River, as it appeared in 1957. Albion King Slade (1823-1909) and his wife, née Mary Bridge Canedy (1826-1882), rented a portion of this house from 1857 to 1861, during which time they frequently harbored fugitive slaves. The structure was later altered with the addition of a tower when it was converted to the First Church of Christ Scientist.

2.1.7 Residence of Dr. Isaac Fiske (1791-1873), 263 Pine Street, Fall River, as it appeared in 2013. A homeopathic physician and Quaker abolitionist who was actively involved in anti-slavery activities in the city, Dr. Fiske often offered shelter to escaping slaves en route to freedom in Canada. According to his daughter, Anna Robinson Fiske (1845-1929), later Mrs. Harry Theodore Harding, "it was not safe to go in the attic, for there might be a runaway slave up there."

2.1.8 The "stone mansion" built in 1843 for Andrew Robeson Jr. (1817-1874) at 28 Columbia Street, in an aerial view photographed during the residency of Friend William Hill (1799-1881), a Quaker abolitionist. The elegant mansion, which was constructed of native Fall River granite, was used as a station on the Underground Railroad by both the Robeson and Hill families.

FALL RIVER AND THE CIVIL WAR

The year 2015 marked the Sesquicentennial of the end of the American Civil War.

On April 9, 1865, General Robert E. Lee surrendered the Army of Northern Virginia to General Ulysses S. Grant in the parlor of the Wilmer McLean house in Appomattox Court House, Virginia.

The war, which began in 1861, ravaged the country for four long years. The conflict was America's bloodiest and still holds many infamous records such as the highest average number of deaths per day (504). The savage combat violence at battles such as Antietam, Gettysburg, and Shiloh, shocked the civilized world.

According to the nonprofit Civil War Trust: "Nearly as many men died in captivity during the Civil War as were killed in the whole of the Vietnam War. Hundreds of thousands died of disease. Roughly two per cent of the population, an estimated 620,000 men, lost their lives in the line of duty."

On April 14, 1865, only five days after Lee's surrender, President Lincoln was assassinated by Confederate sympathizer John Wilkes Booth while watching a play at Ford's Theater in Washington D.C. The man who had faithfully guided the Union throughout the Confederate rebellion would not live to see his dream of reunification and reconstruction.

Massachusetts furnished over 159,000 men to serve in the war, and Fall River did its part.

On April 19, 1861, one week after the Confederacy had opened hostilities by firing on Ft. Sumter, a crowded public meeting in city hall adopted by acclamation an appropriation of $10,000 to aid the families of volunteers. Five days later, the Fall River City Council voted to pay $15 per month to every volunteer.

The city was the third in the state to apply to Governor Andrew for permission to raise military companies and enlistments began immediately. On June 11, 1861, Companies A and B of what would become the Seventh Massachusetts Volunteer Infantry were mustered in.

According to the 1911 *History of Fall River* by Henry M. Fenner, "[*Fall River*] also contributed many men to other regiments and 497 to the navy. In all 1,770 men went to the front, including 820 for three years, 207 for nine months, 192 for three months and 37 for one year."

James Buffington, the first mayor of Fall River, enlisted as a private in Company

A, of the 7th Regiment Massachusetts Volunteer Infantry, serving with that unit until August 24, 1861. Buffington, who served seven terms in Congress from the Second Representative District of Massachusetts, was discharged by the Secretary of War to return to his Congressional seat. According to Nelson V. Hutchinson's 1890 *History of The 7th Massachusetts Volunteer Infantry, 1861-1865*, Buffington's return to Congress allowed him "… to do much for all the soldiers."

Hutchinson's history profiles another local volunteer:

> Sergeant Henry E. Kay was born in Fall River, Mass., May 21, 1836. Was a machinist before the war. He was wounded in the leg at Salem Heights, May 3, 1863, and again in the same leg, a year later, May 5, 1864, at the battle of the Wilderness, one bullet going through the leg below and another above the knee. He is still a machinist, having a manufactory of his own in Fall River, manufactures thread and roll covering machinery, which goes to all parts of the United States and Canada, and even to Scotland. He was a splendid soldier, and is an industrious citizen.

Fall River's Oak Grove Cemetery has an extensive dedicated veterans' area just inside the main gate. The oldest veterans' memorial is an obelisk inscribed with Civil War dead, guarded by four cannons. But perhaps the most notable Civil War grave, standing alone some distance away, belongs to Corporal James Holehouse, another member of the 7th Regiment Massachusetts Volunteer Infantry.

With one glaring omission, Hutchinson's history chronicles Holehouse's service while providing a tender insight into his personality:

> James Holehouse was born in Stockport, England, Dec. 25, 1839. He came to the United States in 1856, and, when the war commenced, was a weaver in No. 1 Union Mill, in Fall River. He enlisted—the twelfth man on the roll of Co. B—April 12, 1861; was mustered June 15, 1861, and served with his regiment faithfully until June 27, 1864; received a slight scratch near the eye-brow at the battle of the Wilderness, May 5, 1864, and the next day a bullet went through his dress coat, leaving a sore spot on his flesh. Comrade Holehouse was a loyal soldier to his adopted country. Exceedingly good natured and witty, his jovial manners and talk kept many of his comrades from an attack of the blues.

The Corporal may have been the life of the party around the campfire but his good humor belied a serious side with an ample dose of courage. Historian Hutchinson somehow overlooks the pinnacle of Holehouse's army career, his receipt of the Nation's highest military honor.

While serving with Company B, Holehouse was awarded the Congressional Medal of Honor for his bravery at Marye's Heights, Virginia, during the May 3, 1863, Battle of Chancellorsville. His official citation reads: "With one companion voluntarily and with conspicuous daring advanced beyond his regiment, which had been broken in the assault, and halted beneath the crest. Following the example of these two men, the colors were brought to the summit, the regiment was advanced, and the position held."

Far from the roar of the cannon and the crack of the rifle, and with no mention of the Medal of Honor award, Holehouse's paragraph in the regimental history ends quietly: "Since the war, has followed the occupation of loom-fixer, until within the past six years has not been able to do any laborious work on account of diseases contracted in the army."

Corporal James Holehouse died on May 20, 1915.

The few secessionist sympathizers in Fall River during the Civil War took their lives in their hands if they were bold enough to speak out for the Confederacy. There were accounts of shops looted, property destroyed, and beatings administered to anyone advocating for the South. Returning troops were treated as heroes and greeted with parades and public speeches by politicians and dignitaries

"The news of the fall of Richmond was announced by the general ringing of bells," writes Fenner in his history, "and when it became known that Lee had surrendered, the bells were again rung, cannon fired, the Light Infantry paraded, schools dismissed, and work generally suspended. A large meeting was held in the city hall in the evening, presided over by the mayor."

Fall River's textile mills flourished during the war and with several infrastructure improvements including an extension of the railroad to Newport, Rhode Island, in 1863, the city was well positioned to take advantage of the post-war prosperity.

The end of the Civil War saw the first great wave of French-Canadian immigrants to come to Fall River and immediately find work in the labor-starved mills. By 1868, the city was operating over 500,000 spindles and had surpassed Lowell as America's pre-eminent textile city.

By 1916, some forty corporations operating one hundred mills employed upwards of 30,000 textile workers in Fall River. A half-century after the end of the Civil War, World War I would breathe a last gasp of prosperity into the city's doomed textile industry. An industry soon to move lock, stock, and loom, to of all places … the American South.

March 1, 2015
Fall River, Massachusetts

2.2.1 Hon. James Buffington (1817-1875) in military uniform, 1861; Fall River's first mayor, he was in office from 1854-1855. A Civil War veteran, he was an Adjutant on the staff of General Darius Nash Couch (1822-1897). He served seven terms as a member of Congress from the Second Representative District of Massachusetts, and, as such, was able "to do much for all the soldiers" during the conflict.

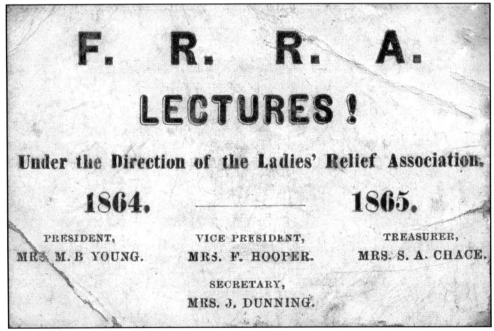

2.2.2 Ticket for Fall River Relief Association benefit lectures, 1864-1865. Formed by a group of the most prominent women in the city on December 9, 1864, "for the purpose of organizing a society for the relief of soldiers' families," the organization provided considerable aid of all kinds to families, widows, and orphans, throughout the war. It was one of several such organizations founded in Fall River during the conflict.

2.2.3 Company F, 26th Regiment Massachusetts Volunteer Infantry, assembled on North Main Street in Fall River, April 5, 1864, while on furlough from New Orleans, Louisiana.

2.2.4 Sgt. Henry E. Kay (1836-1902).

2.2.5 Corp. James Holehouse (1839-1915).

2.2.6 Civil War monument in Fall River's Oak Grove Cemetery. The beautifully carved central obelisk was donated by Col. Richard Borden (1795-1874) in memory of fallen Union soldiers. The Colonel's wife, née Abby Walker Durfee (1798-1884), was a founding member and dedicated worker of the Fall River Soldiers' Aid Society, lauded for her "untiring energy and zeal in behalf of the soldiers of the Union."

2.2.7 Graves of fallen Civil War soldiers in Oak Grove Cemetery, 2008.

FALL RIVER'S AFRICAN AMERICAN PIONEERS

By the mid-nineteenth century, there were two railroads operating in Fall River. One, the Old Colony, carried passengers to and from the waterfront where, boarding luxurious Fall River Line steamships, they continued their journey to New York City.

The other, the so-called Underground Railroad, helped spirit runaway slaves through Rhode Island and Vermont, and on to eventual freedom in Canada.

Several homes in the city's downtown area where abolitionists temporarily sheltered fugitives from southern slave catchers survive to this day. Two well-known safe houses were the 1833 Isaac Fiske House at 263 Pine Street, and the Slade Double House at 286-292 Pine. Probably the best known safe house in Fall River is the Fall River Historical Society mansion on Rock Street. Built by Quaker abolitionist Andrew Robeson and originally located on once-fashionable Columbia Street, the home's movable bookcase opens to a secret underground room once used to hide fleeing slaves.

Although Lincoln's 1863 Emancipation Proclamation and the subsequent passage of the 13th Amendment following the Civil War officially ended American slavery, racial discrimination continued. Beginning in the mid-1870s, former Confederate and many Border States enacted a series of anti-black laws. This rigid racial caste system, collectively called Jim Crow, institutionalized African Americans in a second class citizenship that wasn't to be undone until the Civil Rights Movement of the 1960s.

"Blacks enjoyed a very small window of opportunity in the years immediately following the Civil War," said Fall River historian Dr. Philip T. Silvia Jr. In his 2006 pamphlet commemorating the 20th Anniversary of the Massachusetts Hall of Black Achievement at Bridgewater State University, Professor Silvia recounts, "the story of two black sisters that is inspiring and troublesome at the same time."

In 1873, Mary W. Lewis, a twenty-six-year-old seamstress, married Lewis H. Latimer in Fall River. Latimer, born to former slave parents who escaped a Virginia plantation six years before his birth, would go on to become one of the most preeminent black scientists of the nineteenth century. Among other things, Latimer is credited with preparing the drawings for Alexander Graham Bell's telephone patent. The young inventor also invented an improved filament for Thomas Edison's incandescent light bulb that greatly extended the life of the bulb.

According to Professor Silvia, Mary enjoyed the middle-class security and comfortable lifestyle achieved through her husband's accomplishments in the workplace. Lattimer's work responsibilities required frequent travel, and in a diary begun in 1882 Mary fondly remembers a four-month stay in London, England, with her husband.

Mary would give birth to two daughters, Emma Jeannette and Louise Rebecca, and the couple would live to celebrate their golden wedding anniversary in 1923. Mary Lattimer died in 1924, Lewis Lattimer in 1928. They are buried together in Fall River's Oak Grove Cemetery.

In the immediate post-Civil-War years childhood education took a back seat in the Spindle City. According to Silvia, in 1865 "700 of the city's 1900 children from 10 to 14 were working full time. Only thirty-seven percent of these employees possessed both reading and writing skills in English."

It was different for Mary's older sister, Sarah Anna Lewis. "Defying the odds," writes Silvia, "Sarah had progressed in school and was well prepared to take an exam for admission into the Fall River High School, precursor to Durfee High." After high school, Sarah applied for admission into the State Normal School at Bridgewater, Massachusetts, now Bridgewater State University.

Sarah successfully completed her course of study and along with sixteen other graduates was awarded a diploma in January, 1869. In so doing, Bridgewater Normal was in the vanguard of racial enlightenment. Harvard University awarded its first undergraduate degree to a black student a year later in 1870.

"A Bridgewater degree was held in high repute," said Silvia, and in March of 1869, Sarah was appointed the first full time black teacher in the Fall River school system at the "1ˢᵗ Div[ision] Intermediate" level. She remained a teacher until May 11, 1871, when, according to Silvia, she "chose to do something that was legally taboo." She married.

With her marriage to Edward A. Williams, a cook and baker, Sarah forfeited her professional career because by law only single women were allowed to teach. This had drastic financial consequences for the couple and by 1880 they had taken up residence in Manhattan, New York, reasonably close to Sarah's sister, Mary, then living in Bridgeport, Connecticut.

The couple raised three children, Florence, Ernest, and Harriet. The family subsequently moved to Newton, Massachusetts, where Edward pursued his vocation as a cook until his death in 1902. In 1910, Sarah then moved to Cambridge, Massachusetts, supporting herself as a dressmaker. She later lived in Everett, Massachusetts, with her married daughter Florence, until her death at age ninety-two on January 24, 1939. Sarah and her husband are buried in Oak Grove Cemetery.

"We are left to muse over what her reflections about her life experience might have been by this later date," writes Dr. Silvia. "Would Sarah A. Lewis Williams have dwelled on the irony of having transcended racism in advancing her education, only to be snared by gender discrimination?"

February 17, 2014
Fall River, Massachusetts

2.3.1 Lewis Howard Latimer (1848-1928), circa 1882.

2.3.2 Lewis H. Latimer and his wife, née Mary Wilson Lewis (1847-1924), circa 1920. The couple were married in Fall River in 1873, at which time Mary was working as a seamstress.

2.3.3 Fall River High School as it appeared in 1879. "Defying the odds," Sarah Anna Lewis "had progressed in school and was well prepared to take an exam for admission into the Fall River High School, precursor to Durfee High."

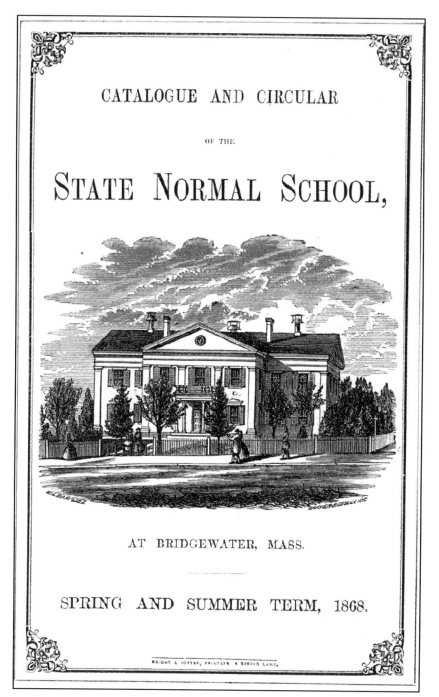

2.3.4 "Catalogue and Circular of the State Normal School at Bridgewater, Mass. for the Spring and Summer Term, 1868," published during Sarah Anna Lewis's student years.

STUDENTS.

SENIOR CLASS.

LADIES.

Ella M. Armes, Barrington, N.H.
Hattie A. Cobb, East Bridgewater.
Laura A. Leonard, South Middleboro'.
Clara F. Leonard, Bridgewater.
Flora McFarland, Fall River.
Mary E. Minter, Plymouth.
Sarah R. Walker, Dighton.

Cora I. Young, Boston.— 8.

GENTLEMEN.

Samuel J. Bullock, Salem.
James A. Francis, Westport.
Noah Hathaway, Freetown.
Walter Hoxie, Newburyport.
Moses W. D. Hurd, Boston.— 5.

SUB-SENIOR CLASS.

LADIES.

Clara A. Armes, Barrington, N.H.
Mary C. Babcock, Natick.
Georgianna Duckworth, Bridgewater.
Olivia S. Holmes, West Bridgewater.
Clara Kenrick, South Orleans.
Susan W. Kirby, Fall River.
Sarah A. Lewis, Fall River.
Lucia Millett, Bridgewater.
Lucretia G. Osborne, E. Bridgewater.
Sarah L. Porter, South Braintree.
Sarah E. Pratt, Reading.

Rosa C. Shaw, Carver.
Abbie Smith, East Bridgewater.
Melora A. Whitcomb, Templeton.—14.

GENTLEMEN.

Merrick J. Fay, Worcester.
Melvin C. French, Berkley.
Philander A. Gay, Rockville.
Hiram L. Hutchinson, S. Danvers.
Nathaniel S. Keay, Rockville.
Thomas H. Treadway, Bridgewater.
Barrett B. Russell, Dartmouth.—7.

2.3.5 "Catalogue and Circular of the State Normal School at Bridgewater, Mass. for the Spring and Summer Term, 1868," listing Sarah Anna Lewis as a member of the "Sub-Senior Class."

2.3.6 Sarah Anna Lewis at the time of her graduation from the State Norman School at Bridgewater, Massachusetts, 1869.

2.3.7 Sarah Anna (Lewis) Williams in the 1920s. Sarah married Edward A. Williams (1824-1902), who was employed as a cook, baker, and caterer, in Fall River in 1871; in the late 1870s the couple relocated to Manhattan, New York.

2.3.8 Mary Wilson (Lewis) Latimer's grave in Oak Grove Cemetery, Fall River. In 1964, the ashes of her husband, Lewis H. Latimer, were combined with those of their daughter, Louise Latimer (1891-1963), and interred in Mary's grave. Also in this plot are the remains of Mary's sister, Sarah, and those of her husband, Edward.

CHAPTER THREE

STONE

BEDROCK

Fred Flintstone and Barney Rubble would have been right at home in nineteenth-century Fall River. The cartoon quarrymen from fictional Bedrock could easily have found work extracting the Spindle City's very own prehistoric bedrock—granite.

From the Latin root word *granum*, meaning "grain," granite is an igneous rock composed primarily of four minerals: quartz, feldspar, mica, and hornblende. Although feldspar can come in many colors, it is this component of Fall River granite that provides its distinctive pink speckling when viewed up close.

In 1841, still using the city's only recently changed name, geologist Edward Hitchcock gave the following description of Fall River granite: "No rock can be finer for architectural purposes than the granite of Troy. The feldspar of this rock is a mixture of the flesh red and light green varieties; the former predominating: the quartz is light gray, and the mica, usually black. It works easily and has a lighter and more lively appearance than Quincy granite."

Quincy, Massachusetts, some forty miles to our north is, of course, "The Granite City." But Fall River could well have appropriated that sobriquet had it not been for one overriding and preeminent use for the rock itself—the construction of cotton mills.

In its history, the city has been home to over one-hundred-and-ten textile mills, approximately two-thirds of which were constructed of granite. Visitors driving through the city for the first time on Interstate 195 are amazed at the number and size of the hulking grey monoliths. Little do they realize, their ranks have already been considerably thinned.

Besides ravaging the city's downtown in the early 1960s, Interstate 195 took out several granite mills, including: the Wamsutta; Troy Mills Nos. 1 & 2; and Union Mill No. 3. Many more city mills, both granite and red brick, have been consumed by spectacular conflagrations. Still others have fallen to the wrecking ball, the latest of which was the original Fall River Iron Works No. 1, on Water Street. As we celebrate the Bicentennial of Col. Joseph Durfee's first mill at Globe Corners, only some sixty of its brethren still stand in the city.

"Many of the granite mills have enormous basements," said Michael Martins, Curator of the Fall River Historical Society. "If they hit ledge while building, they simply quarried on site and used the rock in the construction." But despite the abundance of this natural building material, not all of the city's mills would be built of granite.

With some exceptions, notably the Sagamore Mills Nos. 2 & 3 on North Main Street, most of the "below the hill" mills, such as the Border City, the Mechanics, the Narragansett, and the sprawling Iron Works itself, were of red brick. Because the city's quarries were on the flat ground above the ridge, teams of oxen could easily transport the heavy stone to the nearby construction sites safely and inexpensively.

Moving it *down* the city's many hills however, presented problems. Runaway oxcarts carrying granite blocks weighing up to several tons, could surely maim or kill both man and beast. A massive stone dumped from an overturned or damaged cart was not easily reloaded without the time and expense of a temporary derrick or winching sled brought to the accident site.

Although they did use smaller granite cuttings for sills, lintels, posts, and curbs, the city's waterfront mills instead turned to brick as their primary construction material. Most of this brick came from kilns in Providence, Rhode Island, and Taunton, Massachusetts, transported to the city by barge and offloaded at docks adjacent to the job sites.

During the construction boom of the 1870s when twenty-two new mills were built and many more were enlarged, Fall River's granite quarries flourished. Among others, there were: Maj. Bradford Durfee's Bigberry Ledge, on the shores of the Quequechan near 16th Street; the Earle quarry off Bell Rock Road; Thurston's Ledge, east of Freelove Street; the Savoie quarry on Beauregard Street; and the Ross quarry on Barlow Street, near Watuppa Pond.

But the granddaddy of them all was Beattie's quarry on the northern end of aptly named, Quarry Street, formerly called the Harrison Quarry and consisting of less than three acres; brothers William and John Beattie purchased the site near the end of the Civil War.

By 1910, the pit was the length of three football fields and measured seven hundred feet wide by sixty feet deep. A 1911 United States geological survey bulletin listed an impressive inventory of the plant's equipment including: five derricks, three hoisting engines, an air compressor, fourteen air plug drills, two surfacers, three steam drills, and a stone crusher with a daily capacity of eighty tons.

"Despite their importance to the city's history, the quarries are a difficult subject to research," said the Historical Society's Martins. "Unlike the textile industry, we have few photographs or records in our archives." Of course the most visible and enduring record of the quarries' existence are the buildings and monuments which they helped to construct.

Besides the looming mills, local examples incorporating Fall River's native stone include: the Public Library, built in 1899 of dressed Fall River granite; the YMCA, combining hammered granite with Roman brick; and the Gothic style St. Mary's Cathedral on Spring Street.

Rock Street's former B.M.C. Durfee High School, Mary B. Young's gift to Fall River in memory of her son, was built in the Modern Renaissance style in 1886. Now a courthouse, the restored building has a foundation of the native bedrock, with the upper stories constructed of dressed New Hampshire granite. Off the beaten path but particularly striking is the Fall River Waterworks tower on upper Bedford Street, an elegant example of hand-cut local granite.

The city's one-hundred-acre Oak Grove Cemetery borders the northernmost edge of the former Beattie quarry at Locust Street. Not only does the cemetery contain thousands of fine granite monuments above ground, it also has its share of the bedrock from which they were carved, below ground. This is, of course, a continuation of the same granite deposit commercially exploited just next door by Beattie.

In 1913, Oak Grove managers for the first time used the cemetery's own workforce instead of the usual outside contractors for excavation. In his annual report to the Fall River Park Commissioners, the cemetery's superintendent proudly points out where he's saved city taxpayers some money: "Blow drilling was first attempted upon a section … along the southeasterly line of the cemetery. Here solid ledge predominated, thus giving the desired opportunity of testing the ability of the men to cope with this extreme condition. The excavation proceeded with surprising rapidity…The steam road roller proved indispensable in hauling from the cut huge pieces of rock which would otherwise have entailed much labor in their removal."

"As the cemetery expanded over the years," said Mike Keane, president of Friends of Oak Grove Cemetery, "they were constantly removing boulders and ledge to clear space for additional graves." The cemetery's iconic twenty-five-foot high Prospect Street arch, its buildings, and its perimeter walls, are of course made of Fall River granite. But according to Keane, it would be wrong to assume that it all came from the adjacent Beattie quarry. "Park Commission records show that they asked for bids annually," said Keane, "so year by year as they added holding vaults, installed curbing, and extended the wall in stages, the granite could have come from any one of the city's several quarries."

Quarrying was dangerous work, and Fall River's quarries operated long before the safety and record keeping requirements of the Occupational Safety and Health Administration (OSHA). Unfortunately, injuries were frequent and often crippling.

As big a problem as individual accidents was the threat from the ever present clouds of stone dust from the cutting, grinding, and chiseling of the granite slabs. Without even so much as a simple dust mask, workers were constantly breathing fine particulate, often leading to what we now know as the respiratory disease, silicosis. Obituaries of nineteenth-century stone cutters and quarrymen would routinely and matter-of-factly list the cause of death as "stone consumption."

Long after the city's open quarries ceased operations, they continued to be dangerous, several accidental deaths from falls and drowning have been recorded throughout the years.

As might be expected, several Fall River commercial stone cutters prospered during the late-nineteenth century and into the early-twentieth. Two, with prime locations bracketing the Prospect Street entrance to Oak Grove Cemetery were: Durkin & Co. Granite & Marble Works and Lawson's Granite & Marble Works.

Alexander Lawson, a Scottish immigrant, is credited with the carvings on the Oak Grove entrance arch itself. His company, later run by his son Frederick, was also responsible for some of the cemetery's largest monuments including those of the prominent Stafford and Davol families.

During World War I, when both manpower and the gunpowder used to blow apart the rock were in short supply, granite quarrying slowed, not only here but nationwide. In the 1920s, competing with improved structural steel and reinforced concrete construction methods, demand for granite diminished further, leading to the eventual closure of most of Fall River's quarries.

But recently, the long closed William & J. Beattie, Jr. quarry (John Beattie, Jr. was his nephew), reached forward to once again touch the city. After its abandonment in the late 1920s, the huge excavation at Quarry and Locust Streets began retaining water from natural underground springs and aquifers.

It's axiomatic that nature abhors a vacuum, but apparently so did the citizens of Fall River. In addition to the rising water, they, too, began filling the city's mini-Grand Canyon with trash. During the 1940s and 50s, before the concept of the managed landfill, the yawning pit slowly became an open dump.

In the mid-1960s, the dumping ground was reclaimed with the help of clean fill and subsequently acquired by the Fall River Housing Authority. Oak Village, an apartment complex for the disabled and elderly, built in 1965, stands there today. Somewhat shakily.

According to Housing Authority Executive Director, Thomas Collins, by 2011 there had been an ongoing problem for years with at least two of the buildings' floors cracking and their walls tilting. Not surprisingly, authorities attributed the problem to settling of the stratified and poorly compacted layers of dirt-covered trash filling the old quarry. Engineers advised that there was no cost effective way to stabilize the buildings and they were razed.

Ironically, the Beattie quarry, having furnished its strong and beautiful bedrock to erect so many buildings, played a role in demolishing a couple.

July 4, 2011
Fall River, Massachusetts

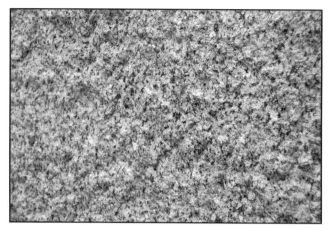

3.1.1 Detail of Fall River granite. "No rock can be finer for architectural purposes than the granite of Troy [*Fall River*]. The feldspar of this rock is a mixture of the flesh red and light green varieties, the former predominating; the quartz is light gray, and the mica usually black. It works easily and has a lighter and livelier appearance than Quincy granite."

3.1.2 Merchants' Manufacturing Company as it appeared shortly after its expansion in 1872; the structure is a stellar example of a mill constructed of Fall River granite. Traces of the city's quarrying industry can be seen in the foreground, which is littered with granite construction material, grade curbing, and water troughs.

3.1.3 Border City Mills, No. 2, as it appeared in 1930; constructed in 1873, the structure is a fine example of one of the mills "below the hill" that were constructed of red brick.

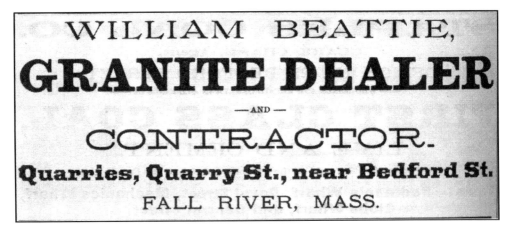

3.1.4 Advertisement from the 1895 edition of the *Fall River Directory* for "William Beattie, Granite Dealer and Contractor."

3.1.5 Quarrymen at Beattie's Ledge, Fall River, in the 1880s.

3.1.6 Quarrymen at Beattie's Ledge, Fall River, 1903.

Granite is quarried, not mined. That is, it is taken out of an open shaft, with no underground shafts leading off from the main opening, as is the case in marble quarries. This view shows a granite pit. The stone is in layers, and is so hard that it has to be blasted loose. The men in the foreground are busy chiseling these stones, preparatory to splitting them into the proper sizes.

The stone is quarried in this manner. A foreman measures out on a layer the shape desired. On the line so laid down holes are drilled and charges of powder are inserted. These charges are set off, hurling a great mass of stone into the bottom of the quarry. The stones are then worked down by drills run by compressed air, and by hand tools such as you see the workmen using. If the grain is straight, steel wedges can be used to block the stone into the desired sizes.

3.1.7 Quarrymen at Beattie's Ledge, Fall River, 1903.

These great blocks of stone are blasted out of the solid seam of granite. What is strong enough to lift it? High up on the edge of the quarry hole there is a huge derrick. One arm of the derrick has been swung out over the quarry. A heavy iron chain hangs from that arm. The other end of the chain you can see fastened around the block of granite. A steam or electric engine pulls the chain up, and so up goes the granite block to the top of the quarry. The rope fastened to it swings it in any direction needed. It is loaded on a flat car and taken to the shed where it is cut and polished.

3.1.8 Entrance gate to Oak Grove Cemetery, Fall River, as it appeared in 1890; the rough texture of Fall River granite furnished an ideal surface for the ivy vines that cloaked it for decades.

3.1.9 Workmen at Oak Grove Cemetery in the early-twentieth century. This photograph clearly illustrates the "difficulties encountered in construction of lots."

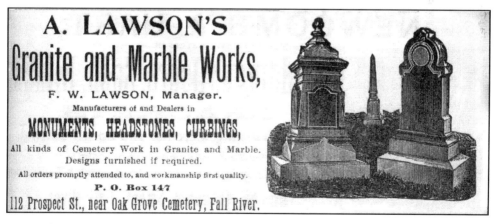

3.1.10 Advertisement from the 1895 edition of the *Fall River Directory* for "A. Lawson's Granite and Marble Works"; the establishment was conveniently situated "near Oak Grove Cemetery" for the convenience of patrons.

FALL RIVER'S FOUNDATION

The word granite is inextricably connected to Fall River and has had a part in naming several local places and structures: Granite Street; Granite Row; two Granite Blocks; and even the accurately if unimaginatively named Granite Mills.

Granite, besides being strong and durable, is also highly resistant to bacteria, second only to stainless steel. The heat, scratch, and stain resistant stone has become the modern day choice for upscale kitchen and bar countertops.

Fall River granite was used extensively outside of the city itself. Examples include: *Chateau-sur-Mer*, one of the first of Newport, Rhode Island's grand mansions; parts of that seaside city's Fort Adams and Naval War College; and the base of the statehouse in New York State's Capital of Albany.

A common misconception is that the base of the Statue of Liberty is made of Fall River granite. Although it *is* Beattie granite, it came from William Beattie's brother John's quarry on Leete's Island in New Haven County, Connecticut.

The Sagamore Mills off North Main Street are one of the few granite exceptions to the red brick mills along the city's waterfront. Sagamore No. 2 was originally constructed of stone from the Assonet Ledge, transported to the site by rail.

Old-timers tell of the caretaker's dog at the Quarry Street dump rooting out rats from the mounds of trash to be picked-off by its master wielding a .22 caliber rifle. The sharp shooting caretaker's name has been lost, but the dog is remembered as "Queenie."

Not all Fall River granite ended up in beautiful buildings or grandiose monuments. Before the successive road building advances of macadam, tarmac, blacktop, and finally, asphalt, granite cobblestones jarred wagons and horseless carriages on most of Fall River's streets. A section of cobblestone can still be seen behind the American Printing Company Mill at Anawan and Pond Streets.

Although some supplies of granite curbing and storm drain capstones remained in Public Works Department inventories after the quarries closed, older city streets usually have the distinctive Fall River pink curbstones. Newer streets and replacement curbs are identified by smoother, grey Quincy type granite.

Several older "granolithic" sidewalks in the city are imbedded with small bronze plaques indicating that they were built by the Depression era, Works Progress Administration (WPA). There are also a few bronze sidewalk plaques bearing the name of Beattie and Cornell, a contracting company offshoot of the Beattie family quarries.

On February 8th, 1872, during the height of the city's cotton mill building boom, Wm. & J. Beattie, Jr., Granite Dealers & Contractors sent the Troy Mill Co. a bill. Itemized on that invoice were: granite window sills, belting, iron clamps, use of tools, and of course, labor for cutting and fitting the stone. The bill totaled $8,600. It was quite an order—in today's dollars it would be valued at about $150,000.

William Beattie purchased a burial plot on a high knoll in Oak Grove Cemetery overlooking his adjacent quarry. Naturally, his wish was to have a large monument of polished granite as his memorial. There was one problem. For all its strength, hardness, and impervious durability, Fall River pink granite refuses to be polished. Nevertheless, William Beattie, the Granite King of Fall River, got his highly polished headstone—made of Quincy granite.

June 21, 2011
Fall River, Massachusetts

3.2.1 Quarrymen at Beattie's Ledge, Fall River, during the late-nineteenth century. The seemingly limitless supply of granite, which forms the city's foundation, furnished an ideal building material for the textile mills of the "Spindle City," as well as countless other structures throughout New England and beyond.

3.2.2 *Chateau-Sur-Mer* was constructed in the fashionable seaside resort of Newport, Rhode Island, in 1852, for William Shepard Wetmore (1801-1862); originally designed in the Italianate style, the mansion was constructed of Fall River granite. In the 1870s, William's son and heir, George Peabody Wetmore (1846-1921), hired renowned society architect Richard Morris Hunt (1827-1895) to redesign the mansion in the French Second Empire style, once again using Fall River granite, finished to match the original structure. George P. Wetmore had a personal connection to Fall River, having been a close friend and traveling companion of Fall River's wealthiest resident, Bradford Matthew Chaloner Durfee (1843-1872), who was known to have spent considerable time in Newport.

3.2.3 Sagamore Mill No. 2, Fall River. Unlike the vast majority of Fall River's textile mills, this structure was constructed in 1872-1873 using stone from the Assonet Ledge in nearby Assonet, Massachusetts, transported to the site at 1822 North Main Street by rail.

3.2.4 A scene on Fourth Street, Fall River, from Hartwell to Pleasant Streets, taken in the 1920s, showing an expanse of cobblestone paved street. Fall River's bustling thoroughfares were once paved with miles of durable granite cobblestone. A section of sidewalk curbing, undoubtedly cut from Fall River granite, can be seen in the lower right corner of the image.

3.2.5 This bronze "Beattie & Cornell" plaque remained in situ on a Fall River "granolithic" sidewalk in 2011.

3.2.6 Advertisement for "Beattie & Cornell, General Building Construction" from the 1927 edition of the *Fall River Directory.* The firm was founded by William Henry Beattie (1864-1935) and George H. Cornell (1864-1943) in 1896 and remained in operation until 1932. In 1921, Michael Joseph Collins (1874-1941), a long-time employee, became a partner in the firm.

3.2.7 Invoice from "William & J. Beattie Jr." to Troy Cotton and Woolen Manufactory, February 8, 1872.

3.2.8 Monument erected to the memory of William Beattie (1829-1915) in Oak Grove Cemetery, Fall River. The city's so-called "Granite King" was interred beneath a memorial carved from highly-polished granite quarried in Quincy, Massachusetts, as opposed to the Fall River granite of which he sold vast quantities: the latter refused to take a polish, making it unsuitable for cemetery markers.

OFFICES

In its textile heyday, Fall River was home to over one-hundred-and-ten cotton mills, approximately two-thirds of which were constructed of native Fall River granite. But whether granite or brick, the city's historic monuments to its former textile supremacy embodied singular features.

Often built with stone quarried on-site, many of these monoliths have basements two and three stories deep. More than a few have attached bell towers, useful as stairwells and for hoisting heavy loads to upper floors. Several mills featured distinctive flare-top chimneys, one prominent example of which survives—albeit marred by cellphone antennae—at the red brick former American Printing Company Mill No.7, on Anawan Street.

Not all mills had elaborate towers or fancy chimneys. Fall River's Foster H. Stafford who built his eponymous mills at the corner of Quarry and County Streets in 1870 wanted neither. Asked why his buildings didn't have towers as did many of his competitors, Stafford famously replied, "Towers don't pay dividends."

But Stafford did build an attractive, free-standing, red brick office building in the Romanesque style on County Street. Rather than an uncharacteristic indulgence in luxury by the tight textile titan, this building was a practical necessity.

Vibrations caused by heavy looms and other machinery were a constant problem for textile manufacturers. The mills themselves were designed to absorb the punishment with deeply driven foundations and ground floor walls between three and four feet thick. Unlike the buildings, the operatives had difficulty absorbing the punishment.

Fall River historian, Alfred J. Lima, describes the effect of these vibrations in his book, *A River and its City*: "The oscillation in the upper story of one Fall River Mill was four inches or more and once so alarmed the help that they left the building fearing for their lives. If filled within six or eight inches of the top, barrels of water in the top floor would spill over."

With vibration came noise, deafening noise. Sound levels in Fall River weave rooms regularly exceeded 100 decibels and it was virtually impossible to converse below a full shout. Partial loss of hearing was widespread among the operatives and total deafness was a commonly accepted price paid for long years of steady employment in the mills.

Combining this perpetual din with the heat, humidity, and airborne cotton dust, a grim picture of textile mill work emerges. It was estimated that one spinner in three died of respiratory disease before completing a decade of employment.

"It's hard to imagine anyone being able to concentrate on a telephone call or performing any kind of office work in those conditions," said Dennis Binette, Assistant Curator at the Fall River Historical Society. True, but like Foster Stafford, Fall River's mill owners found a simple expediency to solve this problem: detached office buildings.

Separated sometimes by only a few yards from the factories themselves, these small, sturdy structures, provided a clean, quiet, vibration-free environment for management, engineering, and clerical staffs. Such distancing added the advantage of shielding the company's vital records from the frequent fires, large and small, that plagued the operations buildings.

Often situated near the main gate of the complex, the offices controlled workforce, vendor, and visitor traffic. According to Curator Binette, these mostly two-story buildings incorporated lots of windows for light, usually situating office and clerical help on ground level and engineering and drafting personnel on the second floor.

Although several mill office buildings were demolished along with their factories, and some, like the King Philip Mills office on Kilburn Street recently destroyed by arson, many examples remain.

In addition to Stafford's management sinecure on County Street, other survivors include North Main Street's Sagamore Mills office, which was newly connected to the adjacent Mill No. 2 in the twentieth century, and the Narragansett Mill office with a separate gate and stairway leading to the "first floor," below street level.

Bay Street offers the yellow brick Algonquin Mills building (now a religious center and school), and the historic 1840 Oliver Chace Thread Mill. In 1867, Chace's building, once part of a much larger complex, became the headquarters of the Mount Hope Mills, and was renamed in 1880 for the successor Conanicut Mills. The two-story rubble-granite structure has now happily gone to the dogs (and cats presumably) serving as a pet service and supply store.

The Flint's Quequechan Valley Mills Historic District provides three detached buildings that depart from the usual two-story architecture more common to Fall River mill offices. These blocky, one-story examples may have been copied by the Germans attempting to defend the Normandy landings. Looking more like bunkers for gun emplacements, they served the Arkwright and Davis mills on Quequechan Street and the Flint Mills on Alden Street, at the foot of Jencks Street.

Arguably, the king of Fall River's detached offices is the two-and-one-half story Durfee-Union Mills building on Pleasant Street. This imposing granite structure sits front and center in the sprawling twelve building complex, restored by the Architectural Conservation Trust in 1983. These huge, unique buildings, once filled with vibration, noise, and cotton dust, live on in several medical, governmental, and commercial capacities.

Originally, just a practical solution to an unpleasant problem, these detached office buildings are symbolic of the class and wealth separation that existed between the city's mill barons and their operatives.

May 25, 2014
Fall River, Massachusetts

3.3.1 Quarrymen at an unidentified granite quarry in Fall River, circa early 1880s. In the photograph are John Lyons (c.1832-1888), seated in the top row, at the far left, wearing a hat, and his son, John P. Lyons (c.1857-1889), seated in the second row from the top, at the far left. Both men are identified in the *Fall River Directory* as "stonecutters," however the attire of John P. Lyons suggests that he may have been employed in a managerial capacity.

3.3.2 Construction workers at a Fall River mill site in the early-twentieth century; an unfinished granite wall is clearly visible behind the workmen.

3.3.3 Construction workers engaged in foundation work on the grounds of the Bourne Mills, Fall River, circa 1900.

3.3.4 Construction workers on the grounds of the Bourne Mills, Fall River, circa 1900.

3.3.5 Construction workers on the grounds of the Bourne Mills, Fall River, circa 1900.

3.3.6 The towering red brick chimney of the American Printing Company, June 28, 1890. The caption penned on the reverse of the image by its photographer, George Pitman Brown (1851-1920), was written sixteen years after the image was taken: "View taken in the forenoon from the pond side of the gas-works. The wooden bridge was replaced some fifteen years later by the present one (1906)."

3.3.7 Foster Hazard Stafford (1815-1891), who curtly avowed: "Towers don't pay dividends."

3.3.8 "Stafford Square, Showing Stafford Mills, Fall River, Mass." depicted in an early-twentieth century postcard; the office building, constructed of red brick, is strikingly situated in the mill yard, dominated by the granite factory walls.

3.3.9 Stafford Mills office building, 62 County Street, Fall River, as it appeared in 2014; the structure was constructed in 1896 in the Romanesque style.

3.3.10 Spooling Room in the Border City Mills, Fall River, in the 1890s: "With vibration came noise, deafening noise."

3.3.11 Weave Room in the Border City Mills, Fall River, in the 1890s: "Sound levels in Fall River weave rooms regularly exceeded 100 decibels and it was virtually impossible to converse below a full shout. Partial loss of hearing was widespread among the operatives and total deafness was a commonly accepted price paid for long years of steady employment in the mills."

3.3.12 Employees in the office of the Fall River Bleachery. Ella Eliza Griffiths (1884-1969), who was employed as a stenographer at the Bleachery from circa 1906 to 1915, is depicted at the far left of the photograph, seated at her typewriting machine.

3.3.13 Sagamore Mills office building, 1822 North Main Street, Fall River, as it appeared in 2014; the structure was constructed in 1884.

3.3.14 Narragansett Mills office building, 1567 North Main Street, Fall River, as it appeared in 2014; the structure was constructed in 1879.

3.3.15 The former Oliver Chace Thread Mill, 505 Bay Street, Fall River, as it appeared in 2014; the structure was constructed circa 1835. "In 1867, Chace's building, once part of a much larger complex, became the headquarters of the Mount Hope Mills, and was renamed in 1880 for the successor, Conanicut Mills."

3.3.16 The former Oliver Chace Thread Mill on Bay Street, Fall River, when it housed the offices of the Conanicut Mills in the early 1880s. The building has survived in a remarkably unaltered state, as is evidenced in the previous photograph.

3.3.17 Arkwright Mills office building on Quequechan Street, Fall River, as it appeared in 2014; the structure was constructed in 1903 in the Romanesque style, and resembles a "bunker for gun emplacements." The building was designed and constructed by Chauncey Howe Sears (1853-1925), a prominent Fall River architect and contractor who made a specialty of mill construction. To facilitate and expedite construction, he also owned and operated his own stone quarries.

3.3.18 Durfee-Union Mills office building on Pleasant Street, Fall River, as it appeared in 2014; the structure was constructed circa 1872 and is the most imposing of all the city's textile mill office buildings.

GRANITE MILL TRAGEDY

On the morning of September 19, 1874, workers on the upper floors of Fall River's Granite Mill No. 1 faced a desperate choice, either jump five stories to the ground, or be burned to death.

At a 2009, symposium held at Bristol Community College and sponsored by the Fall River Historical Society, Bridgewater State University Professor Philip T. Silvia Jr., and retired attorney Jay J. Lambert, Esq., presented a compelling review of the nineteenth-century relationship between capital and labor and the negligent conditions leading up to the tragic fire. The program was part of a series commemorating the 150th anniversary of the Massachusetts Superior Court System.

"In 1874 the typical mill family income was $555 annually," said Professor Silvia, "with fifty-five per cent of that going just to food." As a consequence, in post-Civil-War Fall River, it was common for children as young as eight years old to work in the city's forty-odd textile mills. "Humans were considered just a cog in the machinery," said Silvia. "Without child labor supplied through multiple family contracts," he added, "more than half of the city's families would have been below poverty level."

Although it was illegal to hire children under the age of fourteen, it was estimated that fully twenty-five per cent of the city's mill operatives were younger. "Many parents simply lied about their children's age and the law provided a meaningless penalty," noted Attorney Lambert. "Because of the mill owners' power, most cases were routinely dismissed by the courts," he added. "The family system forced mother, father, and children into the mills."

The day of the fire was a Saturday. Saturday work was popular with the operatives because, unlike weekdays, quitting time was a much earlier 3 p.m. On the fateful day, the Bedford Street mill was running a full shift.

The fire, believed to have been caused by friction generated sparks from a spinning machine that ignited waste cotton, broke out shortly before 7 p.m. on the fourth floor. These fires were relatively common and were usually extinguished quickly by workers dousing them with buckets of water kept at hand for the purpose.

This day would be different. According to the later coroner's report, "the water buckets were empty, and the fire hoses were dry." Finding the holes through which leather belting supplied power to the machines, the blaze quickly spread upwards to the fifth floor and the attic above. There were no fire escapes; the only exit was by the mill's center stair tower. Although most workers on the lower floors made their way to the street, because of smoke and flames in the tower, operatives on the upper floors were trapped.

According to newspaper reports of the day, "a crash of glass was heard" as panicked workers appeared at the windows of the upper floors. Fire department ladders were too short to reach much beyond the second floor. With the flames at their backs, the trapped workers, many of them women and children, took the fearful leap to the ground.

Despite the efforts of nearby residents who spread mattresses on the ground in an attempt to cushion the falls, the official toll was twenty-three dead and thirty-three injured. Later estimates would raise the count to forty dead and eighty injured, caused by both the fire itself and catastrophic injuries from jumping. On a rare happy note, one James Smith, age nine, survived when he landed on a mattress.

Said Attorney Lambert, "There were never any criminal or civil liability consequences as a result of the fire. Although the company paid for some of the funerals, any employees who sued were fired, forced out of their company-owned tenement, and blacklisted. According to Fall River legend," added Lambert, "mill owners bought up whatever photographs of the fire scene that they could find."

At the time of the Granite Mill tragedy, there were no meaningful laws to protect employees from workplace injury or fire. Nevertheless, the conflagration caused Fall River and New England mill owners to at least begin to address fire safety. Many mills began installing alarms and sprinkler systems, holding drills, and providing exterior fire escapes. In 1876, two years after the Granite Mill No. 1 disaster, Granite Mill No. 2 added fire escapes.

One injured survivor of the fire who did sue the company was Ellen Jones, a twenty-year-old operative. Although she won an initial judgment in the lower courts, her case was denied on appeal to the Massachusetts Supreme Judicial Court. In citing the case, Attorney Lambert pointed out that the court found that the empty water buckets and inoperable fire hoses "were a result of the negligence of fellow workers." According to the ruling, a company could not be held liable for Miss Jones' injuries in the same way that it could not be held liable for injuries sustained in a fist fight between two employees.

"From 1908 to 1912, famous photographer Lewis W. Hine toured the country to evoke sympathy for the anti-child labor movement," said Professor Silvia, "and many of his photographs had to do with the Fall River area." According to Silvia, it wasn't until about the same time of Hine's work that public policy and federal and state labor laws finally began to provide meaningful protection to the worker.

April 17, 2009
Fall River, Massachusetts

3.4.1 A scarce, original edition of "History of the Granite Mill Fire," published in Fall River in 1874.

THE GRANITE MILL FIRE. 17

THE DEAD AND WOUNDED.

DEAD.

Honora Coffee,
Catharine Connell,
Albert Fernly,
Ellen J. Hunter,
Arabella Keith,
Bridget Murphy,
Margaret Murphy,
Annie J. Smith,
James Smith,
James Turner,
Mary Healy.

Thomas Caveney,
Maggie Dillon,
Gertrude Gray,
Mary Haley,
Mary Lesondre,
Kate Murphy,
Frederick Portrais,
James Newton,
Victoria Warner,
Margaret Harrington,
(Two missing.)

WOUNDED.

Mary Burns,
Mary Brodeur,
Julia Coffee,
Annie Dailey,
Annie Healy,
Joanna Healy,
Catharine Harrington,
Ellen Hanley,
Joanna Hanley,
Margaret Lanergan,
James Mason,
Julia Mahoney,
Isabella Morehead,
Nancy Mullens,
Annie O'Brien,
Margaret Sullivan,

Hannah Stafford,
Margaret Sullivan,
Catharine Sullivan,
Catharine Smith,
Annie Twoney,
Margaret Twoney,
William Vinnecomb,
Delia Warner,
Mary Wriggley,
Bethiah Wordell,
Ellen Jones,
Delia Portrais,
John Brodeur,
Thomas Gibson,
Edson Keith,
Joseph Ramsbottom,

Annie Sullivan.
Four firemen were also slightly injured.
(The woman who jumped on a man was only injured, and not killed, as was stated on page 6.)

3

3.4.2 List of "The Dead and Wounded" from "History of the Granite Mill Fire."

3.4.3 Mrs. Joseph Freelove, née Roann R. Sanford (1830-1901), as she appeared in the early 1860s. A dedicated diarist, her commentary on the horrors of the Granite Mill fire furnish a compelling, first-hand account:

> The screams of the injured & groans of the dying & of all that had loved ones in the flames ... was sickening in the extreme; men, women & children, crying & running in the wildest confusion; I did not go around to the most heart rendering part of the scene, could see and hear enough at home. Heard the cries & screams saw them carried by, dead & dying. Most were killed instantly or shattered in a terrible way [*and*] a feeling of horror filled every heart.

THE PANIC—ESCAPING THROUGH THE WINDOWS.

3.4.4 "The Panic – Escaping Through the Windows," as depicted in *Harper's Weekly,* October 10, 1874.

3.4.5 "The Fall River Disaster – Great Fire and Loss of Life in the Print Works, Granite Mill No. 1 ... Finding the Bodies of the Victims," as depicted in *Frank Leslie's Illustrated Newspaper*, October 3, 1874.

3.4.6 "The Ruins of the Granite Mill," as depicted in *Harper's Weekly*, October 10, 1874.

3.4.7 View of the Granite Mill fire depicting the south side of the mill, from a point near the corner of Bedford and Robeson Streets.

3.4.8 Horrified spectators watching the Granite Mill fire.

3.4.9 View of the Granite Mill fire.

3.4.10 William Mason (1806-1892). A wealthy Fall River textile entrepreneur, he served as president of the Granite Mills at the time of the disastrous fire.

3.4.11 Ruins of the Granite Mill No. 1, taken from the Crescent Mills on *Eight Rod Way*. "A peculiar effect in the picture may be observed in the upper window at the left, near where most of the unfortunates perished. The charred roof-beams have fallen in such a way as to produce the picture of a perfect cross, which the photograph shows up with striking distinctness."

3.4.12 Detail of the previous photograph, showing "the picture of a perfect cross."

FALL RIVER'S WASHINGTON MONUMENT

His likeness graces currency, stamps, sculptures and paintings. Cities and states and bridges are named after him. The cornerstone of his 555-foot and $5^{1/8}$-inch monument in the Capital was laid in 1848 and, in 1934, his face was carved in stone on Mount Rushmore.

George Washington, farmer, soldier, statesman, and the father of our country, is surely the most recognizable of American icons. But we still have a hard time celebrating his birthday properly.

Based on the Julian calendar then in use in the British Colonies, Washington was born on February 11, 1731. When the Gregorian calendar was implemented by the British Calendar Act in 1752, those born between January 1st and March 25th had their birthdates moved forward one year and eleven days. By the stroke of a quill, twenty-one-year-old George instantly became twenty again, and forever after recognized his equivalent birthdate as February 22, 1732.

Americans had unofficially celebrated our first president's birthday, long before his death in 1799. In 1879, President Rutherford B. Hayes made it official by signing into law a bill adding February 22nd to the existing federal holidays of New Year's Day, Independence Day, Thanksgiving, and Christmas. Washington's Birthday had thus become the first federal holiday to recognize an individual's birthdate.

By 1968, strong support from both business and labor had urged congress to consider standardizing holiday observances to Mondays, thereby creating a three-day weekend.

In May of that year, the Congressional Record noted a three-point benefit package to Monday holidays directed specifically at families:

> Three-day holidays offer greater opportunities for families—especially those whose members may be widely separated—to get together. . . .

> The three-day span of leisure time . . . would allow our citizens greater participation in their hobbies as well as in educational and cultural activities.

Monday holidays would improve commercial and industrial production by minimizing midweek holiday interruptions of production schedules and reducing employee absenteeism before and after midweek holidays.

The implementation of the Uniform Monday Holiday Law in 1971 officially moved the observance of Washington's Birthday to the third Monday in February, meaning the observed holiday can never fall on Washington's actual birthday.

Contrary to popular belief, there is no federal holiday called "Presidents' Day." Although Congress created a uniform federal holiday law, it could not force a uniform holiday title agreement among the states. Although the states dutifully shifted their recognition of Washington's Birthday to the third Monday in February, many chose not to retain the federal title. One of the first was Texas, which shortly after the implementation of the 1971 law, renamed their state holiday President's Day.

In fact, Congress specifically ruled out changing the federal holiday name of Washington's Birthday to Presidents' Day while crafting the final bill.

"It was the collective judgment of the Committee on the Judiciary," stated Mr. William Moore McCulloch (R-Ohio), "that this [naming the day Presidents' Day] would be unwise. Certainly, not all Presidents are held in the same high esteem as the Father of our Country. There are many who are not inclined to pay their respects to certain Presidents."

Among others, the Committee members may have had in mind President Andrew Johnson who was impeached in 1868. But they were prescient concerning the 1974 resignation of Richard Nixon and the 1998 impeachment of William Jefferson Clinton.

Although as far as we know George Washington never slept in Fall River, he nevertheless has found a special place in the city. In 1942, amid the patriotic fervor of World War II, the Catholic school children of the Diocese of Fall River "collected their pennies" to finance the erection of what was then hailed as one of the most beautiful George Washington monuments in the nation.

Renowned sculptor Frederick Warren Allen, head of the Sculpture Department at the School of the Museum of Fine Arts, in Boston, Massachusetts, won a design contest judged by Bishop James E. Cassidy and the architectural firm of Maginnis & Walsh.

The monument, at the corner of Highland Avenue and New Boston Road, is carved from finely textured Deer Island granite, and features a centered heroic portrait bust of Washington atop a tapered pedestal. Curved benches extend outward ending in pedestals upon which sit a boy on the right and a girl on the left.

Allen himself carved the bust, while assistants following the sculptor's clay models worked on the rest. An adjustment to the figure of the boy became necessary when a defect was discovered in the granite. Amid much pomp and ceremony, the memorial was dedicated on July 4th, 1942.

Although the calendar may note next Monday, February 17th, [2014,] as Presidents'

Day, what we're officially celebrating is just one president's birthday, George Washington's.

February 9, 2014
Fall River, Massachusetts

3.5.1 Most Rev. James Edwin Cassidy (1869-1951), Bishop of the Diocese of Fall River, Massachusetts, 1934-1951.

3.5.2 Photograph that accompanied an article headed, "Beautiful Memorial to George Washington Dedicated Here," which appeared on the front page of the *Fall River Herald News*, July 6, 1942.

UNVEILING OF GEORGE WASHINGTON MEMORIAL: The memorial to George Washington, one of the finest in the land, was unveiled just as this picture was taken. The memorial – a bust of Washington atop a 16-foot granite shaft and the figures of a boy and girl at each end of two long seats – was unveiled by three boys and three girls from various parts of the diocese. They represented the donors, the Catholic children of the diocese. Chiseled in granite under the seats is the notation "Gift of the Catholic children of the Diocese of Fall River." Most Rev. James E. Cassidy, Bishop of Fall River, conceived the monument declaring, "Loved, honored, and ever held in sacred memory is and should be the name of the leader of the forces that won us freedom, the first President of the United States, the Father of Our Country, George Washington."

3.5.3 The caption on this 1940s postcard depicting the George Washington Memorial reads: "The memorial is a gift of the Catholic children of the Diocese of Fall River, Mass. It was dedicated July 4, 1942."

CHAPTER
FOUR

BARS, BREWERIES, AND TEMPERENCE

BARS

Like most gritty industrial cities, mid-twentieth-century Fall River had its share of working class bars, clubs, and taverns. In the late 1930s, recovering from the triple whammy of Prohibition, depression, and municipal bankruptcy, the city's watering holes gradually regained their place in the social and cultural fabric of daily life.

From the dine and dance nightclubs at the Narrows, to the bars dotting nearly every corner of Bedford and Pleasant Streets, to the scores of ethnic social clubs, it wasn't hard to get wet. Every neighborhood barroom had a ladies' entrance in the back, but until recent years only men went in through the front.

Although a few remain, most of Fall River's iconic saloons have long disappeared from life's ongoing pub-crawl. Many were taken out when the city was gutted by Routes 195 and 79. Still others have moved, morphed into restaurants, or become otherwise gentrified.

Bedford Street's recently closed Billy's Café may have been the quintessential example of the corner bar. Opened in 1934, only months after the Twenty-first Amendment washed away Prohibition, Billy's attracted a diverse clientele ranging from lawyers, to cops, to laborers and factory workers. With its pitchers of beer and signature Chouriço and Chips dish, the bar became club-like to an army of regulars. No formal membership required, just keep showing up.

Former regular and later bartender, Ron Berube, fondly remembers Billy's for its spirited discussions about politics and sports, the latter especially between Red Sox and Yankees fans. According to Berube, there was only one downside to Billy's dark paneled ambiance: the broom closet sized men's room with the original depression era plumbing. "I don't know how they ever got away with that for all these years," laughed Berube.

> "If I had to live my life over, I'd live over a saloon."
> —W.C. Fields.

In Fall River, especially in the Flint Section, many fulfilled Fields' dream. And if they didn't live over one, they probably lived near one. From the 1930s through the 1960s, depending on which year you took count, there were between twenty-five and thirty-five bars on or immediately adjacent to Bedford and Pleasant Streets alone.

Prior to World War II, an automobile was a luxury beyond the reach of most of Fall River's working class. If you lived any distance from your job, you took a bus. But when you left home heading for the saloon, you walked.

Luckily, there was no shortage of walkable bars available to denizens of the densely packed Flint neighborhoods. Beginning near Bogle Hill and strolling west there were, among others: the Green Lantern; the Beacon; the Webster; and the aptly, if unimaginatively, named East End Café.

Continuing toward downtown there was the Dover Club at Cash Street, the Strand Café at Mason Street, and the Canadian Club around the corner on Jencks Street, where you could shoot hoops on the second floor basketball court warmed by a pot belly stove.

Further along came the Mahogany, the Massasoit, and the Blue Bird at Stafford Square. Before attempting to cross Plymouth Avenue on foot, you could fortify yourself with a stiff one at the Crown Café. Although few arrests were made, in the old days the Flint would have been home to thousands of cases of WUI—Walking while Under the Influence.

One of the Flint's best loved neighborhood bars was the Pleasant Café, presumably named as much for its atmosphere as its address. Opened in the late 1940s on the corner of Quequechan Street, Antone Albernaz, and later his son Manuel, served the shot and a beer crowd from behind the twenty-foot-long mahogany bar until its closure in 1979.

As young boys, Manuel's sons, Richard and Robert, had clean-up chores at the café. "I could barely see over the bar when I started," recalls Richard. Robert, who later tended bar at the cafe, remembers his grandfather and father as sticklers for cleanliness. "They would hide pennies, nickels, and dimes in the corners," he chuckled. "If they were still there after we swept up, we'd catch hell."

Manuel Albernaz' brother Johnny, an early partner in the Pleasant Street operation, continued in the booze business, later owning and operating the King Philip Café at the corner of South Main and King Philip Streets. "It's now Mee Sum's Chinese restaurant," said Robert Albernaz, "and the bar area is still there just like when my uncle owned it."

The Lusitano Restaurant now occupies the site of another former King Philip Street bar, Harold Miller's Tic Toc Café, among the first bars in the city to feature a television set. Tic Toc regulars were known to play softball in the vacant lot across the street, often on Sunday mornings before the bar's "official" noon opening.

> "The difference between chirping out of turn and a faux pas depends
> on what kind of a bar you're in."
> —Wilson Mizner

One city bar where you wanted to keep a low profile, especially if you weren't a regular, was Pleasant Street's Ringside Café. Co-owned by onetime professional boxer Donald "Bobby" Chabot, the Ringside was an informal home to a stable of boxers including well-known local pros Gene LeBlanc and Bobby English.

"Those guys were pretty good," remembers octogenarian Ray "Red" Kitchen, a keen observer of the local fight scene in the 40s and 50s, "they fought some big names." LeBlanc, a lightweight, had a ring record of forty-nine wins (twenty-eight by knockout), thirty-eight losses, and three draws. Perhaps his highest profile fight was a 1950 loss to Connecticut's then undefeated Art Suffoletta, "The Stratford Windmill".

English, who also fought in the lightweight division, had fifty-four lifetime wins including three of five bouts vs. his friend LeBlanc, all fought at the Fall River Casino. Although he lost by knockout in the third round, English went big time in August, 1945, when he fought two-time featherweight World Champion Sandy Sadler in Providence.

With fight promoters keeping club fighters busy filling out undercards, there were no long layoffs between matches. In May of 1947, English fought no less than five times in New York, New Hampshire, Providence, and Fall River. "I don't know how they did it," laughed Kitchen, "they seemed to train on alcohol but they had a fight almost once a week."

Another thematic Fall River bar was Al Petrillo's Roma Café in the Academy Building. With an entrance on Second Street, the subterranean Roma may have been the city's first sports bar. A devoted Yankees fan, Petrillo regularly ran train and bus excursions to New York to see the Bronx Bombers as well as New England's original NFL team, the New York Football Giants.

In the halcyon days of Bobby Orr and the Big Bad Bruins, catching the game on Channel 38's weak UHF signal was no problem at the underground Roma. Petrillo had a special antenna installed high atop the Academy Building roof.

The Roma's Academy Building location had other advantages. In the 1960s when the Academy Theater switched to X-Rated films, patrons would often steal up the Roma's hidden back stairway to catch the show from the theater's balcony section.

"Don't drink at the hotel bar, that's where I do my drinking."
—Casey Stengel

In Post-Prohibition Fall River, through WW II, and well into the 1950s, *the* hotel bar in Fall River was at the Mellen. Billed as "Fall River's Leading Hotel," its stylish art deco style bar was a popular downtown stop after the theater or a movie. "Meet me at the Mellen" meant only one specific spot: the bar. Before the advent of dedicated function restaurants, everything from beauty pageants, to weddings, to graduation parties, were held at the Mellen. Having fallen upon hard times in the 1960s, the hotel closed and served as Fall River's city hall from 1962 until the 1970s completion of the new Government Center.

"Fortune knocks at every man's door once in a life, but in a good many cases the man is in a neighboring saloon and does not hear her."
—Mark Twain

There was at least one Fall River watering hole where fortune frequently knocked and was often heard. North Main Street's venerable Quequechan Club, formed in 1894 by a group of wealthy businessmen, was home to generations of Fall River's industrial, banking, and political movers and shakers.

At the turn of the twentieth century, the club served as a restaurant and banquet hall for male-only members, and it was not until the 1970s that women were permitted to enter the dining room unescorted. It's safe to say that many business deals large and small were consummated over cocktails and cigars at the private club's bars.

As Fall River's old style saloons disappear new versions are springing up to take their place. In addition to the resurgent Quequechan club, and Franklin Street's newly renovated Belmont Club, three new establishments have recently opened in the city. Jerry Remy's and the Red Cedar (succeeded by the Clique Bar in 2016) at Commonwealth Landing, and the Tipsy Toboggan on Ferry Street bring an exciting new vibrancy to the Fall River bar/restaurant scene.

As the city's corner bars near extinction, it's still easy to find your own corner at a Fall River bar.

February 15, 2012
Fall River, Massachusetts

4.1.1 The Rathskeller, 7 North Main Street, Fall River, 1934. The bar was established the year this photograph was taken, and was located in the basement of the Burke Building until 1943.

4.1.2 Manuel "Manny" Albernaz at the Pleasant Café.

4.1.3 The Circus Cocktail Lounge, 85 Bank Street, Fall River, 1957. The distinct neon sign, featuring a clown and seal performance, was apropos to the name of the establishment, which was in operation from 1955 to 1957. The painted "ghost sign," that is visible on the side of the structure, once advertised The Rathskeller, located at 7 North Main Street from 1934 to 1943.

4.1.4 Henry's Latin Quarter – Show Bar, 289 Central Street, Fall River, "In the Heart of Downtown," billed itself as the "Largest Show Bar in New England." The business name changed on three occasions, but always retained the "Latin Quarter" distinction: MacAndrade's Latin Quarter, from 1942-1944; Al & Billy's Latin Quarter, from 1945-1947; and finally, Henry's Latin Quarter, from 1949-1962.

4.1.5 Manuel "Manny" Albernaz tending bar at his Pleasant Café, circa 1950.

4.1.6 A boxing match at the Fall River Casino, 1936. The photograph is captioned: "Many of the men who have won the world's championships in boxing have fought in the Casino ring in Fall River. It is one of the most unusual rings in the country, being made entirely of rope and having no posts."

4.1.7 The Roma Café, 93 Second Street, on the corner of Pleasant Street, Fall River, 1970s; the café, which "may have been the city's first sports bar," was established in 1936 and was located in the iconic Academy Building, closing in 1977. By the 1960s, the Academy Theatre had switched from feature films to X-Rated films and café patrons "would often steal up the Roma's hidden back stairway to catch the show from the theatre's balcony section."

4.1.8 View of the south side of Pleasant Street, looking west, from Third Street, Fall River, 1962. The street was teeming with businesses, including a plethora of bars and cafes, ensuring that "it wasn't hard to get wet." The Yellowstone Café, at 45 Pleasant Street, can be seen in the center of the photograph; the café was in operation at the Pleasant Street location from 1951 to 1966, at which time it moved to Borden Street. The Roma Café was located just a few doors west, at the corner of Pleasant and Second Streets, in the Academy building, visible at the right of this image.

4.1.9 The New Wilbur Café, 31 Pocasset Street, Fall River, on the southeast corner of Second and Pocasset Streets, as it appeared in 1962; the establishment was in operation from 1934 to 1959. The building was originally used as a stable for the Pocasset House, a hotel on Main Street, which was built in 1833 and burned in the Great Fire of 1843. The structure was razed in 1962 to make way for the construction of Interstate 195. McDermott's Diner can be seen at the left of the image.

4.1.10 Hotel Mellen, 123 North Main Street, Fall River, 1927.

4.1.11 The recently renovated façade of the Hotel Mellen Grille, 1936. The photograph is captioned: "Up-to-the-minute designs in store fronts are to be found in all parts of Fall River."

4.1.12 The stately foyer of the Hotel Mellen, Fall River, 1936; the popular "Air-Conditioned Grille and Cocktail Lounge," called the Falcon Room, was located through the first door to the right. The grille could also be entered through an entrance on the corner of North Main and Franklin Streets.

4.1.13 This Hotel Mellen wine list also includes a wide variety of beer, cocktails, and liquor. Likely dating to the late 1930s or early 1940s, the menu was printed after the repeal of Prohibition by the 21st Amendment in 1933, at which time each state was allowed to set its own alcohol consumption law; most established the minimum legal drinking age at twenty-one.

4.1.14 The Falcon Room at the Hotel Mellen, 1936. The room was dominated by an oil-on-canvas mural depicting a bevy of slightly intoxicated medieval revelers, painted by Helen Doak Martin (born 1888); her murals were also featured elsewhere in the structure.

4.1.15 Spring Café, 314 Spring Street, Fall River, on the northeast corner of Spring and Pearl Streets, 1957; the café was in operation from 1934 to 1959. The structure was razed in 1962 to make way for the construction of Interstate 195.

4.1.16 This private residence at 34 Franklin Street became the Belmont Club in 1933, shortly after this photograph was taken. The back and south sides of the Hotel Mellen, and the north end of the Fall River Public Library can be seen at the left. The club is still in operation at this location in 2017.

BREWERIES

Last spring's monsoon rains caused heavy damage in many parts of the city, but in one case the flood helped unearth a piece of history.

The destruction along Mount Hope Avenue just east of Bay Street was particularly severe. In the aftermath, as workers dug a trench to replace a severed gas line to the nearby St. Anne's Fraternity, they were greeted with a surprise. Deep in the ditch glinted the butt-end of a seemingly intact bottle.

"Mike Rua and I were watching the excavation when all of a sudden this bottle appeared," said Fraternity Vice President Donald Arsenault. Rua, the club's President, grabbed a shovel and hopped into the dig to retrieve the find. "Mike carefully dug around it and finally out came what looked like a clear glass soda bottle," added Arsenault. "I originally was going after some colored glass next to it," said Rua, "but it turned out to be only a shard."

After a bit of cleaning and a closer examination the pair were surprised to discover that it was instead a beer bottle, embossed with the profile likeness of an Indian chief and the following nomenclature: *King Philip Brewing Co., Fall River Mass., Registered.* "I'd never even heard of the brand and I've been a beer drinker all my life," laughed Arsenault.

It's difficult to pin down the age of any antique bottle with absolute certainty. But before the turn of the twentieth century, most beer bottles were either brown or green glass and were usually hand blown. This bottle's clear glass, "champagne" shape, brand embossing, and perfectly round unmarked base, points to it being an early machine made example, probably between 1900 and 1910. And, as it turns out, the bottle is a link to Fall River's long-lost brewing industry.

In the latter half of the nineteenth century and well into the twentieth, most beer was dispensed from fifty-four gallon barrels called "hogsheads." Long before the concept of the package store, beer traveled from the brewery by horse drawn wagon to its primary retail outlet, the saloon. Because of the hills, Fall River breweries needed more horsepower, often employing three-horse teams on their wagons rather than the more common two-horse hitch used in other cities.

It's estimated that at the turn of the twentieth century, breweries controlled upwards of eighty per cent of American saloons. Typically, the brewery would finance the saloonkeeper, who in turn would agree to sell only his sponsor's brands. Besides the considerable amount of product consumed on premises, the neighborhood saloon was virtually the only source of beer available for home consumption. Although all manner of pitchers, pots, and jars, were dutifully filled and priced by the bartender, customers generally used tin pails called "growlers" to carry their beer home or even to their workplace for a lunchtime beverage.

Before 1910, there were three breweries in Fall River: Enterprise Brewing Company; Old Colony Brewing Company; and King Philip Brewing Company. In 1894, the original Enterprise Brewing Company began operations at 50 Glasgow Street, a couple of blocks from Brayton Avenue. Old Colony started production four years later at 866 Davol Street. Although King Philip's exact year of origin is unclear, its location was 17 Charles Street, just west of Bay Street, on the site now occupied by Gold Medal Bakery. It is thought to have begun operations circa 1900.

According to contemporary newspaper reports excerpted in Dr. Philip T. Silvia's *Victorian Vistas, Volume III,* King Philip Brewing held a public open house in the late summer of 1907 to showcase a newly installed bottling line. From a September 6, 1907, newspaper: "Half a dozen distinct machines, each one a marvel of mechanical ingenuity and each very costly, compose the bottling plant. It cost the company, complete, $40,000, and will turn out 18,000 bottles, filled with beer, capped and labeled in a day of 10 hours." A reported ten thousand visitors toured the brewery during the event, and according to the newspaper account, "With the eatables were served King Philip lager and ale specially brewed for the occasion."

In 1910, Old Colony Brewing acquired Enterprise Brewing and one year later added King Philip Brewing to the fold. The three consolidated Fall River breweries operated under the Old Colony name with headquarters at Davol Street until the advent of Prohibition. In 1920, like the rest of the country, Fall River's beer taps would be shut off—at least legally—for the next thirteen years.

With the repeal of Prohibition in 1933, the consolidated companies, now renamed Enterprise Brewing Company, resumed operations at the modernized and enlarged Davol Street plant near the bottom of President Avenue. Under the direction of its President, Adolf F. Haffenreffer, Sr., the suds again began to flow.

Although the brewery's flagship brands were Old Tap Ale and Bohemian (Boh) Lager Beer, the company brewed and marketed a number of ancillary labels such as Enterprise Bock Beer, Yankee Trader Beer, and White Seal Ale. Shortly after the brewery's restart in 1934, the King Philip brand was briefly resurrected with offerings of Ale, Beer, and Porter in bottles bearing the familiar Indian chief logo on paper labels. The brand was permanently retired in 1940.

Following World War II, and throughout the prosperous 1950s, the brewing business underwent significant changes. Local breweries, once the staple of the industry, faced increasing competition from regional and national brands with large advertising and marketing budgets—think Budweiser, Miller, Schlitz, Schaefer, etc.—an inevitable consolidation took place and few local and independent brewers survived.

Unable to remain profitable, Fall River's Enterprise Brewing ceased operations in 1963.

July 19, 2010
Fall River, Massachusetts

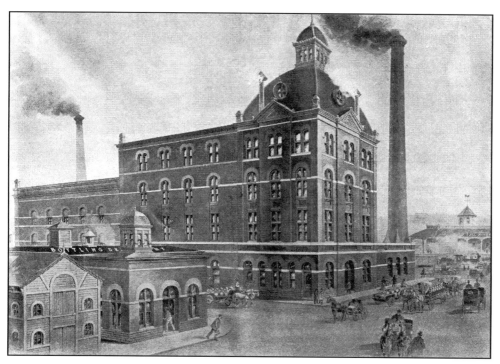

4.2.1 Old Colony Brewing Company, Fall River, 1896.

4.2.2 King Philip Brewery, Bay Street, Fall River, 1909.

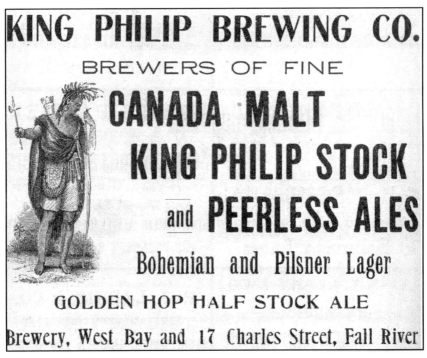

4.2.3 King Philip Brewery advertisement that appeared in the *Fall River Directory*, 1909.

4.2.4 Old Colony Brewing Company delivery wagon, 1890s.

4.2.5 Old Colony Brewing Company delivery van, 1920s.

4.2.6 The Enterprise Brewing Company, 883 Davol Street, Fall River, as it appeared in the early 1930s. The company maintained three addresses at its plant: an office at 866 Davol Street; a brewery at 883 Davol Street, and the Bottling Department at 81 President Avenue.

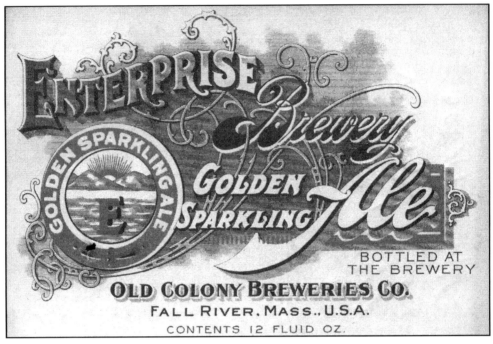

4.2.7 Golden Sparkling Ale label, Old Colony Brewing Company, Fall River, early-twentieth century.

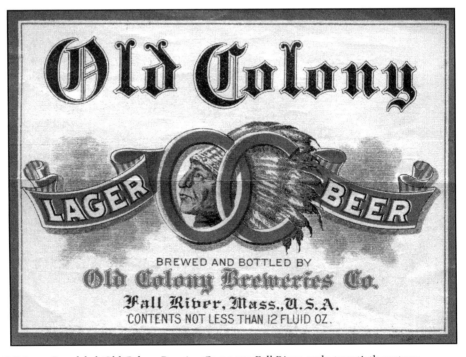

4.2.8 Lager Beer label, Old Colony Brewing Company, Fall River, early-twentieth century.

4.2.9 Old Tap Ale label, Enterprise Brewing Company, Fall River, circa 1937.

4.2.10 Clyde Cream Ale label, Enterprise Brewing Company, Fall River; the product was in production from circa 1934 to the 1950s.

4.2.11 A novelty label for Valentine Beer, Enterprise Brewing Company, Fall River, 1952; the "Rich, Mild and Mellow" product was distributed by the Sterling Beverage Company, Hamden, Connecticut.

PROHIBITION

President Woodrow Wilson advocated temperance over abstinence and enjoyed a "wee touch" of Scotch whiskey in the evening.

But in October of 1919, the United States Congress overrode the veto of America's twenty-eighth president and enacted the Eighteenth Amendment to the Constitution ushering in National Prohibition. On January 16, 1920, the country officially went dry.

Breweries, distilleries, and wineries all across America ceased normal operations and struggled to survive. Many distilleries acquired special "medicinal use" licenses and continued to operate at reduced volume. In the "Roaring Twenties," it helped to have a sympathetic doctor. It's estimated that for the duration of Prohibition, medicinal whisky prescriptions were written for over one million gallons annually.

Wineries with their own vineyards simply sold grapes and made grape juice. Other vintners resorted to making vinegar and altar wine. It was joked that Americans became more religious during prohibition as the demand for sacramental wines spiked upward.

Breweries, because of the sheer volume of their product, had a tougher time. Many simply switched to legal .05% alcohol "near beer" or sold yeast, a key ingredient for home brewing. Some beer makers simply went underground, often bribing officials to continue operating at lower levels. Larger brewers went into the real estate business, selling off their extensive holdings in prime location company-owned saloons to developers. Some, like Anheuser-Busch, even began making soft drinks.

In addition to wholesaling near beer, Fall River's Old Colony Brewing converted part of its Davol Street plant to a bonded warehouse and hired out its beer trucks for cartage hauling. Under the management of Adolf F. Haffenreffer Sr., the company also retrained a portion of its workforce and began manufacturing oil burners on site.

By the late 1920s, with state and local enforcement efforts waning, it was apparent that the "Noble Experiment" was a failure. In 1933, the Eighteenth Amendment became the first and only constitutional amendment ever to be repealed. On December 5th of that year, the nation once again went "wet" just in time for Christmas.

Of approximately 1,300 pre-Prohibition breweries nationwide, the former Old Colony Brewery was one of only 600 to resume production in 1933. Renamed the Enterprise Brewing Company, the Fall River beer maker rehired much of its former workforce and immediately restarted brewing operations. Under Mr. Haffenreffer's direction, the Davol Street plant was enlarged and modernized and was the first brewery in the United States to install then state of the art centrifugal refrigeration equipment.

At full operation in the early 1950s, the brewery's filling line was producing 100,000 containers per eight-hour shift—bottles and cans combined, the beer can having been introduced in the late 1930s. But by the early 1960s, intense marketing by the national mega-brands had taken its toll on sales of Enterprise stalwarts Old Tap Ale and Bohemian Beer. The resilient Fall River brewery had survived Washington's Prohibition only to be done in by New York's Madison Avenue.

Declining revenues and profits forced the Enterprise Brewing Company to permanently shut off its taps in 1963.

December 5, 2016
Fall River, Massachusetts

4.3.1 Pint of Milshire Dry Gin prescribed by Dr. William Edward Synan (1868-1931) to an unidentified patient for medicinal purposes, with instructions to take "as needed." The script was filled at the Mohican Drug Store, 2 North Main Street, Fall River, on August 6, 1925.

4.3.2 Pint of whiskey prescribed by Dr. Mary Wilbur Marvell (1871-1952) to her patient, Norman Salisbury Easton (1872-1957), for medicinal purposes. The fragmentary label indicates that the script was filled at Riddell's Pharmacy, 21 South Main Street, Fall River, on December 6, 1927. The fact that half the contents remain intact may well indicate that this whiskey was, indeed, used for medicinal purposes.

MAYHEM AND MURDER

Life in certain Fall River bars wasn't all merriment; often, there was mayhem, sometimes even murder. It's best to keep a low profile in a bar, especially if you're not a regular. There are legendary stories of alcohol-fueled brawls between members of different branches of the service home on leave during World War II, some of the most memorable at downtown's former Army-Navy café and the Narragansett Room.

Most of the time, the combatants left in a Paddy Wagon or an ambulance with nothing worse than a bloody nose or a black eye. But infrequently things turned deadly as was the case in two of the city's more infamous saloon homicides. In 1963, bartender Eugene Thibeault was murdered during a robbery at Padden's Café on Borden Street, and, in 1972, Thomas F. McCabe, himself the co-owner of a bar on Davol Street, was shot and killed in the Drake Hotel's Camelot Inn.

December 5, 2016
Fall River, Massachusetts

Gunmen Kill Thibeault In Cafe Robbery Here

4.4.1 Headline that appeared in the *Fall River Herald News* on December 28, 1963, reporting details of the murder of Eugene "Jean" Thibault at Padden's Café, 125 Borden Street, Fall River.

4.4.2 The Camelot Inn, 425 South Main Street, Fall River, as it appeared in 1980.

4.4.3 Advertisement for the Camelot Inn that appeared in the 1972 edition of the *Fall River City Directory.*

City Man Shot to Death After Hassle at Cafe

4.4.4 Headline that appeared in the *Fall River Herald News* on October 7, 1972, reporting details of the murder of Thomas F. McCabe Jr. at the Camelot Inn, 425 South Main Street, Fall River.

Temperance

The good doctor wanted Fall River to dry out, so he gave the city a fountain.

Dr. Henry Daniel Cogswell, dentist and temperance crusader, was born in Tolland, Connecticut, on March 3, 1820. Snared by the ubiquitous child labor system of the time, he worked in a cotton mill by day while pursuing his studies by night.

Eventually becoming a school teacher, in 1846 he married Caroline Richards, daughter of Ruel Richards, a wealthy Providence manufacturer. Dissatisfied with teaching, and still in his early twenties, Cogswell entered dental school. Completing his studies in 1847, he hung out his shingle in Pawtucket, Rhode Island.

In 1848, a carpenter helping to build a water-powered sawmill owned by John Sutter on the American River near Coloma, California, discovered gold flakes in the water. As news spread of the discovery, thousands of prospective gold miners set out by ship or wagon train to San Francisco and the surrounding area. In 1848, the non-native population of California numbered less than one thousand, by the end of 1849, that number had exceeded 100,000. Dr. Cogswell and his wife were among them, landing in San Francisco on October 12, 1849, following a 152 day voyage aboard the clipper ship *Susan G. Owens.*

The Cogswells never mined an ounce of gold themselves. Practicing dentistry for the miners instead, the doctor successfully speculated in mining stocks and invested in real estate. An innovator in his field, among other firsts, Cogswell pioneered the use of anesthetic chloroform in dental surgery. His practice, along with his investments, soon resulted in Cogswell becoming one of San Francisco's first millionaires in the day when a million meant something.

Financially secure, and no longer satisfied with just preaching temperance, Dr. Cogswell turned from dentistry to philanthropy. Believing that the availability of clean, cool drinking water from public fountains would deter the drinking man from the "evils of distilled liquors"; he resolved to erect one fountain for every one hundred saloons in the country.

In their book, *Parallel Lives: A Social History of Lizzie A. Borden and Her Fall River,* authors Michael Martins and Dennis A. Binette wrote: "In 1883, the philanthropist Henry Daniel Cogswell of San Francisco, California, a staunch advocate of temperance, found himself appalled by the large number of saloons and liquor retailers in Fall River; that year, 186 such establishments were listed in the city directory." Clearly, Fall

River more than qualified for one of Cogswell's fountains.

In a meeting with the Board of Aldermen on August 13, 1884, Dr. Cogswell offered to give the city a carved and polished granite fountain providing certain conditions were met: "Adopt and pay the cost of an ornamental lantern ($50) which is to surmount this [*fountain*] and keep same lighted whenever lights are required in the city." The city was also required to use Cogswell's method for cooling the water in warm weather which consisted of an ice box through which ran a series of coiled pipes. The city also agreed to supply the ice.

On October 4, 1884, the Cogswell Fountain was set in place at the corner of North Main and Market Streets, near the northwest corner of old City Hall. Dr. Cogswell's gift, no doubt aided greatly by the Fall River chapter of the Women's Christian Temperance Union, formed in 1883, may have had its desired effect. According to authors Martins and Binette, "By 1890, there were only sixty-five establishments in the city exclusive of 'Eating Houses' and hotels that served liquor."

During his lifetime, Cogswell donated thirty-one temperance fountains to cities throughout the country. Among the recipients were: Washington, D.C.; New York City; Boston; Pawtucket, Rhode Island; and of course, San Francisco. The elaborate structures were not always well received. Washington, D. C.'s version was once called "the city's ugliest statue." Many municipalities targeted for a fountain by Cogswell hurriedly established fine arts commissions to screen such gifts.

One Cogswell Fountain city, Rockville, Connecticut, took drastic action. "The Rockville city council was pleased to accept the donation, but once it got a look at the fountain, some townspeople had second thoughts," said town historian S. Ardis Abbott. The anti-alcohol sentiment didn't resonate with the residents who had recently voted against the town "going dry."

"There were something like thirty-three saloons in Rockville," Abbott said. "They were the social clubs of the working people. In the middle of the night one night, someone took down the statue and threw it into the lake."

Fall River's fountain flowed almost continuously until the coming of Route 195 and Government Center Plaza. It survives today—minus its lantern—mostly unnoticed at the northwest corner of North Main and Central Streets. Walk close to it, and you can hear the din of the interstate highway that displaced it. Unlike the many bars and restaurants that still dot the streets of Fall River, Dr. Cogswell's fountain has gone dry.

March 2, 2014
Fall River, Massachusetts

4.5.1 Dr. Henry Daniel Cogswell (1820-1900); this image was among the contents of the time capsule deposited in the base of the fountain in August, 1884. The ephemera and photographs placed in the time capsule are in the collection of the Fall River Historical Society.

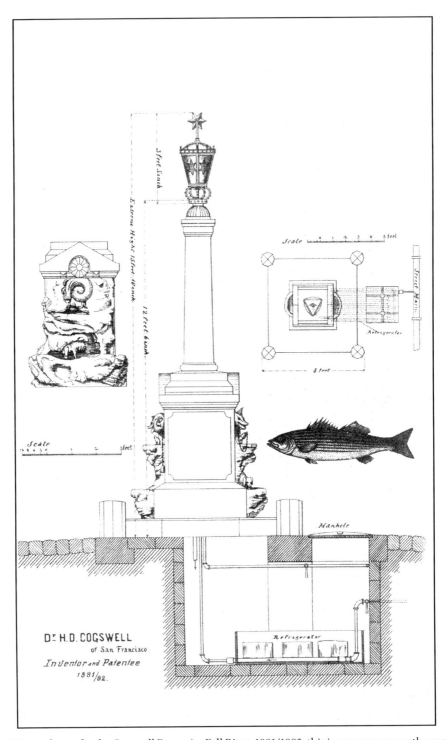

4.5.2 Patent design for the Cogswell Fountain, Fall River, 1881/1882; this image was among the contents of the time capsule deposited in the base of the fountain in August, 1884.

City of Fall River.
MAYOR'S OFFICE.

August 18th 1884

Dr. H. D. Coggswell.
Dear Sir:
We are anxiously awaiting the arrival of your fountain and cannot understand what causes the long delay. In this intensely hot weather it ought to be standing and to be in daily use.
Your draft was hurried nearly a week since. In my judgment the fountain should be located near City Hall.

Truly Yours
Milton Reed
Mayor.

Please hurry it along; we need it every day.

P. S. The above letter from the Mayor refers to the Ice Water Drinking [illegible] donated to the Citizens & Mill Operatives of City of Fall River Aug 15/84 by Dr Henry D. Cogswell

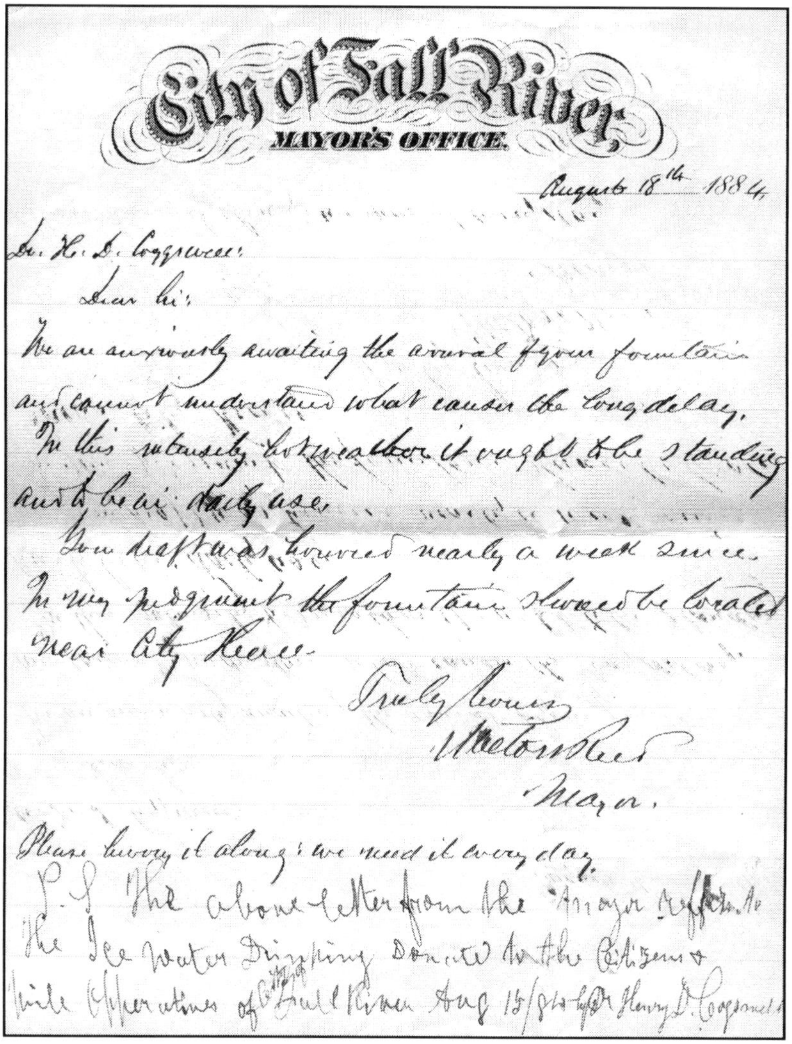

4.5.3 Letter sent by Hon. Milton Reed (1848-1932), mayor of Fall River, to Dr. Henry D. Cogswell, August 18, 1884; this was among the contents of the time capsule deposited in the base of the fountain in August, 1884.

> We are anxiously awaiting the arrival of your fountain and cannot understand what causes the long delay. In this intensely hot weather it ought to be standing and to be in daily use.
>
> Your draft was hurried nearly a week since. In my judgement the fountain should be located near City Hall.
>
> Please hurry it along; we need it every day.

A notation on the bottom of the letter, written by Dr. Cogswell reads:

> The above letter from the Mayor refers to the Ice Water Drinking [*Fountain*] donated to the Citizens & Mill Operatives of City of Fall River Aug 15/84 by Dr. Henry D. Cogswell.

4.5.4 The impressive City Hall, Fall River, 1891, showing the Cogswell Fountain in its original location.

4.5.5 The corner of North Main and Market Streets, Fall River, 1923, with the Cogswell Fountain depicted against a backdrop of automobiles.

4.5.6 The Cogswell Fountain as it appeared in 2014.

CHAPTER FIVE

NEIGHBORHOODS

French Street

As easy as reciting their ABCs, most Fall Riverites can tick off the city's major sections by rote: Border City, Corky Row, the Flint, The Globe, Maplewood, etc.

At the city's zenith as the center of American textile manufacturing during the late-19th and early-20th centuries, the engines of Fall River's enormous wealth, the operatives, lived in cramped, cold-water tenements crowded around the great brick and granite mills in these neighborhoods.

But the possessors of that wealth, the mill owners, lawyers, merchants, and bankers, mostly escaped the city's industrial grittiness by removing themselves to one area, The Highlands, then commonly known as "The Hill." Among the most fashionable streets for the Spindle City's Gaslight Era and post-Victorian affluent were High Street, Rock Street, and, of course, Highland Avenue itself.

On St. Patrick's Day, 1893, Robert Armstrong McWhirr, the founder of the city's iconic department store of the same name, died at the age of forty-three. Within months, the R.A. McWhirr Company was reorganized by a trio of long-term employees affectionately known by their entry-level, original titles: "The Three Cash Boys."

Only a few years later, McWhirrs' ruling triumvirate of President Asa A. Mills, Vice President James H. Mahoney, and Secretary Richard S. Thompson, were living within a half mile of each other in mansions at 851, 606, and 943 Highland Avenue, respectively. By Fall River standards, they had arrived.

But there was yet another street on The Hill that would become home to Fall River's famous and infamous: French Street.

One Lizbeth Andrew Borden had long desired to live on The Hill. Following her 1893 acquittal in the murders of her father and stepmother, Lizzie, along with her sister Emma, left the scene of the crime at 92 Second Street and took up residence in a newly purchased home on French Street. *Maplecroft* as it was later called, was a much larger and more spacious home.

According to *Parallel Lives: A Social History of Lizzie A. Borden and Her Fall River,* by Michael Martins and Dennis A. Binette (2010): "In place of an entrance foyer, the French Street house featured a sizeable hallway, with a high ceiling, natural finished woodwork, and a parquet floor, which gave the impression of a grand space; to the west, a staircase, with a built-in hallway bench, was illuminated by jewel-toned stained-glass windows and, to the east, a mantelpiece that featured elaborate brackets ornamented with applied decorative elements."

The populace surrounding the Borden sisters new home was almost as diverse as their old Second Street neighborhood only decidedly more affluent. With Lizzie's sensational trial still fresh in everyone's mind, many French Street residents had misgivings about their new neighbor. And although not as well-known as Lizzie, many were notable in their own right.

The resident of the large home a couple of blocks west at the corner of French and June Streets probably had no apprehensions about Lizzie's proximity. Atty. Andrew J. Jennings was a member of Lizzie's defense team at her recently concluded trial.

Well into the early-twentieth century, the French Street neighborhood would remain a comfortable enclave for some of the city's more prominent individuals and families. Although Emma Borden would vacate their French Street residence in 1905 after a falling-out with her sister, Lizzie would remain there until her death in 1927.

Here's a partial roster of Lizzie's 1920s neighbors near *Maplecroft*:

> Patrick J. Hurley, 132 French Street, president of Hurley and Brady, cotton brokers.

> Omer Elton Borden, 162 French Street, teller, Fall River Five Cents Savings Bank.

> Elizabeth J. McWhirr, 243 French Street, widow of Robert A. McWhirr, founder of McWhirr's Department Store.

> Everett Cook, 257 French Street, cashier, First National Bank.

> John T. Swift, 294 French Street, a police commissioner and treasurer of the Citizens Savings Bank.

> Emma Lake, 309 French Street, widow of Edward B. Lake, a partner in the wholesale grocery firm of Allen, Slade, & Company.

> Cyrus C. Rounseville, Jr., 364 French Street, the assistant treasurer of the Shove Mill.

And just two houses up toward Highland Avenue from Lizzie lived Phebe Davenport, widow of James Franklin Davenport who served as mayor of Fall River from 1874 to 1877.

Lizzie A. Borden died of heart disease at *Maplecroft* on June 1, 1927, just over a month shy of her sixty-seventh birthday. According to her instructions, she was laid out in the parlor of her French Street home. The Reverend Edmund James Cleveland of the Episcopal Church of the Ascension conducted a simple service at noon on

Saturday, June 4th. Lizzie is buried at her father's feet in the family plot in Fall River's Oak Grove Cemetery.

February 14, 2016
Fall River, Massachusetts

5.1.1 Robert Armstrong McWhirr (1849-1893) attired in the regalia of Chief of Clan McWhirr, circa 1890; he was "a prime mover in the organization," which was named in his honor. A native of Dumfriesshire, Scotland, he immigrated to the United States in 1873, and was the "founder of the city's iconic department store."

5.1.2 Residence constructed in 1889 for Charles Marion Allen (1852-1920), 306 French Street, Fall River, as it appeared in the mid-twentieth century. In 1893, the house was sold to Emma Lenora Borden (1851-1927) and her sister, Lizzie Andrew Borden (1860-1927), and by 1908 had been named *Maplecroft* by the latter.

5.1.3 A view on French Street, Fall River, looking east from High Street, circa 1900. The residence of the widowed Mrs. Robert Armstrong McWhirr, née Elizabeth J. Greggan (1856-1929), 243 French Street, can be seen on the right; the house was constructed in 1897. The residence of Benjamin Cook Sr. (1845-1914), 257 French Street, is visible next door, to the left.

5.1.4 Parlor in the residence of Benjamin Cook Sr., 257 French Street, Fall River, as it appeared in the 1890s; a granddaughter, born in the house in 1899, remembered the rooms as "very stuffy, very Victorian." The interior decoration was typical of the homes of the affluent in that fashionable neighborhood.

5.1.5 Residence of Edward Bennett Lake (1835-1913), 309 French Street, Fall River, shortly after its construction in 1891.

5.1.6 A view on French Street, looking west from Highland Avenue, Fall River, 1891. The residence of the widowed Mrs. Hon. James Franklin Davenport, née Phebe A.B. Ramsay (1833-1924), is the second on the right.

ALMOND STREET

Barring fire, flood, or the bad luck of blocking the way of a new six-lane interstate, neighborhoods are survivors.

Old buildings are razed, new ones are built, people come and go, but traditions and cultural landmarks endure. Having somewhat amorphous borders, neighborhoods defy precise geographical boundaries. But to paraphrase Supreme Court Justice Potter Stewart's famous 1964 pronouncement on a more controversial subject, I know one when I see one.

As easy as reciting their ABCs, most Fall Riverites can tick off the city's sections by rote: Border City, Corky Row, the Flint, the Globe, the Highlands, Maplewood, and so on. But within those relatively large areas are found the real lifeblood of the city—smaller more intimate, often nameless true neighborhoods. One such is what we'll call, simply, Almond Street.

Loosely bound by Ferry Street on the north, Broadway on the east, Kennedy Park on the south, and Mt. Hope Bay on the west, the area forms part of the larger Below-The-Hill section, and remains a working class enclave of mainly traditional two- and three-decker apartment houses.

In the latter part of the nineteenth century, and well into the twentieth, like a procession of ants, the neighborhood's denizens routinely trudged up to two miles round trip, six days a week, to the nearby factories and textile mills. To the north were the American Printing Company complex, the Metacomet Mill, and the Mechanics Mill. Close by to the south were the Wyoming Mills/Marshall Hat complex, the Laurel Lake Mills, and the Globe Yarn Mills.

As in other parts of the city, the Almond Street neighborhood saw an explosion in the construction of company-owned housing during the 1871-72 textile boom when twenty-two new mills were opened citywide. Although gradually transitioning from coal stoves, chamber pots, and outdoor privies—to oil stoves, running water, and indoor toilets—these workers' tenements would remain largely cold-water flats through the 1950s.

But, unlike many crowded tenement blocks, the neighborhood was blessed with the city's largest front yard. Designed in the late 1860s by famous landscape architect Frederick Law Olmsted, South Park—now Kennedy—provided a pastoral refuge for picnics, ball games, and band concerts. The vistas of Mount Hope Bay from the park's rubble-stone pavilion were as spectacular then as they are now, albeit with a few modern eyesores added.

Len Mendoza spent his childhood and teenage years on Almond Street in the 1950s and 60s, and remembers the park fondly. "Now the wading pond is tarred; in the old days it was a dirt bottom, no splashing allowed, but you could get frogs in the cracks around the edge. We'd ice skate in the winter—there were no floodlights—better for making out.

"In summer we'd make wood box cars using roller skates or wheels from old baby strollers. The axle was mounted to a steering board with bent over nails, and then we'd ride the contraption down the park road."

The Almond Street neighborhood with its Beach and Beacon Street components is not to be confused with its eponymous counterparts on the south side of the park. Along with Ash Street, South Almond, South Beach, and South Beacon, that neck of the woods was, ever so subtly, a different breed of cat. Although also a mainly working class neighborhood, the southern side had more single family homes and lacked the saloons, pool halls, and railroad yards found north of the park's natural green buffer zone.

Tommy Medeiros, a neighborhood wag who grew up on Division Street and owned a moving business on Almond Street in the 1970s, had a standard reply to anyone who confused the two areas: "We're not from the wrong side of the tracks, we're just from the wrong side of the park."

Like the popular 1950s TV show of the same name, a good part of the neighborhood was "Industry on Parade." Colliers and tugboat-guided coal barges regularly skirted the granite shoals guarded by Borden Flats Light on their way to Montaup Electric. Freighters of all types maneuvered close to shore to load and land cargo at the piers along Water Street.

In 1937, Firestone Rubber took over the American Print Works complex that now houses the Borden and Remington Company. Soon, huge latex carrying tankers, bearing exotic names and countries of registration, were regularly moored at the plant's dock, their looming sterns only a few yards from the corner of Almond and Ferry Streets.

Before the now departed Quaker Fabric, and until its closure in the late 1980s, Myer and Edwin Jaffe's, J & J Corrugated Box Company, near that same corner, provided steady employment for three generations of workers. On close summer days, the neighborhood even had its own special aroma courtesy of the Kormon Water bleach works on Howard Street.

But the neighborhood's true grittiness emanated from its signature industry, the Almond Street rail yards and roundhouse. In 1854, this was the southern terminus of the Old Colony Railroad, connecting passengers and freight from Boston and points north, to the Fall River Line steamers sailing south to New York.

During the Civil War, the tracks were extended to Newport, and, in 1893, both freight and passenger traffic surged when the line was leased by the New York, New Haven, and Hartford Railroad. For years this was a major marshalling yard where box cars were switched to form trains carrying "King Cotton" and other Fall River manufactured products to market.

Arguably, the Almond Street area was at its most vibrant in the decades spanning the 1940s through the 1960s. Beginning with the immediate post World War II years, the neighborhood grew to become a self-sufficient village with residents seldom having to leave its confines to satisfy the needs of everyday life.

In those pre-supermarket days there were four full-service family grocery stores within easy walking distance: Landry's and Mello's, on opposite corners of Almond and Division Streets; Marques, on the corner of Almond and William Streets; and Campos, on the corner of Division and Howard Streets. Orders telephoned in by housewives were dutifully delivered only hours later by "grocery boys" often pulling sack-filled red wagons behind them.

According to Len Mendoza, Landry's was patronized chiefly by the neighborhood's French Canadians; Mello's, whose proprietors lived above the store, mostly by the Portuguese families. "I worked for Campos Market delivering groceries in their '56 Chevy wagon even after I was married," remembers Mendoza.

Except to trudge to the mills, residents rarely had to leave the neighborhood. Prior to World War II, local boys received their first haircut from either Machado's Barber Shop on Division Street or Richy's Barber Shop on Almond. In addition to the four markets, there were two variety stores: Pat's on Division and Jimmy's on Almond. School children on their way to the Longfellow and St. Louis schools treasured Pat's for its seemingly boundless selection of penny candy. Jimmy's Variety, on the other hand, carried two staples for somewhat older children: Pennsy Pinky balls and loose cigarettes, three for a nickel.

Tony's Spa, at the bus-stop corner of Almond and William, was the pre-Dunkin Donuts answer to the neighborhood coffee shop. "I remember everybody talking about the Brinks Robbery at Tony's in the early 1950s," said Jimmy Tavares, retired owner of the former Jimmy's Texaco on the neighboring corner.

In a rite of passage, neighborhood teenagers graduated from playing the Gottlieb and Williams pinball machines at Tony's and moved south a couple of blocks to July's Pool Room on Division Street. There, they pretended to be more sophisticated by drinking Cokes and smoking cigarettes while playing nine-ball for nickels and dimes.

You could even buy a new car without venturing out of the neighborhood, as long as it was a Plymouth or a DeSoto. The dealership at the corner of Broadway and Bradford Avenue caused a neighborhood sensation in 1956 when it imported Hollywood movie star Aldo Ray for a promotional appearance.

Like a modern mall anchor store, Almond Street's Portuguese American Athletic Club was the neighborhood's mainstay institution. Although less than fifty yards from Division Street's competing Welcome Café, the PA Club, as everyone called it, was worlds apart. "It wasn't just a barroom it was a true club," said former president Don Mays, "it was like a second home."

Throughout the mid-twentieth century, the PAAC, as its name implied, sponsored everything from soccer teams, to volleyball teams, to baseball and softball nines. It even hosted an annual tug-of-war competition among area clubs. "In the 1970s we were one of the first clubs to install lights on our horseshoe pitch," added Mays proudly.

Ric Oliveira, who grew up on Eagle Street, remembers bringing his Columbia Street crew to the court behind the PA Club for home and home basketball games in the late 1950s. "It was an old concrete volleyball court with a single basket in the left hand corner—everybody had to learn to shoot from the right side," he laughed. "Our home court at the old Doran schoolyard wasn't much better," added Oliveira. "If you were shooting at the south goal you were going uphill, but at least we had two baskets."

In addition to the PA Club's lively subterranean bar—into which many a neighborhood housewife would send junior to fetch dad for supper—there was always something going on in the upstairs function hall. Wedding receptions, birthday parties, anniversary celebrations, and, of course, weekend dances. According to old-timers, there were even a couple of wakes held there in the pre-World War II days.

Food was an important part of the Club's culture. Members regularly donated their time to prepare Portuguese specialties priced at cost and served as workingman's lunches on weekdays. On weekends, the kitchen opened to the public and was renowned for its crab boils, at one time reputed to be the tastiest in the city.

Don Mays, a native of Connellsville, Pennsylvania, arrived in Fall River in 1952 as an electrician's mate aboard the destroyer USS Bristol, the first modern naval vessel to dock at the State Pier. "I still remember the juice running down my chin from my first chouriço sandwich," says Mays. "It was at the old Acoreana Club on Broadway, I never tasted anything so good."

True to its name, the PA Club's members were overwhelmingly of Azorean Portuguese extraction. Nonetheless, the club had a small but active Irish minority. In the late 1960s and early 1970s, Mays, along with George Boler, were the first two Irish Americans elected to the club's presidency. Bill Duffy, a native Dubliner, was the club's unofficial Irish mascot. Well into his eighties, Duffy lent a distinctly Irish presence to the club's marching contingent in the Santo Christo Feast processions, proudly wearing his Hibernian shawl and wielding his genuine blackthorn shillelagh.

Mays remembers posting volunteer members to serve overnight fire watches in the club's upstairs hall during religious vigils, guarding against the many votive candles starting a blaze. "The PA Club's members and regulars were always ready to pitch in, we were like a family," said Mays as he ticked off a melancholy litany of nicknames: "there was 'Alabama,' 'Frenchie,' 'Joe Pete,' 'Junior,' 'Tootsie,' 'Mousey,' and 'Wompy,' Almost everybody had a nickname."

Today the Portuguese American Athletic Club is no more. Dwindling membership combined with generational and cultural changes saw the club's fortunes gradually decline throughout the 1980s. An attempt in recent years to reinvent the location as yet another sports bar failed.

Gone also are the markets, the variety stores, the pool hall, and the Welcome Café. The Longfellow school has been replaced by the Frank B. Oliveira apartments. St. Louis Church is gone and the accompanying school stands empty. Tony's Spa has morphed into a "Quick Stop," and Campos grocery has become a convenience store.

Jimmy's Texaco is now an automobile repair shop and no longer sells gas.

Happily, the PA Club building has undergone a reincarnation of sorts since band members of the former Acoreana Club purchased the premises in 2005. Renamed The St. Cecelia Philharmonic Band, the club has gone back to its original Portuguese American roots and has returned vibrancy to the area. Along with its venerable Almond Street neighbor, Richy's Barber Shop, it is again a neighborhood institution as recognizable in the community as its predecessor club was in its mid-twentieth-century heyday.

The Almond Street neighborhood's two and three-deckers are still there, as are a new generation of residents who, albeit now mostly using automobiles, still come and go to work wherever they can find it. Gentrification, in the form of The Landing condominium complex and its adjacent marina, has replaced the bustling rail yards and the quaint Popeye-style fishing shacks that dotted the rocky shoreline along Almond and Bay Streets right up to the 1970s. Two new and popular bars have sprung up and are thriving: Almond Street's Tipsy Seagull, and the Tipsy Toboggan on Ferry Street.

If he were alive today, perhaps the late Tommy Medeiros would agree that the Almond Street neighborhood was no longer "on the wrong side of the park."

October 17, 2010
Fall River, Massachusetts

5.2.1 The Pavilion at South Park, Fall River, 1934.

5.2.2 Mount Hope Bay as seen from the Pavilion at South Park, Fall River, 1934; "the vistas ... were as spectacular then as they are now, albeit a few modern eyesores added."

5.2.3 A view on Almond Street, Fall River, showing the "three-deckers" typical of the neighborhood, 1988; the structures shown were constructed between 1890 and 1897.

5.2.4 Portuguese American Athletic Club, 293 Almond Street, Fall River, 1981; the club featured "a lively subterranean bar—into which many a neighborhood housewife would send junior to fetch dad for supper."

5.2.5 Portuguese American Athletic Club soccer team, 1933; Alvaro Joseph Candeias Jr. (1916-2006) is seated in the front row, second from the left.

RICHY'S BARBER SHOP

In 1878, Rutherford B. Hayes was President, the nation's first telephone exchange began operations, Thomas Edison patented the Gramophone, and a barber shop opened in Fall River.

Yes, there were plenty of barber shops in Fall River in 1878, but this one proved different; it's still there. In continuous operation for 132 years, the shop at 239 Almond Street is easily the oldest surviving institution of the neighborhood, and undoubtedly one of the oldest in the city.

According to proprietor David Candeias, his grandfather Joseph purchased the shop in 1907 and it's been in the family ever since. Although the original owner's name has been lost to history, he was apparently a frugal soul as evidenced from this story passed down to David from his father.

In the early 1900s, despite the presence of a large wood stove, customers would complain about the cold in the wintertime. Patrons were under strict orders from the irascible owner never to touch the stove; that was his job. One winter's day while the owner was distracted, a bold customer stole over to the barely flickering stove and opened the door. "He got a big surprise,' laughed Candeias. "The flicker was coming from a solitary candle perched on top of a coffee can."

David's late father, Alvaro, was an apprentice barber at age fourteen and fully licensed by the age of sixteen. In order to keep the shop running when he joined the Navy during World War II, he made a deal with a rival barber on neighboring Division Street. The competitor, remembered only as Mr. Machado, agreed to close his business and run the Candeais shop until Alvaro came home. In return, the caretaker barber was given a percentage of the profits and was hired as a full-time employee after the war.

In the early years of the twentieth century, the Candeias barber shop featured six chairs, manned by four barbers. "Shaving was a big part of barbering back then," said Candeias. "While four customers were being attended, two more would be sitting in the remaining chairs, faces draped with hot towels softening their beards."

Although King C. Gillette patented the safety razor in 1904, it wasn't until advances in making strip steel for blades that home shaving began to grow. During World War I, Gillette obtained a contract with the Army to equip every Doughboy going "over there" with his razor. "After the boys came back, "said Candeias, "barber shop shaving slowly began to decline and it's almost unheard of today."

Somewhere along the way, Alvaro Candeias acquired the nickname "Richy." Nobody can remember how or why. But from the 1940s on "Richy's Barber Shop" became the Almond Street neighborhood's answer to the nineteenth-century general store; everybody went there, including moms and dads bringing sons for first haircuts.

"I have four regular customers in their nineties, and several more in their eighties," says the third generation Candeias. "Two old timers remember getting their first haircuts here in the 1930s."

Today's Richy's is a sequential time capsule of memorabilia spanning the decades. There's an 1890s pressed tin ceiling, a collection of antique hair tonic bottles, vintage advertising posters from the 1950s, and a montage of photos of family, friends, and customers dating back to the 1920s. There is no television in the shop, only an eclectic selection of magazines and fresh morning newspapers every day.

Although a licensed barber, David Candeias is also a retiree of the Fall River School Department. Nowadays, he opens the shop only four days a week, Tuesday through Friday. "I don't need to, but I enjoy it," he says. "This place has been here a long time and it's nice to keep it going."

October 17, 2010
Fall River, Massachusetts

5.3.1 Richy's Barber Shop, 239 Almond Street, Fall River, as it appeared in the 1980s.

5.3.2 Alvaro José "Joseph" Candeias, Sr. (1876-1942), standing, left, at work in his barber shop, circa 1920; his son, Manuel Joseph Candeias (1907-1972), is standing to his right.

5.3.3 Alvaro Joseph Candeias, Jr. (1916-2006) in a snapshot taken outside the barber shop, 1940s.

5.3.4 David Candeias; the third generation barber at work in 2010.

LEEMINGVILLE

In a neighborhood in Fall River's Highlands, a mysterious symbol repeatedly appears over the front doors of homes. Differing in size only, the distinctive architectural embellishment is nearly always the same, resembling a sunrise with rays bursting forth from a half circle.

"No, it's not a sunburst," said Eldredge H. Leeming by telephone from his Vero Beach Florida home, "it's actually called a fan-transom." Leeming ought to know, it was his company that put them there.

A.H. Leeming & Sons, founded in 1892 by Eldredge's then twenty-five-year-old grandfather, Alfred Hearst Leeming, practically invented the neighborhood distinguished by its trademark "fan-transoms." To this day, residents and real estate agents alike refer to the quiet residential area as Leemingville.

Roughly bounded by Montgomery Street on the north, Eldridge on the east, Albany Street on the south, and Robeson Street on the west, the Leemingville tract purchased in 1920 is almost entirely comprised of single family residences. Not only did the Leeming family build most of the homes in their namesake neighborhood, they lived there as well. "I have nothing but fond memories of Montgomery Street," said Leeming, "we had a great group of neighbors and a wonderful time socializing with our friends."

Curiously, Leemingville's Eldridge Street was misspelled by the city upon acceptance, substituting an "i" for the middle "e" and was not, as one might suspect, named after Eldredge Leeming. "No, it was actually named after my grandmother, Susan Eldredge Peckham," said Leeming.

Another Fall River street with Leeming development influence is Renwood. "They took the last syllable of both my uncle Warren's and my Father Elwood's names and came up with Renwood," laughed Leeming.

The family's Fall River roots trace to Eldredge's great-grandfather, Richard Leeming and his wife Elizabeth, who emigrated from Manchester, England, with the infant Alfred in 1869. Richard found work as an overseer in the city's cotton mills and young Alfred later attended the city's public schools.

In 1885, then seventeen-year-old Alfred was apprenticed to Nathaniel Ford a carpenter, remaining with him for five years. He later became a journeyman for the construction firm owned by Evan Brownell, eventually purchasing the company and laying the foundation for A. H. Leeming & Sons. "Mr. Brownell was in failing health," said Eldredge Leeming, "and he told his wife that she should sell the company to 'that nice young Alfred Leeming fellow.'"

The company survived the depression of 1893 and, by 1897, had participated in the construction of over three hundred buildings. By 1920, A.H. Leeming & Sons— Preston, Warren, and Eldredge's father, Elwood—had grown to over two hundred employees comprising every building trade except plumbing and electrical.

The company was not limited to residential construction. The firm also acted as general contractor for such area landmarks as Swansea's Stevens Home for Boys, the International Garment Workers building on Third Street, and the Hector Belisle School.

In the 1930s, following the decline of the city's textile industry, Alfred H. Leeming augmented his construction business with a sister company called Leeming Realty. The new company's first major project was the purchase and rehabilitation of an empty block of former mill housing on Rodman Street. Leeming Realty continued to purchase and refurbish several buildings in the city including three apartment houses on Winter Street and a parcel on Pine Street near Main.

In 1933, Preston Leeming acquired ownership of the company's Providence, Rhode Island, branch where he continued in residential construction including development in that city's fashionable Blackstone Boulevard area.

In the early 1930s, a connection between A.H. Leeming & Sons and Fall River's infamous Lizzie Borden came to light. Although Miss Borden had died in 1927, a dispute over the disposition of the so-called Henry House, a property just to the east of her *Maplecroft* residence on French Street, had prolonged the probate accounting of her will for several years.

Probate court documents recorded in the years between 1931 and 1933 reveal that, among others, Lizzie had the following debts outstanding at the time of her June 1, 1927, death: A.H. Leeming, carpenter $2317.95; A.H. Leeming, lock $4.35; A.H. Leeming, repair to roof of Henry property $109.95. By order of the probate court, by 1933 A.H. Leeming & Sons had received payment in full for this work.

Long-time Leemingville resident Helen (Carey) Kirkman, who was a year ahead of Eldredge Leeming at B.M.C. Durfee High School, remembers him well. "He was a good-looking fellow," said Mrs. Kirkman, whose Goddard Street home sports a prime example of the Leeming Company's trademark fan transom.

Following his 1941 graduation from Durfee, Leeming began his engineering studies at Massachusetts Institute of Technology. But, as with so many of his classmates, World War II intervened. As a navy pilot, he soon found himself flying combat sorties off the deck of the Casablanca class escort carrier *Petrof Bay* (CVE 80). Affectionately known as "Double 40" by the men who served on her, the *Petrof Bay* saw considerable action against the Japanese in the South Pacific, including the invasion of Iwo Jima.

After the war, Leeming returned to M.I.T., completing his studies in 1948. After a short-lived foray into modular home construction, he found that he "was not impressed with the quality [*of materials*] from the factory," and received the blessing from his father to begin bidding on public general contracting projects for the company's Bank Street mill.

Soon, Leeming began concentrating on private work and the mill quickly became too small for the contracts he was handling. In 1957, having taken over the A.H. Leeming & Sons corporate name, he bought a former Fall River Bleachery building off Jefferson Street. Putting several additions on the site in succeeding years, Leeming and his craftsmen produced the high quality millwork for which the company became famous. "I had a very happy experience until I sold the business in 1983," said Leeming.

The 102-year-old company, renowned for its warm and lustrous woodwork adorning the interiors of universities, private secondary schools, hospitals, churches, banks, and office buildings, closed its doors in 1994.

"It was a darn good business, I enjoyed it," said Leeming, now eighty-eight years old, "I had a lot of very talented people working for me which is always fun." Leeming still sees some of his former employees every summer on an annual trip to Fall River to take the men and their wives to lunch. "We're down to about a dozen now," said Leeming, "but we laugh, have a beer or two together, and really enjoy ourselves."

"Oh, by the way," added Leeming, the M.I.T. engineer, "not all of the fan transoms were half-circles, some were elliptical."

Note: A special note of thanks to former Leemingville residents Sayre and Roseanne Litchman for their remembrances and research that sparked this article.

February 13, 2012
Fall River, Massachusetts

5.4.1 The first advertisement for the firm that became A. H. Leeming & Sons that appeared in the 1893 edition of the *Fall River Directory.* Leeming and Jones, was founded in 1892 by Alfred Hearst Leeming (1867-1952) and John G. Jones (1847-1912); the firm disbanded circa 1901.

SCHEDULE B.

Showing payments, charges, losses and distributions.

1	Ellen Miller, salary	$180.00
2	J. Pemberton "	50.00
3	Ernest Terry "	2380.00
4	Cash for house	135.00
5	Travel, lunches and telephone	7.00
6	Standard Oil, gasoline	425.01
7	Fall River Elec. Lt. Co.	94.31
8	Fall River Gas Co.	796.34
9	N. E. Tel. & Tel. Co.	33.90
10	Water bills	25.21
11	J. E. Winward & Co. undertaker	895.70
12	Potter & Earle, electricians on contract	
13	J. Frier, painting contract	
14	Reed	31.00
15	H. Sears	24.45
16	E. J. Sokoll, cake, etc.	2.60
17	Frigidaire Corp.	7.50
18	Dr. Weeks, dentist	12.00
19	L. Drape market	2.73
20	Quality Market	27.28
21	A. H. Leeming, carpenter	2317.95
22	William Kennedy, plumbing	2181.68
23	J. Deane, groceries	5.25
24	Reed's Tire Shop	8.50
25	J. E. McMahon, masonry	65.60
26	Geo. Pollard, auto repairs	1.10
27	Jordan Marsh Co., mdse.	1.50
28	Reed's	4.00
29	Lawson Granite & Marble Works	80.00
30	D. T. Wilcox	12.80
31	H. Sears, care of lawns, etc.	11.47
32	Staples Coal Co.	57.80

5.4.2 Detail from Schedule B, estate of Lizzie Andrew Borden (1860-1927), listing "Payments, Charges, Losses and Distributions," June 17, 1929, showing debt of $2317.95 due to "A. H. Leeming, carpenter."

5.4.3 Elwood Peckham Leeming (1892-1965).

5.4.4 A view taken in Leemingville, Fall River, 1936.

5.4.5 Eldredge H. Leeming, 1944.

5.4.6 The employees of A. H. Leeming & Sons, Inc. assembled outside the corporate offices and mill, 994 Jefferson Street, Fall River, in the 1970s.

5.4.7 Interior view of the A. H. Leeming & Sons, Inc. mill as it appeared in the 1970s.

5.4.8 An example of the ubiquitous architectural "fan transom" as seen throughout Fall River's Leemingville neighborhood.

A. H. Leeming & Sons Go To Yale

Beginning in the late 1950s, working out of the new Jefferson Street mill, A. H. Leeming & Sons under Eldredge Leeming created architectural woodwork for the interiors of many well-known buildings. Among the prestigious clients were New York's Shea Stadium, The Bank of Boston, Putnam Investments, and Providence, Rhode Island's Fleet National Bank.

"Although it wasn't the largest job we did," said Leeming, "one of the most interesting was one that we did for Yale University."

As Leeming tells it, Pittsburgh industrialist, financier, and philanthropist, Paul Mellon, a Yale alumnus, had a large collection of British art valued at $13 million and was looking for a place to put it. Kingman Brewster, Yale's president in the mid 1970s, agreed to take the collection if Mellon would donate a building to house it. Mellon agreed to finance a building for $13 million, the value of the collection.

To design the building, Mellon hired the world renowned architect Louis Kahn of Philadelphia. "We were called in early in the budgeting process, " said Leeming, "but Kahn's initial figure of $18 million was too high and a lot of things were cut out including some of our woodwork to get it down to $13 million."

On the final drawings that Kahn created, the building was named the Mellon British Art Center at Yale. As Leeming remembers it, President Brewster told Mellon that if he wanted his name on the building he'd also have to establish a perpetual care fund equal to the value of the building. "So here's Mellon giving $13 million worth of art, $13 million worth of building and they want another $13 million to have his name on the building," laughed Leeming.

According to Leeming, Mellon told Brewster that he would like to have his name on the building, mentioned that his father Andrew's name was on the National Gallery in Washington, but replied that he'd have to think about it. "About two or three weeks later," remembers Leeming, "an envelope arrived on Brewster's desk containing a cashier's check for $13 million with a note from Mellon saying he'd like the building to be known as The Yale Center for British Art, period."

"That," said Leeming, "was the ultimate in one-upsmanship."

Leeming remembers that ultimately much of the woodwork that had been omitted in reducing the budget was later restored because Mrs. Mellon wanted it that way. "It wasn't the largest contract we ever had," said Leeming, "but it was the building that gave me the most pleasure."

February 13, 2012
Fall River, Massachusetts

5.5.1 Paul Mellon (1907-1999), "Pittsburg industrialist, financier, and philanthropist."

5.5.2 The Yale Center for British Art, New Haven, Connecticut. "It wasn't the largest contract we ever had, but it was the building that gave me the most pleasure."

CHAPTER SIX

NATURE AND THE OLMSTEADS

COPICUT

Fall River has long been associated with the Wampanoag Indian word Quequechan, or "falling water." But the native Wampanoags had a second word for the area, Copicut, or "deep, dark woods."

Situated in the northeastern corner of the city, the 516-acre Copicut Woods is the southern gateway to the vast wilderness that is the 13,600 acre Southeastern Massachusetts Bioreserve. The area is managed by The Trustees of Reservations. Founded in 1891, the group is a member supported non-profit conservation organization, whose mission is to preserve for public use properties of scenic, historic, and ecological value in Massachusetts.

Once used by the native Wampanoag Tribe as a winter hunting ground and as a route between their settlements on Buzzards Bay and the Taunton River, this network of forests, streams, and swamps is one of the largest protected and unfragmented tracts in the Commonwealth. It comprises the Freetown-Fall River State Forest, the City of Fall River watershed, and 4,000 acres formerly owned by the Acushnet Sawmill Company within the contiguous communities of Fall River, Freetown, and Dartmouth.

In celebration of Biodiversity Day 2008, The Trustees of Reservations sponsored a June 7th nature walk guided by naturalist Linton Harrington, the group's Bioreserve Outreach and Education Coordinator. "Over the past eight years, Biodiversity Day has become a tradition across Massachusetts," Harrington said. "It's an opportunity for the curious of all ages to discover, or rediscover, the amazing creatures that live nearby—birds, trees, mosses, and ferns, furry animals, insects, mushrooms, and even some reptiles and amphibians. Because the Bioreserve is the largest unbroken forest in this area, it supports interior forest species that aren't found anywhere else," he added.

Leading a group of visitors along Copicut's Shockley Trail, Harrington identified various shrubs and trees ranging from Blackberry and Pepper bushes, to Sassafras and Witch Hazel plants. Pointing out a rare American chestnut tree, Harrington explained how blight practically wiped out the native species and described ongoing attempts to revive the population through grafting with blight-resistant Chinese Chestnuts.

Passing a vernal pool—shallow ponds created by spring rains—Harrington's trained eye spotted a green frog peering up at him from just below the surface. With a deft flick of a net, the amphibian was soon housed in a plastic viewing case for closer inspection by the group. In addition to various species of frogs, Harrington explained that these pools are also home to the area's endangered four-toed salamander.

"Wetlands form an important natural defense against flooding," Harrington said as he carved a small but lush green patch of moss from the forest floor, "this can hold forty times its weight in water."

Harrington, who holds a master's degree in environmental education, intrigued the participants by capturing various insects for close-up observation in his magnified viewing box. Among the temporary detainees were a fierce looking—up close, anyway—Wolf Spider and a relatively rare Azure Butterfly.

In addition to blueberry and raspberry bushes, the Naturalist identified and offered tastes of some less known edible flora. The group sampled Indian Cucumber Root, and a mushroom called Chicken of the Woods. Guess what? They tasted just like cucumber and chicken!

Copicut Woods offers miles of hiking trails and footpaths leading through the property and into the greater bioreserve. With winter snow cover, the relatively flat terrain and broad trails are ideal for cross-country skiing and snowshoeing. "Most people have no idea that the Woods are open to public access," said Harrington, "we're trying to raise awareness so that more visitors will come to this beautiful place."

June 9, 2008
Fall River, Massachusetts

6.1.1 An aerial view of Copicut, Fall River, Massachusetts, 1971. "Situated in the northeastern corner of the city, the 516-acre Copicut Woods is the southern gateway to the vast wilderness that is the 13,600 acre Southeastern Massachusetts Bioreserve."

6.1.2 "Bullock Murder Monument" in Copicut, 1930s. John Bullock (1816-1862), a New Bedford, Massachusetts, saloonkeeper was en route to Freetown with a delivery when he was robbed and murdered by Obed Reynolds (1845-1876), on June 19, 1862. The latter, a troubled seventeen-year-old, was intoxicated due to the effects of a mixture of liquor and gunpowder when he committed the crime. The marker documents a little-know aspect of Copicut history.

6.1.3 Linton Harrington, The Trustees of Reservations Bioreserve Outreach and Education Coordinator examines a Green Frog (*Lithobates clamitans*) with Joan O'Beirne.

6.1.4 The edible Chicken of the Woods (*Laetiporus sulphureus*) mushroom.

Winter Watershed Walk

Unlike hibernating woodchucks and brown bats, forty intrepid nature lovers were very much awake during their mid-winter walk through Fall River's Watuppa watershed.

Sponsored by The Trustees of Reservations, and led by the organization's Bioreserve Outreach & Education Coordinator, Linton Harrington, the January 16, 2010, excursion explored the forested shoreline of North Watuppa Pond, an area not normally open to the public. "For over one hundred years this area was closed to protect the city's drinking water supply," said Harrington. "For today's walk, we've received special permission from the Water Department."

Before setting out, the group was treated to a primer on the area's wildlife by naturalist Everett Castro of Green Futures. The stuffed and mounted groundhog he pulled from his bag looked so alive that many thought it was about to bolt back into the woods. Following up with pelts from a fisher cat and a snowshoe hare, Castro explained each animal's behavioral characteristics and their place in the Watuppa ecosystem. "As an old school teacher, I love 'Show and Tell,'" he quipped.

Winding through land once comprising the early-nineteenth-century Blossom Farm, the two-hour trek was punctuated by several stops during which Harrington and Castro offered informational nuggets on various flora and fauna. Referring to the many stone walls, Harrington explained that the now-forested landscape was once completely cleared for farming and grazing. "The walls were formed when the farmers cleared stones and boulders from the fields so the soil could be tilled," he said.

Spotting tracks of red squirrels in the snow, Harrington picked up a pine cone to illustrate how some species survive a seemingly barren winter. "They love to rip apart these cones to get at the seeds inside," he observed. "Although tiny, there are enough of them to make a meal." The group was surprised to learn that flying squirrels also inhabit the watershed. "You don't often see them because they're nocturnal," said Harrington, "I once knocked on the trunk of a hollowed out tree and about six of them glided off in different directions."

Harrington explained that although such animals as squirrels, rabbits, and chipmunks slow their activity during the winter, they are not "true hibernators. The brown bat and the woodchuck are true hibernators. They slow their heart rates to one or two beats and their respiration to only a couple of breaths per minute each," he added.

According to Harrington, many plants and trees in the watershed have medicinal properties. "Scratch the bark of the Black Birch and it smells like wintergreen," he said. "In fact it has similar properties to aspirin." Several of the group scratched away. He was right! "It's the tree's natural defense; if deer were to eat too much of it, they'd get an upset stomach." According to naturalist Castro, the tree was regularly tapped in spring by early settlers for Birch Beer.

All is not well with some of the area's native trees. The American chestnut (*castanea dentate*) and Hemlock are (*conium maculatum*) under attack by the Wooly Adelgid (*Adelges tsugae*), a parasite with no natural enemies. "Forests are always evolving," said Harrington. "Nature hates a void and these trees will be replaced by other species including hardwoods."

Continuing westward through the thicketed path, the group reached the Eastern Shore of North Watuppa, a view of the Pond not many people have seen. Looking across toward the city, not a single building could be spotted along the forested shoreline and beyond. In a sudden, almost reverential quiet, only the faint click of cameras could be heard. "This is how it must have looked to the native Wampanoags," someone remarked.

Note: The Trustees of Reservations was founded in 1891. The group is a member supported, non-profit, conservation organization whose mission is to preserve for public use properties of scenic, historic, and ecological value in Massachusetts.

For more information contact:
The Trustees of Reservations
508-679-2115
www.thetrustees.org

January 17, 2010
Fall River, Massachusetts

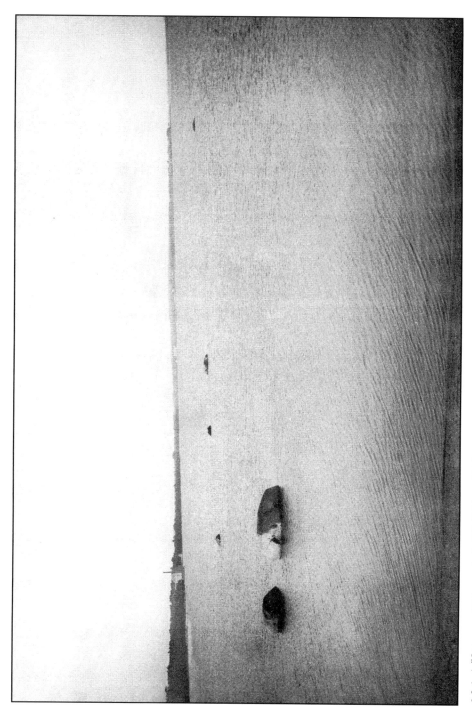

6.2.1 A "Scene on Watuppa Lake," Fall River, 1890.

6.2.2 A "Scene on Watuppa Lake," Fall River, 1890.

ICE

In the nineteenth and early-twentieth centuries, Fall River and surrounding towns eagerly looked forward to harvesting an annual winter crop – ice.

On January 10, 2015, The Trustees of Reservations, the Fall River Water Department, and Bristol Community College presented "Winterlachen," the history of ice harvesting on the Watuppa Ponds, to an overflow audience of history buffs. The program included a rare tour of North Watuppa's *Interlachen* Island and the remains of the Arctic Ice House and Spencer Borden estates.

"Ice was a valuable money crop," said local teacher and historian Bill Goncalo. "The product was basically free and with proper ventilation and drainage, ice would keep for up to two years."

It wasn't until the introduction of Freon in the 1920s that modern refrigeration began to take hold. After the material shortages of World War II were resolved, domestic units with freezer compartments began replacing the venerable but leaky ice box. By the late 1940s, frozen foods—or as the Birdseye brand called them, 'frosted' foods – once a luxury, became a staple in American homes.

According to Goncalo, before refrigeration, ice was also important to many Fall River businesses such as dairies, meat and fish markets. "At one time the city had three breweries and they all used ice to cool the yeast during production. The Fall River Line steamers were also big users of ice," added Goncalo. No doubt first-class passengers enjoyed their Martinis—newly invented in 1911—cold, whether shaken or stirred.

Ice farming usually took place once each winter when the ice was between eight inches and thirteen inches thick. In exceedingly cold winters, there was occasionally a second harvest limited by the amount of storage space remaining in the ice houses.

"The harvest itself was an exercise in geometric precision," said Goncalo. The process began by marking the ice surface in a large grid near an ice house. The lines were three to four inches deep and, until the advent of gasoline powered engines, were made by horse-drawn blades. One job, probably entry level, involved running along behind the horses with shovel and sled scooping up their droppings. Understandably, people preferred clean ice.

Once the grid was complete, men standing on the surface would saw through the marked lines and, using a tool called a needle bar, break off the individual blocks or "cakes." The work started nearest to an inclined conveyor leading to the ice house where teams of workers would slide or float rafts of cakes to the base of the conveyor. A standard cake weighing approximately 500 pounds measured about twenty-four by forty-two inches, dimensions designed to fit on the separate carrying sections of the inclined conveyor belt.

According to Carmen J. Maiocco in his 1992 monologue *The Narrows*: "In 1934 there was a record breaking cold spell that froze the ice on the Watuppa Ponds to a depth of twenty-seven inches. The ice was so thick the run couldn't handle it; the blocks would tumble over backwards as they moved up the incline. The whole operation had to be suspended for a while until the weather moderated."

"A common misconception about ice houses," writes Maiocco, "is that straw or sawdust was spread between the individual blocks of ice. This is not true. Each cake was set on top of each other, ice to ice, with nothing in between. The result was an enormous, solid mountain of ice. Straw or sawdust between the blocks would have produced a mess as the blocks melted while being handled and moved about." According to Maiocco, separating the blocks was hard work called "tonking the ice," and involved the use of large chisels and a tool called a "getting up" bar.

Ice freezing was big news in the nineteenth century. Local newspapers would carry stories about the thickness of the ice and speculate as to when the harvest would begin. "There were numerous ice houses all around the ponds," said Goncalo, "often they would deliberately begin cutting the ice in such a way as to prevent competitors from getting to a harvestable area."

Probably the largest and best known ice house on North Wattupa was the Cook-Durfee facility on *Interlachen* Island; partner William Durfee was nicknamed, "Ice Bill." Comprising several buildings of both wood and Fall River granite construction, it shared the island with the opulent *Interlachen* estate of Spencer Borden Sr. and the merely semi-opulent home of his son, Spencer Jr.

The facility, later to become the Arctic Ice Company, was lost to fire in the 1930s. Remnants of its imposing granite section, built in 1864, can still be seen if you look east on Route 24 North, approaching the President Avenue exit. It's the last vestige of an important Fall River industry that flourished for well over one hundred years.

January 11, 2015
Fall River Massachusetts

6.3.1 Colonel Spencer Borden (1848-1921) and his wife, née Effie Annette Brooks (1847-1923), on the lawn of their estate, *Interlachen*, Fall River, 1906.

6.3.2 Delivery men in front of a Cook & Durfee ice wagon, circa 1870; the photograph was taken on North Main Street, Fall River. The company, founded by Robert Cook (c.1814-1887) and William Durfee (1811-1901), was the city's leading purveyor of ice for many years, supplying "Private Families, Hotels, and others ... at Wholesale and Retail" prices.

6.3.3 A dapper William "Ice Bill" Durfee, as he appeared in the 1870s.

6.3.4 A "Scene on Watuppa Lake," Fall River, depicting William Durfee's Ice House, 1890.

6.3.5 Ice harvesting on South Watuppa Pond, Fall River, 1924.

6.3.6 Arctic Ice Company window card, 1920s; the card was placed in the window to alert the iceman that ice was required in the household. The firm's icehouses were destroyed "in a spectacular blaze of unknown origin" on March 27, 1933.

North Park

Manhattan's Central Park and Fall River's North Park are related; they share the same father.

The designer of New York City's urban oasis, Frederick Law Olmsted, is acknowledged as the father of American landscape architecture. Among many other projects, Olmsted also designed the Capitol Grounds in Washington, D.C., as well as Boston's "Emerald Necklace" park system. Although Olmsted died in 1903, the year North Park's construction began, his son, John C. Olmsted, carried on with a plan embodying the same open space design principles pioneered by his father.

This spring, funded in part by the first installment of a $250,000 grant from the Massachusetts Historical Commission, and with Fall River contributing thirty per cent of the total, the Phase I restoration of North Park began.

"We're going to bring it back as close as possible to the original design," said Fall River Administrator of Parks, Richard Kitchen. "Except for incorporating modern handicapped access, we'll be working off the original Olmsted landscape plans."

To assist with the preservation plan, the city has enlisted the services of Martha Lyon Landscape Architecture, LLC, of Northampton, Massachusetts. The Firm's principal, Martha H. Lyon, is an Adjunct Professor of Landscape Architecture at the University of Massachusetts and specializes in the planning, design, and preservation of historic landscapes.

Around the time of the Civil War, as the city was fast becoming a textile manufacturing center with a burgeoning population, the need for open space began to be recognized. In 1868, Fall River contracted with Frederick Law Olmsted to design two parks straddling the city's center, South – now Kennedy – and Ruggles.

Although North Park's origins go back to the early-nineteenth century when the still unincorporated Fall River acquired the land from the Honorable Thomas Durfee for use as part of its "poor farm," it wasn't until 1883 that the city carved out the parcel destined to become the park. With spectacular views of the Taunton River and upper Mount Hope Bay, the tract was widely acclaimed as one of the most beautiful spots on the city's northern ridge.

Under the direction of the Olmsted Brothers firm, actual construction of North Park began in 1903. The Olmsteds' plan was completed by 1904 and included a gravel music court near the North Main Street entrance, a men's gymnasium, a women's gymnasium, a cinder running track, and a wading pool. The park's activity centers were connected by a network of macadam walkways flanked by shade trees, turf lawns, and ornamental shrubbery.

Traces of long lost aspects of the Olmsted plan can still be found if you look hard enough. At the northeast corner of the park, near the intersection of Highland Avenue and Hood Street, there's an obviously man-made depression in the terrain measuring about one-hundred-yards long by thirty-yards wide. Now used for touch football, kite flying, and Durfee High cheerleader practice, this well-defined space was designed by the Olmsteds as a "cricket crease."

North Park has undergone gradual change over the years. During the Great Depression of the 1930s, laborers supplied by the Works Progress Administration constructed reinforced concrete bleachers at the main baseball field. The park originally occupied twenty-eight acres, but, in 1954, the city razed the men's gymnasium, using approximately two acres for the construction of the Charles V. Carroll Elementary School.

In 1983, North Park was nominated to the National Register of Historic Places within the Highlands Historic District. In the 1990s, the city restored the former wading pool, reopening it as a wintertime ice skating rink.

In addition to its historical significance, North Park has always been an integral part of day-to-day life. In the early part of the twentieth century, with thousands of Fall River's mill workers living in crowded tenements, open recreational space was extremely important. "The [Olmsted] firm's original design for the park was an elaborate one," said consultant Martha Lyon, "serving as testimony to the importance of North and the other Fall River parks to public life in the city."

"These parks [North, South, and Ruggles] were showplaces early in the twentieth century," said Lyon. "The city was tremendously proud of them and what they did to improve the lives of the working people. The fact that the city is now paying greater attention to them is very positive."

Fall River mayor, Robert Correia, had this to say about the project: "Olmstead Parks are a rich part of the American landscape as well as the urban park tradition and history. The City of Fall River is very fortunate to have benefited from the know-how of the great American landscape architect Frederick Law Olmstead. As such, I am extremely pleased that the city received state funds to initiate the Phase I restoration of North Park. In memory of Mr. Olmstead, I find it our duty to continue his legacy and dedication to urban parks by maintaining the grounds and continuing to provide quality places of recreation for people of all ages to enjoy right here in the city."

May 16, 2008
Fall River, Massachusetts

6.4.1 "North Park has always been an integral part of day-to-day life" in Fall River, with "open recreational space ... extremely important" to its citizenry throughout the decades. This circa 1912 photograph, depicting the west side of the park fronting on North Main Street, is captioned: "Front entrance of playgrounds, North Park, Fall River."

6.4.2 This 1936 photograph is captioned: "North Park's natural amphitheater provides an ideal spot for spectacles of athletic and social nature."

6.4.3 "Baseball is played on all Fall River parks. Here is a section of a crowd at a twilight league game at North Park," 1936.

6.4.4 A track meet at North Park, Fall River, 1936; the comfort station is visible in the background.

6.4.5 This 1936 photograph is captioned: "North Park ski trail winds through wooded area of rare beauty."

6.4.6 A view of the wading pond at North Park, looking north toward Hood Street, 1936. The photograph is captioned: "Fall River's parks afford many large areas for ice skating enthusiasts."

SOUTH PARK

Created shortly after the Civil War, Fall River's South Park, since renamed for President John F. Kennedy, has become home to countless concerts, ball games, family outings, and happy public celebrations.

In the third and last of the Fall River Historical Society's summer lecture series held at Bristol Community College on July 30th, 2014, Dr. Stefani Koorey presented, "A History of South Park: Frederick Law Olmsted and the Urban Landscape Movement in America."

According to Koorey, late 1860s Fall River was ripe for the Olmsted movement, named after the acknowledged father of American landscape architecture. "The working class had segregated themselves into a series of different villages stuck together by ethnicity and language," said Koorey. "There were no public promenades or greens."

In 1868, the City of Fall River, Massachusetts, purchased the Durfee/Chace farms—along with their scenic views of Mount Hope Bay—for $1,000 an acre. Only six years earlier, before the 1862 settlement of a boundary dispute by the Supreme Court, this land—and everything south of Columbia Street—was part of Fall River, Rhode Island.

Visiting Fall River with his then partner, Calvert Vaux, for the first time in 1870, Olmsted was taken by the water views from the approximately sixty acres that would become South Park; at the time, the city routinely rented the land to farmers as a cow and sheep pasture. "Because of the spectacular views of Mount Hope Bay," said Koorey, "Olmsted decided that there would be no water in the park itself, and that the public's eyes should be directed towards the natural beauty of the Bay."

In 1871, work commenced on the upper flat portion of the planned three-section park. The upper section was the only part of the park built to conform to Olmsted's original plans. "Unfortunately," bemoaned Koorey, "Olmsted's original design and records were lost in the 1886 City Hall fire."

This upper section between South Main and Broadway was called "The Green" and, according to Olmsted's plan, was to have no structures. His idea was that this area would be used as a parade ground and accommodate concerts, cricket creases, and baseball fields. "Trees were to be planted around the perimeter." said Koorey, "He didn't want park-goers to even know that there was a city around them."

In 1902, the year before Frederick Law Olmsted's death, the city signed a contract with the firm for a revised plan to complete the park. The contract was for $1,800 plus expenses and the work was to be executed by a skilled contractor. "The work ended up being performed by unskilled labor," chuckled Koorey. "The non-union contractor withdrew, citing Fall River as 'a hotbed of labor troubles.'"

By 1904, as the revised plan for park completion began to be implemented, controversy arose. "There was concern that men and boys should not be allowed to play baseball in the upper section." said Koorey, "People were being struck and injured by errant balls. Not only that," added Koorey, "the urinal provided for the male ballplayers wasn't even hidden. Gross!"

As work progressed, boulders were moved and placed in different, "strategic" locations. The city began raising plants for the park in a nursery, and despite the elder Olmsted's wishes, a pond was added to the middle section in 1904.

A bridge was built over Bay Street providing access to the third and final "shore" section of the park. "It was considered the best thing in the park," said Koorey, "as people began to use the beach and the bay."

But unforeseen difficulties soon arose. Odors and floating fecal matter from a nearby sewage pipe made swimming less than desirable. "They finally relocated the sewage outlet further south towards the Staples Coal Company," said Koorey, "but problems persisted for many years."

Over time, the original South Park has continued to evolve and change, not always for the better, in Koorey's opinion. "What a place to put a storage and maintenance shed," she laments, "right at the prominent intersection of Broadway and Bradford Avenue."

"Despite good intentions," said Koorey, "South Park is not the jewel that Frederick Law Olmsted envisioned." In fact, said Koorey, neither Kennedy, Ruggles, nor North Park can really be called "Olmsted parks." "Ruggles Park comes closest," added Koorey, "because the Olmsted sons followed through on the original design."

Nevertheless, concluded Koorey, despite having strayed from the Olmsted's master designs, the parks are valuable public spaces that continue to play an important role in enhancing the quality of city life.

August 2, 2014
Fall River, Massachusetts

6.5.1 Frederick Law Olmstead (1822-1903), "the acknowledged father of American landscape architecture."

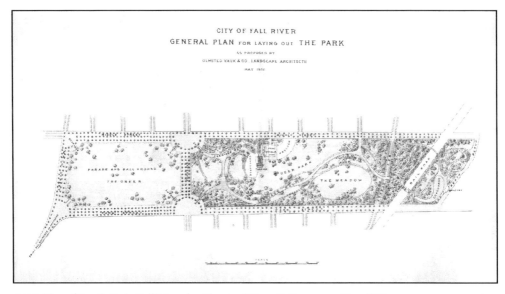

6.5.2 Plan of South Park, Fall River, by Olmstead Vaux & Company, May, 1871.

6.5.3 A view of South Park, Fall River, 1897.

6.5.4 "Front Entrance South Park," Fall River, circa 1912.

6.5.5 A view of the wading pool in South Park, Fall River, looking east, circa 1912; the steeples of St. Anne's Church can be seen on the horizon.

CHAPTER SEVEN

GRAVES AND GRAVESTONES

OAK GROVE CEMETERY

The largest contiguous urban green space in Fall River isn't any of the City's three famous Olmsted parks—it's Oak Grove Cemetery.

In fact, at one hundred acres, the city-owned burial ground is larger than Ruggles, North, and Kennedy combined; Kennedy, the next largest, is just under sixty acres.

"Oak Grove was the precursor to the modern park system and was one of the first to embrace the concept of the 'garden cemetery,' said Mike Keane, president of Friends of Oak Grove Cemetery. "During the Victorian Era, it was common for families to gather in the park-like atmosphere of the grounds for picnics and other recreational activities."

Friends of Oak Grove Cemetery comprises a group of volunteers dedicated to preserving the cemetery's urban park setting. In addition to rejuvenating the site's unique landscape architecture, their mission includes honoring the memories of the over fifty thousand who have passed on and are interred in Oak Grove.

Established in 1855, Oak Grove was designed by local architect Josiah Brown and was modeled after the picturesque Mount Auburn cemetery-park in Cambridge. "These scenic landscapes were intended to provide relaxation for the living as well as rest for the deceased," said Ann Keane, secretary of Friends of Oak Grove. In 1873, a twenty-five-foot-high Gothic Revival granite arch was added to the main Prospect Street gate. Inscribed on the arch in Gothic lettering is: "The shadows have fallen and wait for the day."

Although not officially a city-owned cemetery until 1855, the area was nevertheless occasionally used as a private burial ground well before that with many headstones pre-dating the city's mid-nineteenth century acquisition. In those days, it was also common for wealthy families to disinter relatives from private family plots as well as other cemeteries and relocate them to what they considered a more desirable location. Several of Oak Grove's pre-1855 residents undoubtedly have the distinction of having been buried twice.

So far, the oldest legible headstone discovered belongs to a Joseph Read, who died in 1791. Mystery surrounds the owner of a weather-beaten and partially disintegrated marker on which the only readable information is the tantalizing date "1776."

Perhaps the most illustrious eighteenth-century resident is Thomas Durfee, Esq. (1721-1796). Judge Durfee was a patriot and a friend of Revolutionary War hero

General Lafayette who, it is said, once made a gift of a pair of fine French hounds to the Judge.

During the War of Independence, Judge Durfee kept a large herd of deer in an enclosed park on a tract of land between Main and Rock Streets. Here is an anecdote from *Fall River and its Industries* by Peck and Earl, published by Atlantic Engraving in 1877: "At the time the British troops landed here, and attempted the destruction of the mills on the Run in 1778, the Judge's wife drove the deer into the woods. Soon after the enemy left the town, they returned to the inclosure [*sic*] of their own accord, probably realizing that all danger of being killed and eaten by a British soldier was now past."

Chosen for its natural beauty, elevated topography, and central location, the cemetery site had the added advantage of the nearby quarries destined to provide the granite for its walls and headstones. The irony is not lost that the gravestones of many of the wealthy mill owners buried here were made of the same material used in the construction of their factories and mansions.

To walk through the older sections of Oak Grove Cemetery is to be thrust back in time to Fall River's Gilded Age. Here, under imposing and elaborate granite and marble monuments, lie the titans of the city's once flourishing business and industry.

In the case of Stafford Mills founder Foster H. Stafford, his monument is an elaborately carved miniature stone mill, complete with doors, windows, and a peaked roof. In death as in life, Stafford's "mill" has no tower.

The Braytons, Durfees, Davols, Chaces, and, of course, the first family of Fall River aristocracy, the Bordens, are all here. Familiar names all, after whom factories, streets, schools, theaters, and even city blocks were named. Factions of the Borden family controlled Fall River's mills, foundries, railroads, banks, utilities, and even the fabled Fall River Line Steamship Company.

The grave of mill baron Richard Borden is marked by a twenty-five-foot-tall pedestal and statue of a female figure representing "Hope." His brother, Jefferson, buried nearby, is memorialized by one of the tallest obelisks in the cemetery. "Even into death these members of Fall River's nineteenth-century elite were competing for status," says Fall River historian Dr. Philip T. Silvia Jr.

In another delicious irony, Thomas Evans (1823-1906), a prominent Fall River union leader of the nineteenth century, is buried only yards away from the grand monuments of the wealthy industrialists he undoubtedly antagonized. Evans' otherwise modest headstone is adorned with bas relief miniatures of a textile worker's tools and bears the biographical epitaph: "The Old Agitator."

One of the most beautiful memorials is the classical style mausoleum of Earle Perry Charlton, who died in 1930. Charlton, known as the inventor of the "five-and-dime" store, was a founder of the F. W. Woolworth Co. and a lifelong philanthropist; Fall River's largest hospital bears his name.

A number of politicians are buried in the cemetery, including several congressmen and Fall River mayors. Perhaps the most famous Oak Grove politician is Louis McHenry Howe, known as "the man behind Roosevelt," and acknowledged by Eleanor Roosevelt as "the mastermind of his presidential campaign. "Upon Howe's death in 1936, President Franklin Delano Roosevelt attended his funeral in Fall River, conferring upon him a final title, that of "Devoted friend, advisor, and associate of the President."

Howe, a native of Indianapolis, Indiana, found his way to Oak Grove through his marriage to Fall River native Grace Hartley, a cousin of Lizzie Borden. Shortly after Howe's passing, President Roosevelt appointed Mrs. Howe Postmistress of Fall River, making her the first female in history to hold such a position. She retired from the post in 1951, and died in 1955 at the age of eighty.

The next time you use the telephone or turn on a light bulb, think of Oak Grove resident Lewis H. Latimer. The son of a former slave, Latimer was a prominent scientist who, among other things, is credited with preparing the drawings enabling Alexander Graham Bell to receive the patent for the telephone.

Latimer also invented an improved filament for Thomas Edison's light bulb that greatly prolonged the life of the bulb. The young inventor would go on to work for Edison himself, and in 1918 was named one of the twenty-four charter members—and the lone African American member—of the "Edison Pioneers," a distinguished group of scientists responsible for creating the nation's electrical system.

His connection to Fall River? According to Professor Silvia: "We are not sure how they met, but, in 1873, Lewis H. Latimer traveled from Boston to Fall River to marry Mary W. Lewis, a twenty-six-year-old seamstress." Latimer died in 1928 and is buried with Mary, who preceded him in death in 1924.

Oak Grove's funerary monuments also provide a share of whimsy. Lumber magnate Cook Borden is memorialized by a twelve-foot-high granite tree trunk, complete with intricately carved bark and roots. Sam and Betty Watson's headstone makes a touching allusion to their married devotion: "In this world we jogged along together." And Dwight Mahogany and Elizabeth Greenwood, buried side by side, have gravestones befitting their surnames—twin, carved granite logs.

No roster of Oak Grove residents would be complete without mention of Lizzie Borden. The alleged murderess is buried in the family plot under a small stone that reads simply, "Lizbeth." Nearby, a modest headstone—compared to other Borden monuments—bears the names of the victims of the infamous 1892 murders: "Andrew Jackson Borden" and "His Wife Abby Durfee Borden".

Sometimes forgotten by the casually interested is that Lizzie was acquitted of murdering her father and *stepmother*, not her mother. Sandwiched between the two victims' names on the Borden headstone is "Sarah Anthony Borden, 1823-1863." It is interesting to speculate how history might have been changed had Lizzie's mother Sarah not suffered an untimely death at age thirty-nine from "uterine congestion and disease of the spine."

The decades have not always been kind to Oak Grove Cemetery. The once stately Elms, Beeches, and Oaks that lined its paths and roadways are slowly falling victim to storms, disease, and insect infestation. Where once the cemetery had its own system of greenhouses and a large, dedicated work crew, it now must share the Fall River Parks Department workforce with all the other city parks and cemeteries. With difficult economic conditions and the resulting budgetary restraints, it strains the Department's limited resources to preserve the existing trees and shrubs.

To help fill the void, Friends of Oak Grove Cemetery have worked closely with the Parks Department to develop a plan for restoring cemetery plantings. Established in early 2007, the Friends planted their first replacement trees in May of that year. "Our goal for 2008 was ten new trees," said Friends' President Mike Keane. "With fifteen new saplings currently in the ground, we've already exceeded that."

"Oak Grove Cemetery is perhaps the prettiest and most serene place in Fall River," said former mayor, Robert Correia. "The Friends of Oak Grove Cemetery have brought upon themselves the commendable task of improving on this excellence in design, and the city will always be behind their efforts to make it a more beautiful place."

August 4, 2008
Fall River, Massachusetts

7.1.1 The Trafford family plot in Oak Grove Cemetery, Fall River, 1891. The large plot on Maplewood Avenue, consisting of two lots, numbered 2540 and 2541, is centered by an impressive sarcophagus-style monument cut from a large block of flawless granite. The decorative cast iron urns, once tended by Trafford family gardeners, are no longer in situ.

7.1.2 The plot of Col. Richard Borden (1795-1874) in Oak Grove Cemetery, Fall River, 1897. The plot on Chestnut Avenue, at number 247, is dominated by an impressive monument surmounted by a beautifully carved allegorical figure of Hope. The massive Egyptian Revival style obelisk that marks the adjoining plot of his brother, Jefferson Borden (1801-1887), at lot number 250, can be seen to the right.

7.1.3 The Earle Perry Charlton Sr. (1863-1930) mausoleum in Oak Grove Cemetery, Fall River; the imposing monument on Willow Avenue was constructed from massive slabs of carved granite in the form of a classical Greek temple.

7.1.4 Gothic style receiving vaults at Oak Grove Cemetery, Fall River, 1891; the structure is constructed of both dressed and rough-cut blocks of native granite.

WHITE BRONZE MARKERS

Not all of the grave markers and monuments in Oak Grove Cemetery are actually made of stone. Sprinkled among the thousands of limestone, granite, and marble headstones are a smattering of unusual and beautiful "white bronze" markers.

These relatively rare monuments are actually made of Zinc. The white bronze trade name was merely a marketing tactic designed to attract buyers by making the product seem more exotic. Although found in cemeteries throughout the United States and Canada, it is estimated that these monuments represent well less than one per cent of the countless millions of grave markers in both countries.

Only one firm, The Monumental Bronze Company of Bridgeport, Connecticut, was known to have manufactured these markers. The company's catalogs listed a myriad of sculptures and symbols that could be incorporated on a custom-made memorial, copying the same styles as conventional stone monuments,

A casual observer might walk within a few feet of a white bronze marker without ever realizing its composition. Except for a slight bluish-gray cast, the monuments, which were usually sandblasted, look remarkably like stone with amazingly sharp inscriptions and devices.

White bronze has one major advantage over stone; it is impervious to the lichens and moss that regularly attack and damage conventional headstones. The same zinc oxide coating that gives the monuments their characteristic patina, also serves to repel these organic cemetery pests. Even after over one hundred years, these metal markers are stunningly well preserved.

The Monumental Bronze Company and its Midwestern subsidiaries, marketed white bronze memorials for only forty years from 1874 to 1914. Boycotted by established granite and marble dealers, zinc monuments never gained widespread public acceptance. With the advent of World War I, Monumental Bronze shifted its production to munitions, and except for flat replacement tablets, never again cast a white bronze grave marker. The company ceased operations in 1939.

August 11, 2008
Fall River, Massachusetts

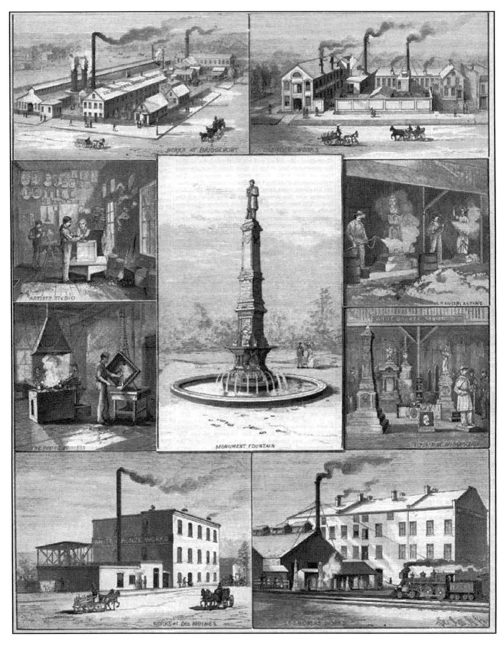

7.2.1 Monumental Bronze Company promotional engraving; the late-nineteenth century piece depicts the company factories, various production departments, and showroom.

7.2.2 Advertisement for Monumental Bronze Company, Bridgeport, Connecticut; produced during the late-nineteenth century, the ad promotes the virtues of "Everlasting White Bronze Monuments."

7.2.3 White bronze monument on the burial plot of the Booth and Wilde families in Oak Grove Cemetery, Fall River.

THE OAK GROVE ECSYSTEM

Fir tree needles are soft and flat; Spruce needles are sharply pointed, square, and can easily be twirled between your fingers.

These and other fascinating tree facts were explained by arborist Dennis Brodeur as he led a group of Friends of Oak Grove Cemetery on a recent tour of the burial ground's flora. "Oak Grove is a large, mature urban setting with some trees over 150 years old" said Brodeur. "A system like this is essentially one organism with an interconnected root system."

According to Brodeur, neighboring trees can actually communicate with one another. "If one tree is under stress, nearby species will try to help it by providing chemical compounds to resist pathogens." Ticking off a list of tree enemies such as fungi, bacteria, carpenter ants, and arachnids, Brodeur identified a few specimens that were "in trouble." "When higher branches begin dying off, it's an indication of root damage," he said.

A disciple of the late Dr. Alex Shigo, who is considered the "father of modern arboriculture," Brodeur was taught to "touch the trees" and learned to identify different species simply by smelling the varying fragrances of their freshly cut wood.

Examining the cemetery's soil, Brodeur proclaimed it basically healthy as evidenced by the presence of various weeds, mushrooms, lichens, and mosses. "Everybody hates dandelions," said Brodeur, "but their roots go all the way down to the subsoil to bring up beneficial minerals."

Oak Grove is home to a dizzying variety of trees, including White Oaks (*Quercus alba*) and Heritage River Birches (*Betula nigra* 'Heritage') not found anywhere else in Fall River. "The people who founded this cemetery were from England," said Brodeur," so they planted trees familiar to their native land such as the Oaks (*Quercus*) and Copper Beeches (*Fagus sylvatica*)."

August 18, 2009
Fall River, Massachusetts

7.3.1 A view in Oak Grove Cemetery, Fall River, 1897; the image illustrates the "dizzying variety of trees ... not found elsewhere in Fall River."

Benjamin Brightman's Gravestone

Sanjay Gyasto's shovel made an ominous clanging sound as he dug the hole where Benjamin Brightman's gravestone would be set. A few more minutes of furious digging revealed, not the feared immovable boulder, but the original brick and mortar base that once anchored Brightman's marker.

"It's very rare to find a brick foundation on a stone this old," said Joshua Craine, Gyasto's employer and project manager of Daedalus, Inc., conservators of sculptures, monuments, architectural ornaments, and historic grave markers. Friday, July 6, 2012, would be the third time that Brightman's slate headstone would be set, and the second time in Fall River's Oak Grove Cemetery.

Benjamin was the father of Captain Henry Brightman, who was famously murdered on the high seas by the pirate chieftain Alexander Tardy. Benjamin died in 1827, the same year his son was stabbed to death by Tardy in the notorious "Brig *Crawford* Affair."

Since Oak Grove Cemetery wasn't opened until 1855, the elder Brightman was obviously buried somewhere else first. "Our records show that the Brightmans came to Oak Grove in 1877," said cemetery manager Tom Eaton, "but the cards don't say where they came from."

In the late-nineteenth century, it was common for prominent Fall River families to disinter their loved ones from family burial grounds and reinter them in the park-like, well-landscaped garden cemetery that was Oak Grove. Brightman's 1877 re-burial fifty years after his death, could explain the brick foundation, probably added to his marker during its second setting.

In 2011, Friends of Oak Grove Cemetery, a non-profit volunteer group dedicated to preserving the cemetery's urban park setting, decided to undertake a headstone restoration program. Benjamin Brightman's marker was to be the first. "While the condition of the slate was good," said Friends of Oak Grove Cemetery President Michael Keane, "the 185-year-old marker had been shattered into multiple pieces."

Early this year, Keane and his group sought the services of Craine's Daedalus, Inc. The Watertown, Massachusetts, firm has a national reputation for its fine art preservation and counts among its clients: the Boston Athenaeum, the Whitney Museum, and the National Gallery of Art. According to Craine, over sixteen man-hours were devoted to the Brightman stone, which was painstakingly restored using metal pins and a polymer mortar, modified to match the texture and color of the original gray slate.

In addition to his September 3, 1827, date of death, Benjamin Brightman's stone carries a beautiful stylistic engraving of a weeping willow and lengthy poetic inscription which reads in part:

> Adieu my friends a long and sad farewell
> A scene more solemn than the passing bell,
> I hope with God in glory I shall bloom
> Where sorrow, sickness, death, can never come.

Through conservator Craine's efforts, the marker was almost completely restored with little evidence of the preservative materials. "Although slate is hard and is resistant to erosion," said Craine, "it tends to delaminate along the layers of its original bedding plane as found in nature. Every stone is different, and sometimes we just have to go by feel while working on them."

According to Friends of Oak Grove president Keane, the group plans to hold an official unveiling and rededication of the stone soon. In addition to the headstone restoration program, the organization continues its work beautifying the cemetery through plantings, dead tree removal, and its path marker program aimed at identifying Oak Grove's many roads with authentic period signage.

July 7, 2012
Fall River, Massachusetts

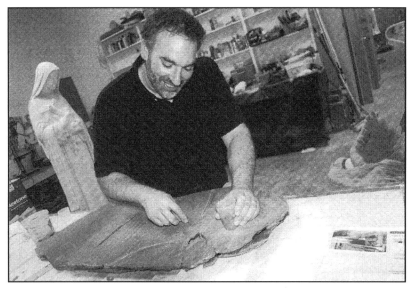

7.4.1 Joshua Crane of Daedalus, Inc., Watertown, Massachusetts, photographed in 2009 while undertaking the restoration of the slate headstone of Benjamin Brightman (1763-1827).

7.4.2 The restored headstone of Benjamin Brightman, Oak Grove Cemetery, Fall River, 2017.

CHAPTER
EIGHT

CENTER CITY

DOWNTOWN

Amazon.com and its internet brethren are doing to suburban malls what those malls once did to downtown shopping districts.

After World War II, through the 1950s and even into the urban renewal ravaged 1960s, Fall River enjoyed a vibrant center city. Added to an extensive and diverse array of shopping, downtown offered restaurants, food markets, drugstores, tobacconists, beauty parlors, and theaters. One could even find education, either in the many bars, or more soberly, with a library card at The People's University on North Main Street.

There was even a shoe shine parlor inside the Pocasset Street entrance of the Academy Building. Although you can still find a piazza, a parlor, and an occasional pay phone, try finding a bootblack in today's Fall River.

According to Fall River's Joyce B. Rodrigues, who frequented downtown with her parents during her late-50s early-60s high school years, Main Street was a community of people and businesses, a symbol of community pride and a piece of community history.

"There was much pedestrian traffic and serendipitous connections on the sidewalks," remembers Rodrigues. "Crowds of shoppers, especially during the holiday season, were sometimes so dense that I would step down from the curb into the street to get around them."

"The value of these connections was social, something that knits together a community," adds Rodrigues. "One does not get that by working in a building in an office park. Nor does one get that by driving up to the door of a retail business or professional business in a strip mall."

The boundaries of Fall River's downtown were amorphous—some East End provincials considered the Flint as their "downtown" and rarely ventured elsewhere—but the artery serving the heart of the city was South Main Street.

Beginning roughly around Morgan Street and running north, South Main was nothing less than Fall River's elongated town square. The activity only began to peter out a couple of blocks after it crossed Bedford Street and became North Main. The library, of course, survives on this brief stretch, but once neighboring institutions now gone were: Rogers Cigar Store, the original China Royal Restaurant, and the Durfee Theater.

The R.A. McWhirr Company, Fall River's iconic department store, which closed in 1975, was the centerpiece of downtown shopping.

Like most retailers of the 1950s, the concept of political correctness was still foreign to McWhirr's. A 1957 ad for the store's exclusive line of clothing for "plump" girls, called "Chubbettes," proclaimed: "Your chubby lass can be the belle of her class." The phrase "plus size" hadn't yet entered Madison Avenue's lexicon.

But the store was only trying to help. With every Chubbette purchase came a free booklet: "Pounds and Personality—a booklet for parents of a chubby girl."

If McWhirr's didn't have it, or you were shopping for price, there was always J.M. Fields. Sears Roebuck, on the other hand, added automotive and tools to the department store mix.

Second only to McWhirr's in its downtown presence, Cherry and Webb was the high end lady's apparel store. "Cherry and Webb stored an aluminum Christmas tree on the roof of the building," said Rodrigues. "The tree was the length and width of the building from the roof to the display windows. Lowering the tree meant that the holiday season had begun in Fall River."

Cherry's, as the store was affectionately known, had two display windows facing South Main Street and two within its entrance foyer. An atomizer situated above the main door periodically emitted a burst of perfume. This sneak attack on the olfactory sense of unsuspecting shoppers successfully pushed sales of the store's "fragrance of the week."

On the block between Anawan and Pocasset Streets were the three five-and-ten-cent stores: J.J. Newbury, Co.; Woolworth's; and S.S. Kresge. Joanne Rago remembers her mother getting her hair done upstairs at Woolworth's. "That was a big deal for me, as we would get lunch at the counter, break a balloon and get a sundae for the price inside the balloon," remembers Rago. "Those were the days. Lots of good memories downtown."

Kresge's had a pet department at the rear of the store that featured a large goldfish tank. It was rare that any parent accompanied by a child could escape the store without a twenty-five-cent goldfish carried home in a small white cardboard carton.

Nancy Sayward Boardman loved watching Woolworth's donut machine. "It somehow dropped donut shaped dough into oil and when one side was cooked it would flip to cook the other side." Balloons are also a part of Boardman's memories: "I'd sit at the ice cream fountain trying to decide which balloon to ask the waitress to pop to find out how much I would have to pay for a sundae—anything from a penny to $.25!"

But Main Street wasn't just about the big stores; you could get just about anything you wanted downtown.

Adams Drug was the forerunner of today's big-box pharmacies and sold everything from prescriptions to perfume. It carried practically every magazine published and was the go-to place for kits for building model airplanes and ships.

Always emanating the tantalizing aroma of fresh brewed coffee, Main Street shoppers likely enjoyed a whiff of Van Dyk's luncheonette before they saw it. Besides its S.S. Pierce line of specialty foods, Van Dyk's had huge homemade muffins and the best deli sandwiches on South Main Street.

Speaking of whiffs, who can forget the aroma of fresh roasted nuts at the Mr. Peanut store on North Main Street; Mr. Peanut himself—in mannequin form—greeted customers at the front door.

Had a sweet tooth? No problem. Downtown featured Hilton's and the Terminal bakeries as well as the Fannie Farmer candy store. Everything could be washed down with a coffee cabinet at Walter Nichipor's Main Drug while waiting for the bus in the Granite Block building.

Allen's Cut Rate, at 135 South Main Street, was a small outlet densely stocked with everything from alarm clocks to suppositories. Many a teenage girl bought their first tube of lipstick and their first makeup compact from Joey. In 1965, you could still buy tins of Polident tooth powder on sale for forty-nine cents, and probably pay for it with the now vanished half-dollar coin.

Depending on style preferences and budget, men had a wide array of sartorial options. Main Street clothing stores included: Tom Beedem Company; Bond's; Burke's; Empire Men's Shop; Tom Ellison Men's Wear; Freed's Men's Shop; Silkson's Clothing; and Paul Woltman's. Just off the main drag was S. Gourse & Sons, The Hub Clothing Company, at the corner of Pleasant and Troy Streets.

The younger set preferred the legendary Sawyer's Campus Shop. It was an unofficial Fall River ordnance that all teenage boys own a tan Baracuta jacket and Sawyer's enforced it.

In addition to Cherry's, women sought the latest fashions at boutiques like Lenor's, Wilbur's, Kitty Michel's Bridal Salon, Louise's, Angie's Fashions, and Milady's Dress Shop.

For preppy teens the Victory Shop had the sought-after "collegiate" look: pleated skirts, knee socks, peter pan collar blouses, Shetland cardigan sweaters, circle pins, and crew-neck sweaters.

"My maternal grandmother paid for my senior prom dress," remembers Joyce Rodrigues. "My dress came from Lenor's—a pink organdy appliqué cocktail dress. This was the first time that anyone I knew had bought a dress from Lenor's. I had made it into the adult world of fashion."

Rodrigues, project director of the Fall River Historical Society's oral history project, *Women at Work: An Oral History of Working Class Women in Fall River*, funded by Mass Humanities, particularly remembers two women's shops: "One ladies' specialty store was Angie's Fashions. I mention this shop because the owners were two sisters, Angie and Mary Vasconcelles, who were religious education teachers [*catechism*] at my parish. Like Rose Coury of Milady's Dress Shop, Angie and Mary represented successful women in retail sales at a time when that was an accomplishment and breakthrough for women in business."

No survey of mid-twentieth-century Fall River would be complete without mention of the downtown theaters. From south to north along Main Street were the Capitol, Center, Empire, Academy, and Durfee theaters. The Embassy was on Franklin Street, just a block off North Main.

Going to the "show" in the vernacular of the period, was a three-to-four-hour escape from reality. In addition to a double feature, the moviegoer was treated to a couple of cartoons, a newsreel, and an adventure serial. The theaters even had flashlight wielding ushers in military style uniforms to guide you to an empty seat.

Modern day malls are probably more efficient but, compared to Fall River's mid-twentieth-century South Main Street, they seem antiseptic and sterile. The Amazon.com's of the world now take shopping even a step further, no face to face human contact necessary. Sadly, Fall River's one time equivalent to the town square has disappeared into the suburbs and cyberspace.

January 31, 2015
Fall River, Massachusetts

8.1.1 Cherry & Webb Company, "Women's, Misses', Junior Misses', Girls', Children's, Infants' and Junior Boys' Wear," 139-149 South Main Street, Fall River, 1940s. The company also sold accessories and shoes, and featured a beauty salon, a photography studio, and fur storage vaults. It was noted for offering "the high end of lady's apparel" in addition to more affordably-priced merchandise. The ever-popular W.T. Grant Company, at 149 South Main Street, occupied the lower southern portion of the building.

8.1.2 South Main Street, Fall River, looking north toward City Hall, 1959; "There was much pedestrian traffic and serendipitous connections on the sidewalks."

8.1.3 James Van Dyk Company, 198 South Main Street, Fall River, circa 1930; "always emanating" from the store was "the tantalizing aroma of fresh brewed coffee."

8.1.4 The interior of James Van Dyk Company, 198 South Main Street, Fall River, circa 1930. The store offered a wide variety of tea, coffee, spices, and other products, in addition to fine specialty foods from the venerable Boston, Massachusetts, firm of S.S. Pierce Company.

8.1.5 A 1965 advertisement for Allen's Cut Rate, 135 South Main Street, Fall River. Allen's was the go-to store for cosmetics and toiletries during the 1950s and 1960s.

8.1.6 A Christmas window display at Allen's Cut Rate, 135 South Main Street, Fall River, 1935.

8.1.7 The Hub Clothing Company, 162 Pleasant Street, Fall River, 1928; the city's many men's clothing stores featured "a wide array of sartorial options," with The Hub being one of the more upscale emporiums.

McWhirr's

The muffled swish of the revolving door instantly silenced the din of South Main Street, the floorboards creaked underfoot, and the lunch counter aromas sent tantalizing signals to your stomach. You were in a different world; you were in McWhirr's.

The R.A. McWhirr Company, Fall River's iconic department store, which closed in 1975, less than two years short of its one-hundreth birthday, was a Mecca to generations of area shoppers.

Before the proliferation of cookie-cutter suburban malls, downtown—as it was called in Fall River—was *the* shopping destination, and borrowing a term from modern-day mall-speak, McWhirr's was the "anchor store." According to Fall River Historical Society curator, Michael Martins, "Everybody has a McWhirr's story."

Robert Armstrong McWhirr first sailed into New York harbor aboard a Cunard liner from his native Scotland in 1873. Relying on his retail experience with a Glasgow merchandiser, the twenty-three-year-old easily found employment with fellow Scotsmen at the Callender, McAusland, and Troup, department store in Providence, Rhode Island.

Despite the camaraderie of his countrymen, it took less than year for the young McWhirr to determine that his prospects were limited at the large Providence store. Restless and ambitious, in 1874, he quickly moved on to a job with Fall River retailer, E.S. Brown Co. It was there he met Sarah E.R. Ramsay, the store's manager of ribbons and lace goods and a popular church singer in the city.

Soon, McWhirr discovered that his business ambitions were only exceeded by Ramsay's, and in 1877, they bid goodbye to Mr. Brown and immediately became his competitors. The lady received top billing as Ramsay and McWhirr set up shop in an 1100-square-foot rented storefront on Charity Lane, only a few yards removed from their former employer's South Main Street location—Charity Lane, also known as Chapel Street because of the proximity of the nineteenth-century Church of the Ascension, extended west from South Main Street to Pearl Street.

The joint venture was short lived. Only four years later, although remaining an employee of the company, Miss Ramsay retired from the partnership. In 1882, McWhirr took on a new partner in Alexander Thomson, an experienced retail manager from the dry goods firm of Stewart and Hammerton. Renamed McWhirr and Thomson, the new partnership expanded their floor space that same year with a brick addition to the rear of the wood framed store.

In 1886, perceiving the city's population expanding northward, E.S. Brown moved his department store, then the city's largest, from its South Main Street location to new quarters at the corner of North Main and Pine Streets. Skeptical of Brown's perceived population shift, Robert McWhirr convinced his new partner that this was a golden opportunity for expansion. Soon, they were installing their first fixtures in the newly vacated building even as Brown was removing the last of his. The upgrade tripled McWhirr's floor space in what would become the store's last and permanent address, 75 South Main Street.

On St. Patrick's Day, 1893, forty-three-year-old founder, Robert Armstrong McWhirr died. In May of that year, the R.A. McWhirr Company was re-organized by a trio of long-term employees affectionately known by their entry-level, original titles: "The Three Cash Boys."

Ten years later, under President Asa A. Mills, Superintendent James H. Mahoney, and Secretary Richard S. Thompson, the store continued its expansion by leasing Robert McWhirr's original building back across Charity Lane. Only one year later, in 1904, after extensive litigation and contentious negotiations with abutting property owners, McWhirr's acquired Charity Lane from the city. The entire street soon disappeared into the McWhirr footprint as the firm again expanded by erecting an uninterrupted storefront along newly joined South Main Street.

Surviving both the devastating 1916 fire to its south, and the 1928 conflagration that consumed much of the city's business district to its north, McWhirr's continuously remodeled throughout the early 1900s. In its familiar, final configuration, the five story, white terra-cotta fronted building, eventually comprised 166 feet of frontage, housing over 120,000 square feet of floor space.

Lillian Toulan worked in McWhirr's silverware department when in her twenties during World War II. "There certainly was no comparison to today's Wal-Mart," says the former salesgirl. Toulan fondly remembers overnight buying trips to Boston, Massachusetts, with her department manager, a Mrs. Mary Bassett. "We'd meet the buyers from Filene's, Jordan Marsh, and Gilchrist's," says Toulan. "We always stayed in a nice hotel and ate at the best restaurants."

In Toulan's day, the workweek on McWhirr's retail floor was Monday through Saturday, with Wednesday afternoons off, and a Saturday closing of 9 p.m. "Since we had an hour for lunch," laughs Toulan, "in the summertime we'd sometimes sneak up to the roof to get a suntan."

For almost seventy years, Toulan has kept a small manila pay envelope for the week ending August 1, 1942. In neatly penciled figures is her net pay for the week— $13.86 after fourteen cents was deducted for "Federal Old Age."

According to Toulan, McWhirr's silverware department always had a special role to play whenever dignitaries visited Fall River. "When big shots came to town," she says, "their welcoming gift was usually sterling silver flatware in a nice chest." Toulan specifically recalls such presentations made to President Harry S. Truman and Congressman Joe McCarthy.

Toulan has fond memories of McWhirr's management. "The floorwalkers watched you all the time," she says, "but you couldn't help but like the bosses." One boss in particular, Norman F. Thompson, whose father Richard was one of the original "Cash Boys," seemed to have caught young Lillian's eye.

"One day I told a couple of the girls that I was thinking of inviting Mr. Thompson home for dinner," she says. Apparently this was quite an unusual step for a lowly salesgirl and Lillian's co-workers were predictably dismissive. "They didn't think I'd do it," says Toulan, "and if I did, they didn't think he'd accept. Well, I offered, he accepted, and my father cooked us pork chops. We had a lovely time; Norman was really down to earth."

Long-time McWhirr's customer, Ruth Hurley vividly recalls the store during the 1950s and 1960s. "My cousin, Eleanor R.M. Shea, was a buyer for some of McWhirr's basement merchandise," recalls Hurley. "Downstairs was an active place because many people entered and left the store through the back door off Pearl Street." According to Hurley, McWhirr's employees never used the words "seconds" or "discounts" when referring to the basement store. Rather, she says, McWhirr's basement was simply the home of "less expensive lines."

Before the advent of credit and debit cards, Hurley remembers the McWhirr's in-store credit system. "Customers had these little metal discs about the size of a fifty-cent piece," she says, "on one side was embossed "McWhirr's" and on the other side was stamped a two, or three digit number. All you needed to do was show your disc to the clerk and the amount was added to the bill you received at the end of the month."

"My cousin Eleanor told me that the employees often recognized regular customers by their numbers more than their names," Hurley chuckled. It's been said that like Massachusetts' license plates, having a low numbered McWhirr's charge disc was a Fall River status symbol.

"If you bought something at McWhirr's in the morning you could have it delivered to your home by the afternoon," adds Hurley. "They would even deliver wedding presents right to the reception on the day of the wedding." In the 1950s, McWhirr's operated a fleet of four vans traveling over 1600 miles weekly and averaging 10,000 deliveries monthly within a twenty-mile radius of the store.

Mike Walsh worked on McWhirr's wrapping desk for a year in the early 1960s between his graduation from Durfee High School and his enrollment in Providence College. "As a store service, gift wrapping was free," says Walsh. "I think somebody could have walked in with a package off the street and we would have wrapped it for them, no questions asked."

"There was one guy who bought the cheapest matzoh balls we had at the cookie counter and had them gift wrapped for shipping every month," remembers Walsh. "We always thought the wrapping paper was worth more than the matzoh balls."

As a gag one morning before the store opened, Walsh secreted himself at the top of the chute leading to the basement shipping table. Closing the cover over him and folding his arms across his chest, there he lay when his co-worker, Emma Janson, opened the lid to deposit a package left over from the previous day.

"I laughed so hard at Emma's surprise that I slid all the way down the wooden chute," says Walsh, "I had to call my mother to take me to the emergency room to have the splinters removed from my rear end."

In the mid-twentieth century, downtown Fall River was a busy retail destination all year round and McWhirr's was the centerpiece. At Christmastime, when the hustle and bustle was at its peak, the magnificently decorated store seemed to radiate a magical holiday aura. Ask anyone who visited the store's North Pole Workshop, there was little doubt about one thing—sitting here on his elevated chair, more like a throne, actually, McWhirr's Santa Claus was *the* real one.

Or maybe not. Like most Fall River children, long before he worked at the store, Mike Walsh visited the legendary McWhirr's Santa during the Christmas holidays. "I once showed my uncle a photograph of me sitting on Santa's lap," says Walsh. "He takes a close look at it and says, 'Hey, I know that guy, he does painting for me in the summer.'"

"Christmas was special at McWhirr's," remembers Lillian Toulan. "Mr. Burns always had the store decorated beautifully."—John S. Burns was the store's display manager during the 1940s and 1950s. "We even had a competition with Cherry's next door to see who had the most attractive Christmas windows."

Ruth Hurley also remembers a cherished McWhirr's Christmas tradition. "Every year," says Hurley, "the salesclerks would sew original Christmas costumes for dolls to be displayed in the store's windows on either side of the main revolving door entrance." According to Hurley, prizes would be awarded for the best dressed, and after the holidays, the moppets would be donated to charity, usually St. Vincent's Orphanage or the Children's Home on Robeson Street.

In recent years, part of the McWhirr's Christmas tradition has been rekindled by the Fall River Historical Society. Since 2007, Curator Michael Martins and his staff have recreated the popular McWhirr's candy counter in one of the Rock Street. mansion's upstairs rooms. Including the store's original candy scale and candy display stand, the display features such nostalgic delights as lumps of coal, Boston fruit slices, peppermint pigs, and that perennial Fall River favorite, nonpareils.

McWhirr's boasted services simply not found in today's big box mall department stores. Among many unique features, the store had its own United States Post Office branch as well as an extensive private lending library.

"My mother always went to the lending library just beyond the sewing machine department," remembers Betsy Moore. "I got interested in supplementing my wardrobe by making my own clothes, so she bought a White machine for me— on time, of course—for my thirteenth birthday. Not only did McWhirr's sell us a machine, they gave me lessons, too, and I was on my way," adds Moore.

Pneumatic message tubes were introduced into department stores in the 1880s by John Wanamaker, the Philadelphia retail magnate. By the early 1900s McWhirr's had installed its own elaborate air-actuated system that rapidly transferred cash and charge slips from the sales counters to the third floor offices. Except for the toy department, watching the "flying canisters" was often the highlight of a child's McWhirr's visit.

The store even had its own radio studio. Throughout the 1940s and 1950s in-house announcer, Ed Burke, would broadcast a midday program liberally sprinkled with store advertisements over local station WSAR.

Times have changed. In today's big-box superstores, paperless computer networks have rendered pneumatic tubes obsolete, electronically coded credit cards have replaced numbered metal discs, and tiny digital surveillance cameras have all but driven the floorwalker to extinction.

Arguably, the modern retail environment is more efficient, but it all seems so coldly impersonal. More than merely a department store, R.A. McWhirr's was a Fall River institution, a warm and friendly place where a sales clerk often knew your name, and in some cases, your number.

April 1, 2011
Fall River, Massachusetts

8.2.1 The exterior of the R.A. McWhirr Company, 165-193 South Main Street, Fall River, as it appeared in the 1920s; the iconic department store was housed in the Mills Building, named for the store's president, Asa Adam Mills (1864-1941).

8.2.2 The R.A. McWhirr Company candy department decked out for Valentine's Day during the 1920s; always well-stocked with a wide variety of sweets and nuts, the department was one of the store's most popular.

8.2.3 A 1920s R.A. McWhirr Company Christmas window display featuring a newfangled Hoover electric vacuum cleaner, with the catchy sales pitch: "Give her The Hoover and you give her the best." For a down payment of $2.25, a husband could delight his spouse by giving her, according to the McWhirr's advertising department, "What Every Woman Wants."

8.2.4 A 1950s advertisement for the "Chubbettes" line of clothing; Fall River's R.A. McWhirr Company sold the popular line, which was designed exclusively for the "chubby lass."

8.2.5 Michael T. Walsh interviews with the R.A. McWhirr Company Santa, "the real one," in the late 1940s; he worked briefly for the store following his 1961 graduation from Fall River's B.M.C. Durfee High School.

McWhirr's Musings

The downtown Fall River flagship store wasn't the McWhirr's only retail venture. In 1890, founder Robert McWhirr, along with a partner, opened a dry goods establishment in Tampa, Florida. The store was forced to close less than a year later because of an outbreak of yellow fever in the area.

In 1898, McWhirr's branched out to neighboring New Bedford, Massachusetts, where it opened the New Bedford Dry Goods Co., later to become The Star Store. In 1918, the store, at the corner of Union and Purchase Streets, became the first in the country to install an escalator. The Star Store closed in the 1980s.

1909 saw McWhirr's extend its reach northward when it acquired Owen, Moore and Co., a dry goods store in Portland, Maine, purveyors of "needlework, chinaware, cut glass, toys, clothing, & more."

If you were a Boy Scout in Fall River, you had no choice but to make a visit to McWhirr's. The store was the only authorized supplier of official Scout uniforms, equipment, and handbooks in the area.

In 1890, McWhirr's inaugurated a free delivery service using a two-wheeled wagon drawn by a "spirited mare," purchased from the Stanley Brothers of Somerset, Massachusetts.

In the 1920s, McWhirr's boasted the largest private branch telephone exchange in the city of Fall River.

In addition to stocking a wide variety of art supplies, McWhirr's in-house art and advertising staff offered free drawing lessons by appointment to customers.

The store employed a female floorwalker who, in addition to her security duties would double as a personal shopper for customers who ordered items by telephone.

For the convenience of toddlers, McWhirr's third floor ladies restrooms featured a working miniature toilet twelve inches high.

During the great hurricane of 1938, Elizabeth Mills, daughter of McWhirr's executive Everett B. Mills, survived a harrowing experience. She and her caregiver, Mary Black, were caught unaware in the family's Westport Harbor home and were swept away by the storm's huge waves. Elizabeth alone survived by swimming to safety as the hurricanes' tidal surge abated.

From the 1950s until McWhirr's 1975 closing, shoppers were greeted on the store's manned elevator by genial operator Howie Duffy. Acknowledging everyone with a smile, the affable Duffy would announce the various departments floor by floor. After the store's closing, Howie would continue his ups and downs at the controls of elevators at both the Academy and Hudner buildings until his retirement.

April 4, 2011
Fall River, Massachusetts

8.3.1 In addition to being the "only authorized supplier of official" Boy Scout uniforms in Fall River, the R.A. McWhirr Company also capitalized on other specialty merchandise that appealed to boys. In the 1930s, the store's display manager "constructed" a log cabin, to effectively advertise Tom Mix merchandise.

THE DURFEE THEATER

Leaving aside the unfortunate, short-sighted placement of Interstate 195 in the 1960s, the Great Fire of 1928 was the biggest disaster ever to befall downtown Fall River.

On a frigid February 2nd evening, workmen were busy demolishing the recently closed Pocasset Manufacturing Company. While warming themselves with a portable heater, they inadvertently started a blaze which soon engulfed the entire monolithic mill complex. Quickly realizing the enormity of the situation, Fire Chief Jeremiah F. Sullivan sounded multiple alarms and requested assistance from neighboring towns as far away as Boston.

Record low temperatures froze hoses, frustrating fireman in their attempts to limit the flames to the sprawling Pocasset Street complex where the fire had begun. Driven by strong and changeable winds, the flames first jumped north over Central Street, then west crossing North Main, and finally south across Bedford Street. Although there were no fatalities and only a few injuries, by the time the smoke cleared on February 3rd, five city blocks had been reduced to smoldering rubble. The lead of a March 3, 1928, article in New York's *The Syracuse Herald* put it succinctly: "The business district of this city, one of New England's greatest mill centers, lays in ruins today."

City Hall was saved—temporarily—but many important buildings were lost, including the Central Police Station, the Mohican Hotel, and the Granite Block. But one casualty of the conflagration was to become the silver lining in this smoky cloud. The totally destroyed Rialto Theater would become the site of its even grander successor, the Durfee.

The Durfee Theater, opened on August 29, 1929, eighteen months after the fire that destroyed its predecessor, and only weeks before the stock market crash that would usher in the Great Depression. Built by Nathan Yamins and William Durfee, Sr., it was leased to the operating company, Yamins Theatrical Enterprises, Inc. The opening feature was the Marx Brothers' film, *The Cocoanuts*.

Designed by renowned Fall River architect Maude Darling Parlin, the Durfee was patterned after elements of the thirteenth-century Alhambra Palace in Granada, Spain. The lobby's Moorish influences included colorful tapestries, tiles imported from Seville, and a floor of black and gold marble. A bubbling sunken fish pond, near the candy counter, was a required stop for children and adults alike before entering the theater proper.

Considered the crown jewel of Fall River theaters, the Durfee had a capacity of about 2300 and the preferred loge seats could be reserved for a premium over the regular admission fee. As attendance waned during the depths of the Depression, management swallowed their pride by introducing "dish night" on Wednesdays to pump up the house. Week in and week out, housewives would collect a piece of chinaware from an usher after the show until they had a complete set. For many young, Depression-era families, it was the first dinnerware they would ever own.

During World War II the Durfee was patriotic. Theater buff Gerald DeLuca, writing on the website Cinema Treasures, observed the following: "On December 7, 1941, the movie *Birth of the Blues* was interrupted and the manager requested all military personnel present to return to their bases. Noisemakers and paper hats stored for the 1942 New Year's Eve show were thrown out because they were labeled 'Made in Japan.'"

The Durfee is remembered, of course, as Fall River's primary source of first-run films. But in the 20s it was built to accommodate the stage show as an equal partner to the fledgling movie industry.

Following up on its successful 1950s run of TV personalities and Hollywood talent in summer stock at the Somerset Playhouse, Yamins Enterprises decided to bring Broadway back to the Durfee. In 1965, the Broadway cast of *The Sound of Music* came to 30 North Main Street.

The 1969-70 season was particularly memorable opening on October 16th, with the musical *I Do, I Do* starring Phil Ford and Mimi Hines. Ferrante and Teicher, billed as the "world's most popular piano team," performed in concert for a one-night stand the following November. The Jerome Kern musical, *Show Boat* gave two performances on February 2 and 3, 1970.

In April of that year, the long running musical, *Cabaret*, starring Tandy Cronyn and Franklin Kiser, played to a packed house, only to be followed by two equally sold-out performances of *Mame*, starring Sheila Smith, on May 20th and 21st.

Times have changed, including the conventions of theater going. "In those days you dressed-up to go to a live show," remembers Donald Arsenault who, along with his wife, attended the 1970 performance of *Mame*: "I came out of the theater in a pouring rain wearing a suit and tie and had to change a flat tire on my car parked on Central Street."

Times eventually caught up with the Durfee, too. Television's advancing popularity and the advent of suburban mall cinemas with their ample parking gradually strangled the stand-alone center city theaters. In September, 1971, the Durfee went dark. Its last movie—Disney's *The Barefoot Executive*.

In another example of unfortunate short-sightedness, injury was added to insult when, in 1973, the Durfee was razed to be replaced by a bank. Unlike the visionary restorations of the Providence Performing Arts Center—formerly Loew's Movie Palace—and New Bedford's Zeiterion Theater, the curtain will never again rise at the Durfee. Maude Darling Parlin, who died in 1979, was said to have wept at the passing of her creation.

July 7, 2013
Fall River, Massachusetts

8.4.1 The northwest corner of North Main and Central Street, Fall River, 1946, showing the Durfee Theatre, "the crown jewel of Fall River theatres."

8.4.2 The North Main Street entrance of the Durfee Theatre, Fall River, late 1940s; the elaborate interior, inspired by the thirteenth-century Alhambra Palace in Granada, Spain, was indicative of the impressive movie palaces erected during the Roaring Twenties.

8.4.3 The magnificent lobby of the Durfee Theatre, Fall River, late 1940s. Decorated in the Moorish style, the grand space featured handmade tile imported from Saville, Spain, a floor paved in black and gold marble, a sunken marble fish pond, and elaborate tapestries.

8.4.4 The stage of the Durfee Theatre, Fall River, late 1940s; the theatre "was built to accommodate the stage show as an equal partner to the ... movie industry."

THE DURFEE'S INFLUENCE

The Rialto—formerly the Savoy—wasn't the only theater destroyed in the Great Fire of 1928; the neighboring Premier Theater also succumbed to the flames.

Besides the Durfee, Maude Darling Parlin designed many well-known Fall River buildings. Among them: the Mills Building, which housed the R.A. McWhirr Co.; the Women's Club; Temple Beth El; and the Eagle Restaurant.

The Eagle Restaurant, directly across North Main Street from the Durfee, was designed to replicate the elegant dining rooms of the opulent Fall River Line steamships. In November, 1929, the restaurant and the theater staged a combined "grand opening" event.

In addition to movies and stage shows, the Durfee was for many years the site of graduation ceremonies for its namesake high school, as well as Diman Vocational High School and Bristol Community College.

Through the 1950s through the early 1960s, movie ticket prices at the Durfee increased gradually from twenty-five cents to one dollar. From 1965 to 1967, a matinee ticket to a Durfee Broadway stage show held steady at a mere $1.50.

The adjacent China Royal Restaurant enjoyed a symbiotic relationship with the Durfee. Theater patrons frequently combined pre-show and post-show cocktails and meals at the popular eatery.

July 7, 2013
Fall River, Massachusetts

8.5.1 The Rialto Theatre, 55 North Main Street, Fall River, 1924; the structure was destroyed in the Great Fire of 1928.

8.5.2 The Eagle Restaurant, 33 North Main Street, Fall River, 1933; noted Fall River architect Maud Frances (Darling) Parlin (1884-1979), designed the interior of the restaurant "to replicate the elegant dining rooms of the opulent Fall River Line steamships."

THE CAPITOL THEATRE

On the night of February 1, 1926, braving freezing temperatures and wind-swept sleet, nearly 4,000 theater-goers converged on South Main Street near the corner of Morgan. Set against the background of a giddily rising stock market and the raucous indifference to Roaring Twenties Prohibition, Fall River's Capitol Theater opened its doors for the first time.

Learning that the sparkling new theater's 1600 seats were sold out, upwards of 2000 would-be patrons nevertheless crowded the lobby and spilled into the street, hoping that timid ticket holders would be deterred by the weather. As a squad of eight policemen struggled to keep order, the press of the throng was so great that one of the theater's plate glass shadow boxes lining the lobby was accidentally shattered.

The audience—including representatives from Hollywood filmmakers, Metro-Goldwyn-Mayer, United Artists, and Paramount Pictures—was first treated to several numbers by Roy Frazee on the theater's new $25,000 Wurlitzer organ. In opening remarks, Mayor Edmond P. Talbot congratulated the Capitol's owners, saying that the theater "indicates the faith of its builders in the future of the city."

The opening night bill included: a newsreel; a Mack Sennett comedy; a dance drill by the "Nine Tiller Girls" from Miss Katherine Ney's School of Dance; and Al Bradbury, "The Singing Cop," with a rendition of "Pal of My Cradle Days." The night concluded with the feature silent film, *Just Suppose*, starring the immortal Richard Barthelmess. For those left out in the cold, they could cozy-up in their homes and listen to the entire program broadcast over Fall River radio station WTAB, 1130 on the dial.

The majestic new Capitol was designed by noted Fall River architect Joseph M. Darling. The actual construction was supervised by his architect children, Maude and George, after Darling died on April 15, 1925, the very day ground was broken for his new showplace. Darling's design included orchestra chandeliers, an ornate lobby featuring a terrazzo marble floor, and the largest solid mirror in the city at eight by fifteen feet.

In addition to the several, smaller neighborhood playhouses such as the Globe's Park Theater, the Capitol immediately went into competition with the city's established downtown houses: the Academy; the Bijou; the Empire; the Rialto; and the Plaza. The elegant 2200 seat Durfee, sporting its gleaming marble fish pool in the lobby, would be built three years later in 1929.

Bowing to the decline in movie attendance, caused in large measure by the tidal wave of television entertainment, the Capitol operated for only thirty-one years, closing its doors in 1957. In the ensuing decades, a series of indignities have been visited upon the once grand art deco playhouse. At one time or another, it's been a bowling alley, a social club, a game room, and a furniture store. In 1976, vandals added injury to insult by setting fire to a section of the theater's balcony causing over $10,000 worth of damage.

Against all odds, some eighty-five years after the spectacular glow of its opening night, the Capitol still lives—barely. The building housing the theater was purchased by entrepreneurs Glenn and Donna Viveiros in 2004, with much of the space being used for the couple's cable television sales and installation business.

Touring the darkened, dusty theater, with its high walls and cavernous ceiling, is comparable to an archeologist entering a tomb undisturbed for decades. No mummies are entombed here, only memories. Despite the years of grit and cobwebs, vestiges of the theater's original glory shine through. A faded tapestry, a bas relief balcony façade, an intricately carved wall sconce, all this and more, waiting patiently for resurrection.

"The night we discovered all this was still here," said Donna Viveiros, "my husband and I sat in the balcony and celebrated with a bottle of champagne."

"Luckily, the tenants who came after the theater just dropped the ceilings and raised the floors," said Viveiros, "they never really destroyed anything." Much of the Capitol's original floors, walls, and ceilings remained hidden behind a façade of plywood and sheetrock erected to accommodate furniture showrooms. "It was like a treasure hunt," exclaimed Viveiros, "I had my carpenter cutting random holes in the new walls to expose the original beauty of the theater."

Help for the last of the city's grand playhouses is on the way. Led by University of Colorado associate professor and Fall River native, Bob Flanagan, thirteen of that school's graduate students devoted their spring, 2010, semester to formulating a redevelopment plan for a performing arts complex with the Capitol as its centerpiece.

Using the resources of the university's school of architecture, the grad students have created impressive drawings and scale models of their vision of the Capitol restored to its former elegance. The concept goes beyond the theater itself, envisioning a five-to-six-block cultural center including connecting the nearby N. B. Borden school, constructed in 1867, as a venue for teaching the performing arts.

"It's a beautiful building and the students have a great plan to restore it," said Jim Rogers, a member of the non-profit's board of directors. "We're hoping the community will get behind us and support the effort. It could become a focal point for the rebirth of downtown."

All that's missing now is money. "Our contractor tells us that it will cost a minimum of $5 million for complete restoration," said Viveiros, who purchased the building housing the theater for $600,000 seven years ago and has put another $100,000 into it since. Viveiros and her husband have formed the *Capitol Theater Performing Arts Center*; a non-profit whose immediate goal is to spur interest in the overall project's potential by first restoring the front entrance and grand hallway of the majestic theater.

"We have only one more step in our application for listing in the National Register of Historic Places," said Viveiros. Last fall, the project fell just short of garnering enough on-line public support to qualify for a $250,000 grant from the Pepsi Corporation. "We're in the process of reapplying for this year's grant," added Viveiros. "The voting begins on October 1, and we'll be advertising details of how the public can help through their emails and texts to Pepsi."

Viveiros, who has a love of history and a particular passion for old buildings, is determined to save the Capitol. "Kids today have no clue what these places looked like," she says, "I'd like to be able to say that I preserved this for my children and grandchildren."

August 28, 2011
Fall River, Massachusetts

8.6.1 The brightly lit marquee of the Capitol Theatre, Fall River, 1937.

THE LOST STREET

In the early 1960s, as the pounding of the pile drivers signaled the coming of the Braga Bridge, the very heart of Fall River blocked the route of the highway it would carry. When Interstate 195 rudely cut the city in half, it took out not only neighborhoods and buildings, but whole streets.

Just north of the stately nineteenth-century City Hall, itself soon to be sacrificed to the wrecker's ball, lay ancient Market Street. No thoroughfare, Market Street ran from South Main to Second Street, only a few hundred feet of downtown history. But what a busy and useful little street it was.

Not only did it abut City Hall, the street was the shortest connection between two iconic center city landmarks: Main Street's Granite Block Building and the Second Street Post Office. The original ornate Post Office and Custom House, built in 1873, was replaced by the current Post Office in 1932. It survived I-195—the Granite Block did not.

As did the city as a whole, Market Street saw many changes over the years. Home to everything from pushcarts and barber shops, to banks and pool halls, the street hosted a couple of food trucks for the late-night crowd during the Roaring Twenties.

In the nineteenth century, the street had become the home of a unique Fall River monument, the Cogswell Fountain, donated by Dr. Henry Daniel Cogswell, a wealthy temperance crusader.

On October 4, 1884, the ornate—some would say garish—Cogswell Fountain was set in place at the corner of South Main and Market Streets, near the northwest corner of old City Hall.

No doubt preventing Dr. Cogswell from a few spins in his grave, his elaborate fountain was saved from the ravages of 1960s urban renewal. After a few years of nomadic storage, it now sits at the northwest corner of South Main and Central Streets.

As for Market Street itself? Like much of the former downtown, it's gone. The space it once occupied now a barren concrete plaza in the shadow of the Brutalist architecture of Fall River Government Center.

January 18, 2015
Fall River, Massachusetts

8.7.1 Market Street, from South Main to Second Street, Fall River, as it appeared in the late-nineteenth century.

CHAPTER
NINE

BASEBALL

BASEBALL'S BEGINNINGS

If you think Abner Doubleday invented baseball you're probably committing an error, but if you think it was A. J. Cartwright, you may have a hit.

"The story that Doubleday invented baseball in 1839 is a myth," declared local historian Dr. Philip T. Silvia Jr.

In "Base Ballists," the last of the Fall River Historical Society's Summer Lecture Series held at Bristol Community College on August 6, 2013, Professor Silvia painted a vivid picture of the game's nineteenth-century dead ball era and the colorful characters who inhabited it.

"A form of the game called 'rounders' brought over from Britain by colonists was played in Pittsfield as early as 1790," said Silvia, "and the game evolved gradually over time." Henry Chadwick, a New York sportswriter, often called the "Father of Baseball," is credited with developing the box score in the 1860s. But it was another New Yorker, A. J Cartwright, who, in 1849, actually wrote down the fundamental rules including: foul lines; three strikes per out; three outs per inning; and the visionary, enduring metric of ninety feet between bases.

"When it comes to the origin of baseball," said Silvia with a laugh, "the evolutionists are winning out over the creationists."

"By the 1870s, baseball was big in Fall River," said Silvia. Bill "Gunner" McGunnigle, who would go on to play four seasons in the major leagues, invented the catcher's mitt while playing for Fall River in 1875. Catching barehanded—as all players did in those days—was murder; fielder's gloves wouldn't save broken fingers until the 1890s. McGunnigle decided to do something about it. Borrowing a pair of thick bricklayer's gloves, he tried them out during warm-ups but found that he couldn't throw properly with them on. Taking a jackknife, he cut the fingers off the right-hand glove and the catcher's mitt was born.

"McGunnigle was a character," said Silvia, "he wore lavender colored pants and occasionally somersaulted across home plate while scoring a run."

Maine's George "Piano Legs" Gore, who starred for the New York Giants and other major league teams, got his start in the New England League batting .319 for Fall River in 1877. "Gore was probably baseball's first contract hold-out," said Silvia. In 1879, A.G. Spalding, owner of the Chicago White Stockings, offered him $1,200 for the season but Gore refused, demanding $2,500. Eventually they compromised, and

Gore began his fourteen-year big league career at a salary of $1,900 annually.

In 1880, Gore led the National League in hitting with a .360 average. "But it was in runs scored that he really excelled," said Silvia. "He averaged 1.02 runs per game over his career. Think about that: The great Ted Williams only averaged .78 runs per game."

Another Hall of Famer with a local connection is Ned Hanlon, who before beginning his thirteen-year Major League career, starred in 1877 for the Fall River Cascade, of the six-team New England League; the league's other teams included: the Rhode Islands; the Manchester Reds; the Lynn Live Oaks; and the delightfully named Lowell Ladies Men. According to Silvia, Hanlon was a teammate of Fall River's most famous major leaguer, Charlie Buffinton, on the 1887 world champion Detroit Wolverines.

Roger Connor, whom Silvia termed "The Babe Ruth of the 1880s," served as player-manager for the Fall River Indians after the last of his eighteen major league seasons in 1896. Every baseball fan worth his pine tar knows that Hank Aaron broke Babe Ruth's career home run record, but few remember that it was Ruth who broke Connor's record. "Connor at six foot three inches and 230 pounds, had exceptional size for a baseball player of that era," said Silvia. According to Silvia, he also differed from most of his contemporaries in that he was a quiet family man who did not smoke, drink, or swear.

Portraying nineteenth-century baseball as a rough and tumble game, Silvia noted that, in 1877, the president of Harvard University publicly sniffed that the sport had "barbarous qualities." In that same year, Fred "Tricky" Nichols introduced a curveball in a game against Harvard and, according to Silvia, the university called the move "a low form of cunning," adding that "Harvard was not in the business of deception."

Professor Silvia described a different era, when money changed hands on the outcome of games between fans and players alike. According to Silvia, visiting teams not only battled the home nine, but had to contend with the "Tenth Man" – the home town umpire.

Traveling by train from town to town, veteran players were on a first name basis with madams and managers of brothels and saloons. The curse of performance-enhancing drugs was still years away, but alcohol was a factor in many games. "Owners hired private detectives to shadow the lushes," said Silvia. "Sometimes the bases were loaded and so was the pitcher."

August 9, 2013
Fall River, Massachusetts

9.1.1 William Henry "Gunner" McGunnigle (1855-1899), striking a dashing pose on an Old Judge cigarette card when manager of the Brooklyn National League Team, 1887. A noted "character," he "invented the catcher's mitt while playing in Fall River in 1875."

FALL RIVER'S BASEBALLISTS

Stand in the batter's box at Fenway Park today and you'll face a pitcher sixty feet, six-inches away, throwing a baseball at speeds of between ninety and one hundred miles per hour.

Now imagine standing only fifty, or even forty-five feet, away. Intimidating. But, until 1893, these were the distances faced by batsmen—and often barehanded catchers—during the gritty era of nineteenth-century Major League baseball.

It wasn't until 1883 that catcher Jack Clements of the Philadelphia Keystones first wore a chest protector, and it took until 1907 for the Giants' Roger Bresnahan to adapt leg guards used in cricket into the game's first shin guards. "Today we call catchers' equipment the 'tools of ignorance,'" laughed historian Dr. Philip T. Silvia Jr. "Back then it was definitely better to be a pitcher than a catcher."

In "Fall River's Homegrown Professional Baseballists, 1880s – early 1900s," the second of the Fall River Historical Society's summer lecture series held at Bristol Community College on July 23, 2014, Professor Silvia highlighted area natives who played major league baseball in the late-nineteenth and early-twentieth centuries— chief among them, the great pitcher and Fall River native, Charlie Buffinton.

"Following the Civil War, baseball was catching on with the public and by the 1870s had become big in Fall River," said Silvia. In 1876, the Fall River team won the New England championship. But only two years later, in 1878, said Silvia, "the city of irregularities," as Fall River was then known for labor and economic reasons unrelated to baseball, saw most of its star players pirated by the New Bedford nine.

In 1877, the Fall River Cascade of the New England league had no fewer than seven players who would go on to play in the major leagues: George Gore; Mert Hackett; Ned Hanlon; Steve Libby; Bill "Gunner" McGunnigle; Ed Rowen; and Chelsea, Massachusetts, born, manager Jim Mutrie.

In 1880, wealthy Fall River industrialist John S. Brayton donated a plot of land for a ball field at the corner of North Main and Hood Streets. In 1881, the field was enclosed and teams played winner-take-all for the gate receipts. "There were also considerable sums bet on the side," said Silvia.

For several seasons in the mid-1880s, Fall River native and shortstop Frank Fennelly teamed with fellow Cincinnati Red Stockings' second basemen Bid McPhee. "They were the premier double play combination of their day," said Silvia.

But, by far, the most famous and accomplished Fall River born major leaguer was Charlie Buffinton.

Beginning in 1882, Buffinton played eleven seasons in the majors, including five with the Boston Beaneaters, three with the Philadelphia Quakers, and one each with the Philadelphia Athletics, Boston Reds, and Baltimore Orioles. Almost exclusively a pitcher, Buffinton had a career record of 233 wins against 152 losses for a winning percentage of .605.

In 1883, Buffinton won twenty-five games against fourteen losses for National League pennant-winning Boston. The American Association champion Philadelphia Athletics lost their first eight post-season exhibition games resulting in the cancellation of a "World Series" against Buffinton's Beaneaters. The following year, again with National League Boston, Buffinton went an astounding 49-16.

Blacklisted by owners for union activities in 1890, Buffinton joined the hastily formed Player's League where he would win nineteen games for the Philadelphia Athletics. The following year with the Boston Reds of the American Association, he won twenty-nine games while losing only nine, leading the league with a .763 winning percentage. "He was the best pitcher in baseball for the 1891 season, despite pitching in a hitter-friendly ball park," said Silvia.

On July 12, 1884, during a storied six-game home and home series against the Providence Grays, Buffinton struck out thirteen batters while gaining a 7-1 decision over the Beaneaters' hated rivals. "During the series, Fall River fans stopped a game in Providence, Rhode Island, to present Buffinton with a basket of flowers just as he came to bat," said Silvia. "Unfortunately, he popped up."

The Grays, led by Hall of Fame pitcher Charles "Old Hoss" Radbourn, who won a world record fifty-nine games that year, would go on to win the National League pennant and defeat the American Association's New York Metropolitans two out of three in what is considered the game's first post season series.

At six foot one inch and 180 pounds, Buffinton could also field his position. According to Silvia, observers of the day called him "quick as a cat." Apparently, he wasn't bad at the plate either. "In the last game of the July, 1884, Grays' series, he got three hits off the fabled Radbourn," added Silvia.

Contemporaries of Buffinton said that he was "cool and collected" with a "puzzling delivery." "He was said to have a perplexing curve and a drop pitch that 'fell off the table,'" said Silvia. According to Silvia, Buffinton was sometimes called the "Christy Mathewson of the 1880s," referring to the great Hall of Fame pitcher with 373 lifetime wins.

> Unlike the majority of pitchers, when about to deliver the ball, (Charlie) Buffinton squarely faces the batsman. Holding the ball in both hands at arm's length before his face, he nervously twists the sphere about for a moment or two. Then tossing his hands above his head he lifts his left foot from the ground and hops forward on the right. Swinging his right arm down to his side he sends the ball in with but little effort, but with considerable force."
>
> —*New York World* "How Men Pitch Base-Ball," 1886

Charlie Buffinton pitched his last game on June 28, 1892, retiring at the age of thirty-one. Reflecting on Buffinton's baseball career in 1912, a Boston sportswriter wrote: "It was clear that Buffinton had all the best of it."

Fall River's Charles G. Buffinton died in 1907 at the age of forty-six, and is buried in Oak Grove Cemetery.

July 27, 2014
Fall River, Massachusetts

9.2.1 Fall River native Charles "Charlie" G. Buffinton (1861-1907) depicted on an Old Judge cigarette card when a member of the National League Philadelphia Quakers, 1887.

9.2.2 Charles "Charlie" G. Buffinton poses on the mound for a Kalamazoo Bats cigarette card, 1887; he "was said to have a perplexing curve and a drop pitch that 'fell off the table.'"

9.2.3 Charles "Charlie" G. Buffinton's grave marker in Oak Grove Cemetery, Fall River.

Nap Lajoie

Baseball, in a rudimentary form often called "town ball," had been played in America long before the Civil War.

But it was the war itself, coupled with the completion of the intercontinental railroad in 1869, that spread the sport from coast to coast. Games among soldiers in army posts and even prison camps were popular on both sides of the Mason-Dixon line. Returning veterans enthusiastically brought the game back to their home towns.

By the 1890s, the game was rapidly blossoming into our "national pastime."

"1893 Fall River had a remarkable culture of leisure and social activities, in contrast with the immediate post-Civil War years," said historian Dr. Philip T. Silvia Jr., in a July 22, 2015, Fall River Historical Society sponsored talk at Bristol Community College.

Entitled "Glory Days and the 'Big Frenchman': Fall River's Professional Base Ballists of the mid-1890s," the presentation, replete with hundreds of vintage photographs, vividly recalled the period when baseball was a rough and tumble, often alcohol-fueled passion, for both players and fans.

Baseball was a big part, but not the only part, of the city's 1893 leisure and athletic activities. Calling it an "age of joiners," Professor Silvia recounted the numerous organizations available and calling for active participation. Among them was: the Fall River Cycle Club; the Fall River Athletic Club; the Rover Football Club; the Bowling Green Club; the Cricket Club; not to mention four yacht clubs and seven billiard halls. It was easy to work-up a sweat in the Spindle City, both in the mills and in whatever leisure time was left.

It was a period when all of Fall River followed the national pastime, but according to Silvia, "the Flint was crazy about baseball."

The city's nineteenth-century baseball grounds had its ticket booth at the corner of Bedford Street and Oak Grove Avenue. The right field foul line and parallel grandstand ran easterly along Bedford Street toward what is now Savoie Street, then just an unaccepted line on a map. Left field stretched north along Oak Grove with the city's granite water tower visible in the distance.

Among the great and near-great to have worn spikes in the city was New Bedford native Harry Stovey. After retiring from the majors, Stovey later played for Whaling City teams in informal games against Fall River. During his fourteen-year career with stops in Philadelphia, Baltimore, and Boston, Stovey led the major leagues in home runs five times. Sometimes called "nineteenth-century baseball's forgotten superstar," upon his retirement in 1893, he was the all-time home run leader *and* the all-time stolen base leader.

"Stovey invented the feet-first pop-up slide and sliding pads, and over a five-year period from 1886 to 1890, averaged seventy-five steals a year," marveled Silvia.

From 1893 to 1896, the Fall River Indians were the class of the highly regarded New England League winning the pennant four years running. Competing against, among others, the New Bedford Whalers, the Brockton Shoemakers, and the haughtily named Bangor Millionaires, the Indians went 257-143 for a gaudy .643 winning percentage.

The 1896 champions would feature ace pitcher Fred Klobedanz hurling thirty-two of their ninety games, pacing the staff with a sparkling twenty-six wins against a mere six losses. "Kloby" would go on to pitch in the majors for five years where he would post fifty-three career victories against only twenty-five defeats for the delightfully named National League Boston Beaneaters.

Klobedanz married Fall River's Annie Durfee in 1895, and, in 1897, would lead the major leagues in winning percentage with a 26-7, .788 line for the Beaneaters. "In those days it was common for major leaguers to hold off-season jobs," said Silvia. "Kloby did winter carpentry for the teams he played for."

Already riding a streak of three straight New England League Championships, the Fall River Indians would add "The Big Frenchman" to its roster for the 1896 campaign. Napoleon "Nap" Lajoie, was born in Woonsocket, Rhode Island, on September 5, 1874, and in his early twenties had already established a reputation as an up and coming star.

Playing eighty games for Fall River, Lajoie would bat a league leading .429, and hit fifteen round-trippers. In one home and home series against New Bedford, he would win the away game with a dramatic tenth inning home run clearing the fence at the park's deepest point. In the next day's home game, he would pace Fall River's easy win with two doubles and a triple.

The Boston Globe called Lajoie "The most promising player in America," and "The batting phenomenon of the season." "Lajoie was already being scouted by both Boston and Pittsburgh," said Silvia.

Led by "The Big Frenchman," the 1896 Fall River Indians, with a record of sixty-eight and thirty-four, would fly the New England League pennant for the fourth straight year. Local sports reporters would call them "the city's best team ever."

Lajoie played his last game for the Fall River Indians on August 11, 1896, banging out three hits: a single, double, and triple. The next day, he booked passage on the Fall River Line boat/train to Philadelphia, Pennsylvania, where he would play seven seasons with the Phillies and Athletics before moving on to the eponymous "Naps" in American League Cleveland for thirteen years.

On September 15, 1903, Lajoie and his Major League Cleveland "Naps" came to Fall River for an exhibition game won by the home town team 6-2. But beyond the game itself, up to 7,000 fans turned out just to see the return of the legendary Lajoie.

One newspaper blared that "Big Chief Lajoie would raise the roof from the top of the Water Works Tower every time he came to bat."

Lajoie said it felt like a homecoming to him to play again in Fall River. The National League batting champ had a quiet day at the plate, but the crowd didn't care. A newspaper said that the occasion took on "the nature of a love feast."

Napoleon "Nap" Lajoie captured five batting titles, including a modern-era record .426 mark for the Philadelphia Athletics in 1901, won the first Triple Crown in American League history, and finished with a lifetime .338 batting average. He was elected to Baseball's Hall of Fame in 1937.

Professor Silvia attributes the following quote to the immortal Cy Young; "Lajoie was one of the most rugged players I ever faced. He'd take your leg off with a line drive, turn the third baseman around like a swinging door, and powder the hand of the first baseman."

The Sporting News once wrote that Lajoie had a "wolfish thirst for liquor."

"I never took any pledge," Lajoie was quoted as saying, "I always liked a glass of beer and never made any secret about it."

According to Silvia, Lajoie, a good pool player, loved the predominantly French Canadian Flint section of the city and frequented its saloons and pool halls. "Imagine the lost barroom stories," he lamented.

July 26, 2015
Fall River, Massachusetts

Note: The topics for the three articles in this chapter were presented by Dr. Silvia at the Fall River Historical Society's annual lecture series, generously sponsored by the Grimshaw-Gudewicz Charitable Foundation.

9.3.1 Napoléon "Nap" Lajoie, aka Larry Lajoie, "The Big Frenchman" (1874-1959), poses in his Major League Cleveland Naps uniform, 1903.

9.3.2 Napoléon "Nap" Lajoie autographed this vintage Goudy Gum Company baseball card in 1936, the year before he was elected to the National Baseball Hall of Fame.

CHAPTER TEN

PEOPLE

BILL TORPEY

If nothing else, beginning a radio career by interviewing The Three Stooges will teach a broadcaster not to take himself too seriously. But in the summer of 1950, fresh out of Washington D.C.'s National Academy of Broadcasting, that's exactly what Bill Torpey found himself doing.

Torpey, was in character as "Uncle Bill" on a Saturday morning children's show for radio station WOCB in West Yarmouth, Massachusetts, when The Stooges came to town to entertain the troops at nearby Camp Edwards. Good thing it was radio and not TV. "The first thing they do when they show-up is take their pants off to have them pressed for the performance," says Torpey. "They did the whole interview standing there in their skivvies. I was laughing so much I could hardly get the questions out."

Five years later, after presumably working with fully clothed people in stints with two other area radio stations and news assignments at the *Taunton Gazette* and *Fall River Herald News*, the affable Torpey decided on a career change. Signing on as general manager of the fledgling Fall River Line Pier, Inc., Torpey would oversee the growth of the quasi-public, non-profit corporation for almost four decades until his retirement in 1992.

Chartered in May 1948 and funded by a one million dollar state revenue bond, construction of the facility's terminal building, bulkheads, and roadways began in 1951, culminating with the State Pier's official opening on February 1, 1955.

"At the time it seemed like an oddball career for me," says the self-described non-mariner. "I wasn't a sailor and I didn't even have a powerboat." But seeing the potential of the city's deep water harbor, only an eighteen-mile traverse from the open sea, the broadcaster/journalist turned manager embraced the challenge that would transform Fall River into the fifth largest cargo port in New England.

In 1968, the United Fruit Company, the largest banana grower in the world, had just begun using the port of Providence, Rhode Island, to ship its fruit to its lucrative northeast United States and Canadian markets. After only two voyages, the Chiquita Brand managers realized that the Rhode Island port's lack of an adequate on-site weighing capability was a problem.

Having received a call from the company's local executive director asking about the State Pier facility, Torpey invited him to Fall River. "Over lunch in a downtown restaurant I learn that this guy's also the mayor of his town," says Torpey, "so I excuse myself, find a phone, and call my friend Mayor Nick Mitchell at nearby City Hall."

"Nick," I say, "we've got a great opportunity here for some port business; just get down here, walk through, say 'Hi,' and I'll do the rest." Predictably, the two mayors found common ground and got along fine, but more important, Bill Torpey got the information he wanted.

"Believe it or not," says Torpey, "the biggest thing we had going for us was our on-site Toledo electronic truck scale." Because bananas are sold by weight, every truck loading at the Providence terminal had to drive several miles to an independent scale to certify their load. "Our set-up saved a lot of time," says Torpey. "The empty truck would drive up, get its tare weight, and get re-weighed after taking on the bananas, and drive away."

Soon, United Fruit's "Great White Fleet" of banana boats—ships, really—began their regular weekly run from Central America to Fall River. Every Thursday during 1968 and 1969, about one hundred stevedores swarmed the State Pier to unload thousands of boxes of the still green fruit. "The operation derived a substantial amount of revenue from the relationship," Torpey says proudly.

The city's period of banana prosperity lasted two years, ending when a hurricane wiped out the plantations in Guatemala and Honduras, cutting the supply line. "While it lasted it came at a good time for the city," says Torpey. "It coincided with the ongoing telephone company strike and we had plenty of willing workers."

Although Torpey ended his official involvement with the Fall River Line Pier over eighteen years ago, its mission is still dear to his heart. He sees untapped potential for both the State Pier and the port of Fall River in general. "I've always been disappointed that over the years we were unable to convince the various governmental agencies to provide funding to dredge the ship channel to forty feet," he says. Although authorized to a depth of thirty-five feet, Torpey maintains that it's now shallower in many sections, inhibiting the passage of larger, deeper draft ships.

According to Torpey a major problem is the environmental regulatory agencies' refusal to approve a disposal site for the dredge sediment. "I understand the concerns of environmental activists like Save the Bay, but sometimes they go too far," says Torpey. He also expressed surprise and concern over the recent designation of the Taunton River as "Wild and Scenic," seeing no need for it. "There's no reason there can't be a balance among environmental, recreational, and economic concerns," he adds.

Torpey also decries what he describes as the City of Fall River's "lack of unified interest" in the waterfront. "There's no effective Port Authority," he says. "As far as I know, they don't even hold meetings." For years, Torpey has called for port promotion and outreach through the establishment of a Fall River Harbor Association comprising both public and private waterfront interests. "You're never going to get business to come to the waterfront by sitting at a desk," he says.

Nevertheless, Torpey is buoyed by the tourism and recreational activity he sees at Battleship Cove and Bi-Centennial Park. As general chairman and organizer of the Save Battleship Massachusetts committee in 1964, he was instrumental in bringing

"Big Mamie" to the city and was pleased with the recently announced plan to install a living history group on the ship. "I think it's terrific," he said.

In 2011, Bill Torpey will retire again; this time from thirty-five years of service as the Deputy Pilot Commissioner of the Port of Fall River. He recently submitted his letter of resignation to Governor Deval Patrick and is awaiting appointment of his successor. "It's been a privilege and an honor," says Torpey, "but it's time for somebody else to take over."

Supervising ten licensed ship's pilots, in one of only four such positions in the state, Torpey's office is responsible for the safe maneuvering of ships up and down Mount Hope Bay and the Taunton River.

Because he continues in his capacity as a state official until replaced, Torpey declined to comment directly on the shipping aspect of the current liquefied natural gas (LNG) controversy. But speaking of local maritime hazards in general terms, he's of the opinion that for safety reasons, the Brightman Street Bridge should be completely demolished, including its hidden underwater footings. "No court in the land will allow that bridge to remain standing." He says, "You cannot block a navigable waterway under any circumstances."

During his tenure, the waterway has enjoyed an exemplary safety record which Torpey attributes to the expertise of his pilots. "They're a skilled group, on call twenty-four hours a day," He says, "They're highly paid and they deserve every penny of it."

Over the years, Torpey has unselfishly given of himself to many civic groups and professional organizations. Among the positions he has held are: president and honorary life member of the North Atlantic Ports Association; chairman of the New England River Basins & Port Operators Committee; and port director of the Emergency Port Planning Committee, Port of Fall River. In 1984, Torpey was selected as "Outstanding Citizen of the Year" by the Fall River Chamber of Commerce.

Despite his many marine and port management accomplishments, Torpey counts his long association with Charlton Memorial Hospital as a trustee and past chairman of the board as one of his most satisfying and rewarding experiences. "It's been one of my passions," says Torpey. "The experience truly moved me."

Normally, a retiring port commissioner would be described as "sailing off into the sunset" or some such appropriate nautical reverie. But given his self-proclaimed non-mariner status, Bill Torpey will most likely just walk off instead.

There is, however, one direct, personal nautical connection to his beloved waterway that Torpey will admit to. He remembers that years ago he had a small outboard skiff. He doesn't remember how big, maybe sixteen or eighteen feet. According to Torpey, in good weather he'd sometimes use it to commute to the State Pier along the river from near the bottom of his street in Somerset.

Torpey recounts the following anecdote from his boating career: "One summer I had my cousin visiting from Cleveland. She was an Ursuline Order Nun, the principal of a Catholic high school. One day I ask if she'd like to go to work with me to see the Pier. 'Sure,' she says, so the next morning off we go in my little open boat.

"Here we are, slowly chugging down the river under both bridges; I'm dressed for work in a suit and tie, with Sister Mary Dolors sitting primly up front wearing her full habit. I thought a couple of cars were going to drive off the Brightman Street Bridge gawking at us. We must have been quite a sight."

January 30, 2011
Fall River, Massachusetts

10.1.1 William "Bill" J. Torpey (1927-2016), standing at left, oversees the unloading of a packing crate on the City Pier, Fall River, January 3, 1961.

10.1.2 Bill Torpey photographed at his home, 2011.

Maria Altmann

It took almost seventy years but in 2006 an octogenarian with a Fall River connection finally reclaimed family heirlooms seized by the Nazis during World War II.

The recent hit movie *Woman in Gold* recounts Maria Altmann's struggle to retrieve several valuable paintings from the Austrian government through legal battles lasting eight years. Renowned actress Helen Mirren is luminous as Altmann in this intimate true story of justice delayed but ultimately achieved.

In 1998, Altmann, who had lived in Fall River in the 1940s, tried direct negotiations with Austrian authorities but her proposals for recovery were refused. In 1999, she sought to sue the government of Austria in an Austrian court but could not afford the $1.5 million filing fee calculated as a percentage of the $150 million value of the five paintings in question.

After filing a lawsuit in United States District Court under the Foreign Sovereign Immunities Act, the case, *Republic of Austria vs. Altmann*, reached the United States Supreme Court, which in 2004 ruled that Austria was answerable to the suit. Spurred by this decision, Austria agreed to binding arbitration and in January, 2006, a three-judge Austrian panel ruled that Austria was legally bound to return the artworks to Altmann in Los Angeles, California. In terms of value, it was the largest single repatriation of Nazi-stolen art in Austria.

"The paintings have been in Vienna for sixty-eight years, and people in Europe saw them all the time," said Altmann. "I thought it would be a beautiful thing to show them in this country."

In 1938, after Nazi Germany's annexation of Austria, Maria Altmann's wealthy uncle, Ferdinand Bloch-Bauer, was forced to flee the Nazi persecution of Jews leaving behind a collection of artwork by the Austrian master Gustav Klimt, including two portraits of his wife, Adele. The paintings were soon looted by the Nazis.

Ferdinand died in 1945 leaving his estate to a nephew and two nieces, one of whom was Maria. In the confusion following World War II, five of the paintings ended up in the possession of the Austrian government.

In 1937, Maria Bloch—the family name was changed to Bloch-Bauer after her birth—married Frederick "Fritz" Altmann. Soon after their honeymoon in France, Frederick was arrested and interned in the Dachau concentration camp to pressure his brother Bernhard, who had already fled to safety in Paris, to sign over his successful textile business to the Nazis.

After the confiscatory turnover of Bernhard's factory, Fredrick was released and he and Maria, as depicted in the movie, made a harrowing escape from house arrest under the Nazis. Traveling first to Holland, they then reunited with Bernhard Altmann who had started a textile business in Liverpool, England.

England passed the Enemy Alien Act in 1939, and all nationals from enemy countries were forced to move from coastline cities during wartime. Bernhard then immigrated to the United States where he started yet another textile company, this time in Fall River.

In 1940, Maria and Frederick again followed Bernhard and were soon living in Fall River, with Frederick working in his brother's factory. The 1941 *Fall River City Directory* lists "Fritz" as a "textile worker." The following year he got a promotion, with the 1942 directory listing him as "production mgr."

Both city directories list the Altmann's address as 629 Highland Avenue, a three-decker, then and now one of the more modest houses on that iconic Fall River street.

Details are sketchy, but it's known that in 1941 Bernhard Altmann lost control of his Fall River business and moved first to New York City, and then to Texas, where he opened a knitting mill in 1947. It was a great success. In the 1950s, it was estimated that one-third of all cashmere sweaters sold in the United States came from Altmann's Texas factory.

Frederick and Maria Altmann moved to Los Angeles in 1943, where Maria started her own successful clothing business selling Bernhard's sweaters.

Bernhard Altmann died in 1980, Frederick "Fritz" Altmann died in 1994, and Maria Altmann died in 2011 at the age of ninety-four.

May 31, 2015
Fall River, Massachusetts

10.2.1 Maria Victoria (Bloch) Altmann (1916-2011) holds the famed portrait of her aunt, titled *Portrait of Adele Bloch-Bauer*; the portrait was looted by the Nazis and featured in the motion picture, *Woman in Gold*. The masterpiece was painted by the Austrian symbolist artist Gustave Klimt (1862-1918) between the years 1903 and 1907.

10.2.1 Maria and her husband, Frederick "Fritz" Altmann (1908-1994), resided in this house at 629 Highland Avenue while in Fall River during the early 1940s. *Massachusetts Historical Commission Form B., January 13, 1981.*

HORTENCIA RIBEIRO

She's ninety-eight years old, and despite her diminutive size has a memory like an elephant.

Mrs. Manuel Amaral, born Hortencia "Ester" Ribeiro during President Woodrow Wilson's administration, was the first person interviewed for a study called *Women at Work: An Oral History of Working Class Women in Fall River 1920 – 1970.* Some excerpts:

"When the teacher called me Hortencia at the Mount Hope School," remembered Amaral, "I wouldn't answer; I said that's not my name." At home, she was known only as Esther to her parents and four siblings. "I still haven't forgiven my parents for that first name," laughed Amaral.

Before retiring in 1978, Amaral worked for eight different companies in and around Fall River including: Center Garment, Firestone, Gamma Leather, Lynn Sportswear, Maplewood Yarn, Raytheon, and United Rayon. "I started at the Bourne Mill off Shove Street when I was 15 years old," said Amaral.

Amaral remembers her mother putting money away every week to be able to pay the $45 for a ton of coal that would have to last all winter. She recalls her father digging clams, quahogs, and periwinkles off Bay Street to supplement the family's meager depression era diet. "That's probably why I still love seafood even today," said Amaral wryly.

When Ester was a little girl, the family lived in the Bourne Mill Blocks. "I always wanted to help my mother cook," said Amaral, "but she was a little chubby and the kitchen was so small we both couldn't fit at the same time."

Like most families of that era, Esther and her three brothers and one sister handed over their wage packets directly to their father on payday. But just once Esther defied the system. "My mother had only these old housedresses and I promised her that when I started work at the Bourne Mill I would give her my first pay so she could buy a nice new dress," said Amaral.

"When my father asked if I was going to give him my pay I said, 'No, I promised it to momma so she could buy a new dress,'" remembered Amaral. "And I kept my promise." According to Amaral her mother bought her new dress and her father said no more about it.

Funded by a $5,000 grant from Mass Humanities, *Women at Work* is the brainchild of Fall River Historical Society (FRHS) member Joyce B. Rodrigues, who spearheaded the application process. Mrs. Amaral's interview was conducted and recorded by Ms. Rodrigues at the Society's headquarters at 451 Rock Street, Fall River, on November 12, 2014.

The study will document the lives of women who worked in Fall River's textile mills during the period of decline and made the transition to the needle-trades, or who began careers in the city's garment industry during the early years of its establishment.

Mrs. Amaral's recorded interview lays the cornerstone for an important archive of primary source material for the benefit of present and future generations. An archive of pertinent family papers and photographs will also be established for each interviewee, providing an important visual aid and furnishing material for exhibition and publication. Interviewers and consultants on the project include the FRHS curators, humanities scholars, educators, and others, all of whom have a keen interest in the multi-faceted goals of the project.

Note: Hortencia's interview, together with those of nine of her contemporaries, can be seen in the online exhibit *Women at Work: An Oral History of Working Class Women in Fall River, Massachusetts – 1920-1970*, viewable on the Fall River Historical Society's website, fallriverhistorical.org. The profusely illustrated 412-page companion volume, published by the Fall River Historical Society Press in 2017, is also available.

November 16, 2014
Fall River, Massachusetts

Addendum: According to her obituary, published in the *Fall River Herald News*, on October 25, 2017, Hortencia Amaral "... died peacefully at home in her sleep on October 22, 2017." Hortencia was 101 years old.

10.3.1 Mrs. Manuel Amaral, née Hortencia "Ester" Pacheco Ribeiro (1916-2017), in the 1940s.

THIS IS EASY: Hortensia Amaral operates a new machine designed to coat the underside of pillow sections with cement preparatory to their being pressed together. The machine is new to Department 5.

10.3.2 Hortencia at work at Firestone Rubber & Latex Products Company, Fall River, during the late 1940s or early 1950s. In response to a Firestone "big boss" who said that she seemed to like her job she said: "No, I don't …. I have to do it, so I am doing it. It isn't because I like it."

10.3.3 Hortencia posing with a negligee set in salmon rayon satin trimmed in beige machine-made lace that she wore in the 1940s; she donated the garment to the Fall River Historical Society in 2013.

ANDY BISHOP

Fall River's Roger Levesque wanted to be a pro boxer. He had talent, heart, and determination. All he needed now was an alias.

One of ten children, young Roger probably was forced to begin his fighting career at the family dinner table. Beginning his boxing career at the tender age of fourteen, the 118 pound Levesque experienced a meteoric rise through the amateur ranks with knockouts of such notables as Providence's Roland Madore in October, 1944.

On March 20, 1945, only days before his fifteenth birthday, Levesque defeated Eddie Bonnetti of Dorchester, Massachusetts, at the Boston Arena, to capture the New England Amateur Athletic Association bantamweight crown. Just two weeks later on April 2, Levesque lost a hard fought battle for the National A.A.U. Championship to Amos Aitson of Oklahoma City, Oklahoma.

Too young to legally engage in public boxing events either amateur or pro, Levesque decided to adopt the identity of his older brother Henry who was eighteen, the legal age. A New England Amateur Athletic Union registration with a date of October 25, 1945, bears Henry Levesque's name and an April 29, 1926, birth date. But a smiling fifteen-year-old Roger looks out from the attached official photo.

"He was determined to be a boxer no matter what," said Levesque's daughter, Denise Amaral, keeper of a detailed scrapbook compiled by her father himself. "Even as a young girl I remember him holding me up so I could punch the speed bag he kept in our cellar."

As World War II drew to a close, boxing entered a Golden Age both nationally and locally. Soon television would help transport the "sweet science" from small smoke-filled arenas like the Fall River Casino, to even larger smoke-filled arenas with cameras, like New York's Madison Square Garden. Nevertheless, in the late 1940s through the early 1950s, the local boxing scene remained vibrant.

Fall River's Ringside Café, co-owned by one-time professional boxer Donald "Bobby" Chabot, was an informal home to a stable of boxers including well-known local pros Gene LeBlanc and Bobby English. "Although my father never drank alcohol his entire life," said daughter Amaral, "he knew all those guys. I even remember meeting Bobby English at the Ringside when I was much older."

"It's unclear why my father chose the ring name Andy Bishop," said Amaral. "He had an older brother named Andrew so that's part of it. But as for Bishop, it must have had some significance but we don't know what it was."

Levesque's pro career had an inauspicious start. Fighting as "Andrew Bishop" he lost his May 1946 debut when he was KO'd in the fourth round by Jimmy Cleary at Hartford, Connecticut. At least Levesque could say he lost to an undefeated opponent; Cleary had a grand total of four pro bouts, winning them all.

After a second Hartford loss in August, 1946, this time on points to Al Girard, Levesque broke his maiden with a six-round unanimous decision over Gene Gomes of Boston. A Boston sports page gave this account: "Bishop did a good deal of the offensive work all the way through and landed quite a number of blows on the head and body of his opponent."

After a draw with Enos Tebo only two weeks after the Gomes win, Levesque lost again, this time to Jerry Lavigne at the Fall River Casino. This would be Roger's, Henry's, Andrew's, or Andy's last sanctioned fight for eleven months. The Massachusetts Boxing Commission had finally caught up with Levesque's aliases and age falsification and on January 27, 1947, suspended him from fighting indefinitely.

The Commission would lift the suspension on December 18, 1947, and on that very night the now fully-accredited Andy Bishop would defeat Frankie Fay on points in a four-rounder at the Fall River Casino. The win would start Bishop on a string of ten straight starts without a loss (nine wins—one draw).

Having decidedly shaken off the rust of inactivity, in the year following his suspension, Bishop would fight twenty-one times compiling a stellar record of 17-3-1.

Andy Bishop's last bout in that stretch was against fellow Fall Riverite Tony Ferry, the brother of Fall River Casino matchmaker Johnny Farias. In the weeks before the 1949 match, Ferry and Farias took to the newspapers to accuse Bishop and his manager, Anthony LeBlanc, of "dodging" Ferry.

Boxing promoter Sam Silverman was quoted as saying of LeBlanc: "I consider Andy Bishop one of the most promising young fighters in the game today, and it's too bad he is handicapped by such inept management." LeBlanc countered by saying; "We have nothing to gain by meeting Tony Ferry and everything to lose. Andy is entitled to a shot at bigger game."

In the days leading up to the January 6, 1949, fight, in a newspaper interview Ferry boldly predicted that he'd knock out Bishop. "I really don't expect any trouble with Bishop and I'm looking ahead to that January 20 bout for the New England featherweight championship." The winner of the Bishop-Ferry fight had been guaranteed a shot at Timothy "Buddy" Hayes, the reigning New England Featherweight Champion.

The bout was billed as the Featherweight Championship of Fall River and drew one of the best fan turnouts of the year. The fight itself wasn't much of a contest. The taller Bishop had a decided reach advantage over the five foot two inch Ferry and the shorter boxer simply had to absorb too many shots before he could get close enough to do any damage to Andy. Referee Ed McDonald stopped the fight on a TKO with one minute gone in the fifth round. Ferry had been floored twice, his left eye was badly cut, and he was simply defenseless and out of steam.

Featherweight Andy Bishop would get his shot at the championship of New England.

The championship bout went off before a packed Fall River Casino crowd on February 10, 1949. Although Andy fought gamely, he was clearly outclassed by the champion "Buddy" Hayes who up to that point had over one hundred fights under his belt. The plucky Bishop recovered from six knockdowns only to sustain a seventh and final flooring in the fifth round from which he couldn't recover.

Andy Bishop, who streaked to contention for the New England Featherweight Championship, would fight twelve more times. He would win only once.

Roger Levesque married Olivia Camara in June of 1950. "After he met and married my mother, he lost interest in fighting," said daughter Denise Amaral. "I just don't think he cared anymore."

The Levesque's would raise four children and Roger would enjoy a long career with the Fall River Housing Authority. Roger Levesque, husband and father, died at age seventy-one on September 27, 2001. Andy Bishop, the championship caliber boxer with the deceptive record of 19-18-2, had "died" many years earlier.

Note: After this article was originally published, the writer and Denise Amaral discovered why her father probably chose the alias "Bishop." It seems that the surname Levesque translated from old French means "solemn or reverent person," hence, a "bishop."

May 3, 2015
Fall River, Massachusetts

10.4.1 Roger Levesque (1930 – 2001), fighting under the pseudonym "Andy Bishop," and New England Featherweight Champion Timothy "Buddy" Hayes (1926-1990) pose for a publicity shot before their 1949 title fight.

10.4.2 This circa 1949 newspaper clipping is captioned: " New contracts for the Buddy Hayes – Andy Bishop bout for the New England championship at the Casino, February 10 ...."

10.4.3 Andy Bishop and Buddy Hayes in a circa 1949 newspaper cartoon.

Dr. Irving Fradkin

In 1958, Dr. Irving Fradkin started his optometry practice to help patients with their vision. His own vision—Dollars for Scholars—now helped educate 1.5 million people.

After an unsuccessful run for the Fall River School Board in 1957, Dr. Fradkin decided to challenge the community to support a scholarship fund to help send the city's youth to college. A half-century later, the local Fall River program has grown into Scholarship America, with over 1300 chapters both nationally and internationally.

On February 19, 2008, Mayor Robert Correia hosted a Fiftieth Anniversary celebration for the organization in Government Center's Fall River Room. "When I began teaching school just after Dr. Fradkin started his program," the Mayor said, "the annual teacher's pay was $3,800. Even one dollar went a lot further in those days and Dr. Fradkin's scholarships helped many Fall River families."

After reading a 1958 letter from former First Lady Eleanor Roosevelt who gave him his first donated dollar, Dr. Fradkin said, "I was foolish enough not to even save it; I just put it in the general fund. It's amazing," he added. "Who knew it would ever get this big. If you give people hope, a chance at their dream, it can change them forever."

Remembering that he used to telephone former President Eisenhower collect about the program, Dr. Fradkin said, "It's amazing the chutzpah you get when you do things for others."

Mayor Correia presented Dr. Fradkin with a mayoral citation commemorating the program's anniversary and announced plans to rename the square at President Avenue and Elsbree Streets, Dr. Irving Fradkin Square. City Council Vice President Pat Casey also presented Dr. Fradkin with a citation, calling him "The Pride of Fall River." A third citation was presented by Colonel David Gavigan on behalf of the Bristol County Sheriff's Department.

Several Dollars for Scholars recipients joined in honoring Dr. Fradkin including Mrs. Pauline Sardinha who attended nursing school with the help of a scholarship. When Dr. Fradkin suffered a heart attack in 1988, Mrs. Sardinha was instrumental in nursing him back to health. "If it wasn't for her, I wouldn't be here today," Dr. Fradkin said.

Ms. Sharron Machamer, President of the Fall River Educators' Association, began her journey to several advanced degrees with the help of a $250 scholarship in 1973. "I had my eye on a Smith Corona, model 2200, electric typewriter," she said. "I don't know what I would have done without it."

City Corporation Counsel, Attorney Arthur Frank, said the $250 scholarship he received after graduating from Durfee High School in 1975 made it possible for him to attend Brown University. "It may not seem like much now, but that $250 was something my school teacher parents didn't have to take out of their budget."

Fall River native Robert Struminski, now Principal Support Specialist for Providence, Rhode Island, schools, said his $400 scholarship paid half of his first year's tuition to Boston University. Mr. Struminski promised Dr. Fradkin that he would help extend the program to the Providence school system.

Before cutting a Dollars for Scholars Fiftieth Anniversary cake with his wife Charlotte, Dr. Fradkin, who turns eighty-seven in March, 2008, promised to continue his work. "We have a gold mine in the minds of young people," he said. "This program can make a difference and that's why I do what I do."

Note: Dr. Fradkin passed away peacefully at his home in Fall River on Saturday, November 19, 2016, at the age of ninety-five.

February 20, 2008
Fall River, Massachusetts

10.5.1 Dr. Irving A. Fradkin (1921-2016).

10.5.2 Dr. Irving A. Fradkin's office, 290 South Main Street, Fall River, 1959; the office was located in the Manchester Building.

Judge Morton

We're tearing down Judge Morton's school. But we're building a new one; right on the same spot and we're even going to keep his name on it.

After a couple of generations, historically named monuments, buildings, and streets become like so much wallpaper. They're always there but we just don't see them as memorials any more.

It's hard not to think of these places in the abstract. After all, it would be impossible to put say, Messers. Brayton, Davol, and Robeson's full resumes' on their street signs.

But like them, James Madison Morton was a real person, and there was a reason why the once and future Morton Middle School was named after him.

Born in Fairhaven, Massachusetts, on September 5, 1837, his family moved to Fall River while he was a child and he was to spend the rest of his life in the city. Educated in public schools, he was graduated from the city high school—predecessor to B.M.C. Durfee—in 1856.

Upon graduation from Brown University in 1859, Morton went on to Harvard Law School where he was graduated in 1861. He immediately entered into private practice in Fall River for a brief time in partnership with Attorney John S. Brayton.

In 1876, Morton formed a partnership with Andrew J. Jennings, a recent graduate of Boston University Law School who had been studying under Morton since 1874 – Jennings went on to a distinguished career in the Massachusetts House and Senate, and is best remembered as Lizzie Borden's defense counsel at her sensational trial and acquittal in the murders of her father and stepmother.

The civic-minded Morton was for several years the City Solicitor of Fall River as well as a trustee of both the city's hospital and public library. Morton business affiliations included the presidency of the Union Mill as well as counsel for two of Fall River's iconic institutions: the Old Colony Railroad and the Watuppa Reservoir Company.

In 1890, Morton relinquished his business relationships and was appointed by Governor John Quincy Adams Brackett as Associate Justice of the Massachusetts Supreme Judicial Court where he served for twenty-three years until 1913. During the 1917-1919 state constitutional convention he was chosen as Chairman of the Committee on the Judiciary and was credited with guiding the often acrimonious debates with a skillfully firm hand.

Judge Morton died in Fall River on April 19, 1923. At a subsequent memorial tribute attended by the entire Supreme Judicial Court, Chief Justice Herbert Parker was quoted as follows:

> His physical appearance arrested attention. He was tall and slender and exceptionally erect of figure. His abundant white hair gave him a venerable aspect in all his later years. It would be difficult to find his superior as a trial judge. He had keen intuition in searching out the truth. His most signal characteristics were sound judgment and practical sagacity.

Morton Junior High School was dedicated to the Judge in 1925. As is his protégé Andrew Jennings, and Lizbeth Borden, Jennings' infamous client, James Madison Morton is buried in Oak Grove Cemetery.

September 25, 2011
Fall River, Massachusetts

10.6.1 A portrait engraving of Hon. James Madison Morton (1837-1923).

10.6.2 James Madison Morton Junior High School, 362 President Avenue, Fall River, 1934; the building was dedicated in 1925.

JOHN GOLDEN

The largest monument in St. Patrick's Cemetery fittingly belongs to a man who was a giant in the American labor movement.

Blacklisted because of his union activities in England's cotton mills, John Golden, an Irish Catholic, immigrated to Fall River from his native Lancashire in 1884 at the age of twenty-two. Easily finding work in the city's mills in his trade as a mule spinner, Golden's leadership skills quickly led to him becoming treasurer of the National Mule Spinners Organization of the United States and Canada.

This was a time when Fall River's textile industry was in its ascendancy, when immigrant workers crowded into factory-owned tenements, when the workday was from dawn to dusk, when children as young as eleven or twelve years old labored in the mills, and when the average wage was about six dollars a week.

Only a few years later, at the turn of the twentieth century, Fall River boasted a textile industry employing over 26,000 workers. In 1901, Golden's union joined with four others—the loom fixers, carders, slasher tenders, and weavers—to form the United Textile Workers of America (UTW). Elected to the presidency of the UTW in 1903, Golden would serve nineteen consecutive terms ending only with his death in 1921.

According to Fall River historian Dr. Philip T. Silvia, Jr., in his manuscript, "The (John) Golden Rule." In a weak union industry, Fall River was by far the best example of textile labor solidarity. By 1904, about one in five Spindle City mill workers had organized, making up approximately one half of 10,500 textile worker unionists in a nationwide industry with 300,000 employees.'

John Golden was a sometimes controversial leader even among fellow unionists. During the infamous Lawrence, Massachusetts, "Bread and Roses" textile strike in the winter of 1912, he opposed the "radical" tactics of the 20,000 strong International Workers of the World union (IWW) saying in the aftermath that they had "poisoned the minds of these poor people." Not surprisingly, Golden was labeled by IWW leaders as a "tool of management."

Attempting to protect the interests of the skilled craftsmen in his Lawrence local who were idled when the city's unskilled operatives struck, Golden offered to present alternative craft union demands to management in an effort to force the IWW into a strike-ending compromise. This plan failed when the skilled workers demands turned out to be greater than those of the unskilled.

Nevertheless, when the strike ended in March of 1912—with most of the workers' demands having been met—Golden asserted that he and the UTW initiatives were largely responsible for the favorable settlement. Indeed, the short term effects of the settlement reverberated throughout New England's textile mills including Golden's home community of Fall River. In his excellent book on the Lawrence strike, *"Bread and Roses," Viking Penguin, 2005*, author Bruce Watson tells of the mill owners' reaction: "Some boosted wages without even being asked, others to settle strikes in the making. All that coming week the bricks fell; In North Adams, Massachusetts, in Greenville, New Hampshire, in Providence, Rhode Island, and in Biddeford, Maine. They even knocked over the toughest textile town of all, Fall River, Massachusetts."

Golden's conservative approach to unionism led to a close association with Samuel Gompers, president of the American Federation of Labor and generally regarded as the father of the American labor movement. Both men vigorously opposed the socialist philosophy of the IWW "Wobblies" and, according to Professor Silvia, "Before, during, and after World War I, Golden and his labor officer colleagues murmured not a word of protest when the Catholic Irish-American chief of police interfered and prevented IWW speaking engagements throughout Fall River."

Although attacked by radical elements of Labor as insensitive to the needs of the common worker, Golden was undeterred. In the years following World War I while still living in a tenement house in Fall River's Flint section, he embarked on an intensive organizing campaign aimed at America's southern textile mills. Golden's efforts met with significant success and soon the UTW counted over one quarter of their membership from the South.

As president of the American Federation of Labor affiliated United Textile Workers, Golden wielded considerable political and social influence not only in his adopted home town of Fall River, but on a state-wide level as well. Among other labor initiatives, he used this influence to foster the betterment of working-class children. Golden served on several boards and committees including the powerful Massachusetts Child Labor Commission and was described by the *Boston Globe* as a "bitter opponent of child labor."

Widely regarded as a determined adversary of management when fighting for the wellbeing of his UTW membership, Golden also knew how to compromise when not doing so might mean economic hardship to the workers. "I'll go ten miles out of my way to avert a strike," he was quoted as saying.

Although the IWW gradually faded away never having achieved their dream of "One Big Union," the UTW under Golden's leadership continued to grow and was at its apex at the time of his death in 1921. As Professor Silvia puts it, "In one way, he was fortunate in not being around for the remainder of the 1920s to witness labor's problems as the textile 'sick industry' became depressed, with negative consequences for its factory hands."

Richard Pavao of Fall River, a great-grandson of John Golden, recently came into possession of a pocket watch presented to his great-grandfather at the 1917 British Trade Union Congress at Blackpool, England. Mr. Pavao credits the watch with spurring him to learn more about his illustrious forebear. "It seems strange," he said, "but my family really never talked about him much when I was a child. It's only through my own research and the help of Dr. Silvia that I've come to learn what an influential figure he was in the labor movement."

"It seems to me that he was a dedicated leader with the courage of his convictions. His were stressful times but he stood by his principles knowing that he couldn't please everybody," Mr. Pavao added.

John Golden died on June 8, 1921. His funeral, attended by numerous dignitaries and officials from several national unions, was held in Fall River three days later. "In death, as in life," says Professor Silvia, "the social divisions of his adopted city were glaringly apparent. No self-respecting Catholic at that time would be buried in the public (read Protestant) cemetery, final resting place of the old Yankee families who by common perception within the Irish community had been all powerful oppressors."

Instead of the city-owned Oak Grove burial grounds, Golden would be interred in St. Patrick's Roman Catholic cemetery. His imposing polished granite obelisk towering over twenty feet tall would be the equal of any of the mill barons buried at Oak Grove.

Engraved with the clasped hands seal of the United Textile Workers of America, John Golden's monument bears the following inscription: "What greater sacrifice could a man make than to lay down his life for the sake of labor and humanity."

October 26, 2008
Fall River, Massachusetts

10.7.1 John Golden's grave marker in St. Patrick's Cemetery, Fall River. The monument, which is the largest in the cemetery, bears the inscription: "What greater sacrifice could a man make than to lay down his life for the sake of labor and humanity."

THE DOUGHBOY ARTIST

2014 marks the one-hundredth anniversary of the start of World War I. It was once called the war to end all wars. Sadly, it didn't live up to its billing. But it did forever change the way wars were fought and in the process realigned the political landscape of Europe and the Middle East.

"The Great War" introduced aerial dogfights, airborne bombing, tank warfare, and chemical weapons. It lasted four-and-a-half years, killed nine million combatants, and gave rise to the condition we now know as post-traumatic stress disorder—"shell shock."

In September of 1917, New England's 26th Infantry Division, nicknamed the "Yankee Division," became the second major unit of the American Expeditionary Force to be deployed in the theater. Seventeen year-old Private Frederick L. Mayo of Fall River arrived with them.

"My father spent twenty-six months over there," said Mayo's seventy-eight-year-old son, John, "mostly as a liaison runner, one of the most dangerous jobs you could have." Mayo, who died in 1969, earned several citations for gallantry including the French Fourragère cord, the Verdun Medal, the Silver Star, and the French Croix-de-Guerre (twice).

Private Mayo was like a lot of other American "doughboys" with one important difference, he was an artist.

"He was always sketching something, even when he was a kid," said John Mayo of his father. Frederick Mayo's pictorial diary of his WWI experiences is an amazingly vibrant, museum quality portal into the brutal combat of the Great War.

John has lovingly preserved and professionally copied his father's two volume sketchbook containing scores of colorful battlefield scenes. "He made covers for the books out of a leather saddlebag he took off a horse killed in battle," said Mayo.

Frederick Mayo's officers suggested that he destroy his drawings, warning him that if he were captured the information they portrayed about the enemy could cause him to be executed as a spy. "He told me that after all the work he'd put into them, there was no way he was going to get rid of them," said John Mayo.

Although Private Mayo sketched constantly, even during the constant shelling, he was there to fight, and fight he did.

"One day my father and his messenger partner, a fellow remembered only as Ramsey, ran into a sizeable force of German soldiers probing behind American lines," said Mayo. Having only their rifles and seven hand grenades between them, the pair retreated to a nearby unoccupied bunker and began firing and tossing the grenades at the advancing Germans.

"Near the end of the skirmish, an enemy soldier entered the bunker and bayoneted my father in the arm before being shot by Ramsey," said Mayo, remembering his father's account. "According to my father, he turned to his buddy and said, 'That guy was trying to kill me.' 'My father never forgot Ramsey's simple reply: 'We're at war.'"

Both Ramsey, who was wounded by shrapnel, and Mayo would receive Purple Hearts as a result of the encounter.

Fredrick Mayo would survive the war and participate in the Allied occupation before returning home in 1919. "My father remembered thinking that he'd never live to see Fall River again," said John Mayo. "He told me that he had tears in his eyes as he rode the trolley into the city atop the old Slades Ferry Bridge."

October 26, 2014
Fall River, Massachusetts

10.8.1 A World War I German fighter plane goes down in flames in an illustration by Pvt. Frederick L. Mayo; he captioned the image: "*Elle Laisee Tomber* (She has fallen)"

Mayos in the Military

Four of Frederick L. Mayo's sons carried on their father's tradition of military service.

Frederick Mayo Jr., served as a radioman aboard the U. S. Navy Cruiser Atlanta during World War II. He lost his life when the ship was heavily damaged by Japanese naval gunfire during the November 1942 battle of Guadalcanal.

Army Sgt. Major Frank Mayo served his country in three wars; surviving World War II, Korea, and Vietnam.

Seaman Charles Mayo served aboard U. S. Navy aircraft carriers in the 1950s.

Army National Guard Lt. Colonel Leonard W. Mayo was a graduate of Massachusetts Military Academy and once served as Commanding Officer of

Co. "D," 109th Combat Signal Battalion headquartered at Fall River's Bank St. Armory. Col. Mayo was tragically killed in a vehicle accident while on duty at Fort Drum, NY in 1985.

"Because I was married and had a child," said family historian John Mayo, "I was never drafted but I'm here to tell their stories."

October 26, 2014
Fall River, Massachusetts

10.9.1 Private First Class Frederick L. Mayo (1898-1969), 'The Doughboy Artist" of World War I.

CHAPTER ELEVEN

LIZZIE

Lizzie Borden Bed and Breakfast

Last Monday, on the 122nd anniversary of "The Fall River Tragedy," the Pear Essential Players presented Lizzie Borden Crime Scene Investigation, a spirited dramatization of the events in the immediate aftermath of the murders on that fateful day.

Director/script writer Shelley Dziedzic and her cast have been annually reenacting the horrific events of August 4, 1892, at The Lizzie Borden Bed and Breakfast at 92 Second Street, since 1998. "We started out with four actors and we're now up to seventeen, about half of whom are also employees of the house," said Dziedzic. The actors remain in period character during the eight hour-long tours throughout the day.

The troupe's name comes from Lizzie's alibi for the time of the murders. "Lizzie said she was in the barn eating pears when Andrew and Abby were murdered," said Dziedzic. "We needed a name so we said why not?"

Dziedzic, who is an expert on textile history, sews many of the Victorian era costumes worn by the players. "We also shop for period props all year," she added. Her interest in the Borden murders began in 1991 when she saw Elizabeth Montgomery in the 1970s movie *The Legend of Lizzie Borden*. "That's when I took the plunge and got busy with Lizzie," she laughed.

"We have lots of fun," said Dziedzic. "We've discovered that currant jelly works best to simulate the blood stains from the murders." According to Dziedzic, members of the cast take turns spattering the jelly using a fork. "The blood spatter patterns are historically correct in both the amount and the position," she adds.

Carol Ann Simone brings Lizzie herself to life as she's interviewed by police. "Mrs. Borden is my stepmother, not my mother," she replies acidly to a question put to her by the uniformed Officer Harrington, played by Rick Bertoldo. Lizzie's sister Emma, her friend Alice Russell, and attending physician, Dr. Seabury Bowen all make appearances.

Debbie Stellhorn, who with her husband came all the way from Beachwood, New Jersey, also took the House's regular tour the day before. "I started reading about Lizzie at about age nine," said Stellhorn, "but by actually visiting I've learned that there are more theories about the murders than I thought."

Self-described "psychic consultant" Glenn Teza of Woodland Park, New Jersey, has taken the tour five times. He's stayed overnight in the house and exhibits photos that he claims shows "spirit energy." "I slept in the basement one night and got some

Polaroid instant shots that clearly show the spirit presence." Even skeptics might be impressed by his photos that do exhibit some mysterious looking cloudy forms.

The investigative tour concludes in the cellar of the 1845 home where with the help of nineteenth-century Detective George F. Seaver, played by Michael Shogi, the group examines an axe and part of a hatchet as possible murder weapons. With prodding from Detective Seaver, various theories about the identity of the murderer are bandied about. The consensus? Lizzie did it.

August 4, 2014
Fall River, Massachusetts

11.1.1 The Andrew Jackson Borden residence, 92 Second Street, Fall River, as it appeared in the winter, 1892/1893.

Lizzie's Lost Letters

She was accused of two brutal murders, yet as she languished in jail awaiting trial she revealed a surprisingly warm and melancholy side.

Lizzie Borden spent almost ten months imprisoned in a Taunton lock-up prior to her June 1893 trial. A rare collection of Lizzie's personal correspondence, including four letters written while incarcerated, are currently on exhibit for the first time at the Fall River Historical Society.

The recently acquired collection consists of six letters Lizzie penned to her close friend, Mrs. William Lindsey Jr., who she called "Annie."

Written in a flowing cursive hand, the letters provide insight into Lizzie's jailhouse mindset following her arrest for the murders of her father Andrew J. Borden and stepmother Abby Durfee Borden. "I see no ray of light among the gloom. I try to fill up the waiting time as well as I can, but every day is longer and longer," she told Annie in a letter dated May 11, 1893, less than a month before her trial would begin.

Previously held in a private European collection for many years, the letters were tracked down through painstaking detective work by Fall River Historical Society Curator Michael Martins and Assistant Curator Dennis Binette as they researched their book, *Parallel Lives: A Social History of Lizzie A. Borden and Her Fall River*. The curators established a relationship with the owner, a descendant of Mrs. Lindsey, who gave permission for the five letters she had in hand to be published for the first time in *Parallel Lives*.

"She felt very strongly that Lizzie's letters belong at the Fall River Historical Society," Martins said. When she decided to sell the letters earlier this year, she contacted Martins. "She also had some interesting news: she had recently come across a sixth letter Lizzie sent to her ancestor. That letter has never been published, and none of the letters have ever been exhibited."

"We were presented with a very exciting opportunity to purchase the letters before they were sold on the open market," said Martins. And thanks to the generosity of the Oliver S. and Jennie R. Donaldson Charitable Trust and donations from Fall River Historical Society members, we were able to acquire them."

"Examples of Lizzie Borden's letters are extremely scarce in general, but the ones she sent Annie from jail are especially important," added Martins. "They are the only known correspondence that reveals Lizzie's state of mind as she awaited her fate and the content is both poignant and surprising. She poured her heart out to Annie and she was clearly frightened."

According to Assistant Curator Binette, we learn from her writings that she adopted a jailhouse cat named Daisy (later determined to be male) and grew strawberries on the window sill of her cell.

"Lizzie's lawyers were pessimistic about her chances at trial and gave her little hope," said Assistant Curator Binette. "Despite this she was not cold, unemotional, and somber as she's often portrayed. The letters tell a whole different story."

The Fall River Historical Society maintains the world's largest collection of artifacts and material pertaining to Lizzie Borden's life and trial, including the alleged murder weapon and other forensic evidence, rare photographs, and examples of Lizzie's personal possessions. The Lindsey letters [were] on display at the Society through September, 2015.

Note: The highly anticipated *Parallel Lives: A Social History of Lizzie A. Borden and Her Fall River* was published to much acclaim in 2011, and received a coveted *Kirkus* Starred Review, and was also named among the "Best of 2012" by *Kirkus Reviews.* The 1,138-page volume, published by the Fall River Historical Society, is currently available.

August 16, 2015
Fall River, Massachusetts

11.2.1 The Fall River Historical Society, 451 Rock Street, Fall River. The museum is recognized worldwide as the central repository for material pertaining to the Borden murder case and the life of Lizzie Andrew Borden (1860-1927); it houses the most significant collection of such artifacts extant, including the letters Lizzie penned to her dear friend, "Annie."

11.2.2 A regal Mrs. William Lindsey Jr., née Anne Eliza Sheen (1863-1943), as she appeared in the early-twentieth century, habitually bedecked in couturier gowns and valuable jewels. By the time this photograph was taken, the former Fall Riverite had adopted the name Anne Hawthorne Lindsey, stating: "Annie Eliza Sheen sounded too much like a kitchen maid." As one of Lizzie A. Borden's closest friends and confidants, Anne was the recipient of several poignant letters penned from Lizzie's cell at the Taunton Jail.

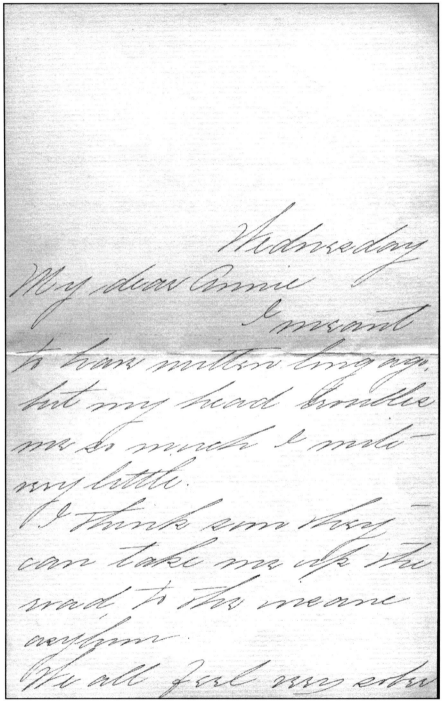

11.2.3 Letter from Lizzie A. Borden to Mrs. William Lindsey Jr., January 18, 1893; "I think soon they can take me up the road, to the insane asylum."

CHAPTER TWELVE

ROCKS

DIGHTON ROCK

It could have been Vikings, Crusaders, or even ancient Phoenicians; nobody knows for sure who put the strange markings on Dighton Rock. "We're pretty certain it wasn't aliens," said Fall River Historical Society Board Member Bob Kitchen with a laugh.

On July 16, at Bristol Community College, Kitchen presented: "Dighton Rock: Catalyst to Discovery?" the first in the Society's summer lecture series.

Since its existence was first recorded by the Reverend John Danforth in 1680, the enigmatic forty-ton boulder, with its curious carvings, has mystified archeologists, historians, and scientists alike. According to Kitchen, Danforth's detailed drawings of the markings, now at the British Museum, verify the authenticity of the petroglyphs on the rock. "Although they had no written language, the native Wampanoag Indians certainly could have put many of the various symbols on the rock," said Kitchen.

Calling it a "glacial erratic," Kitchen said that the rock was probably deposited in the shallows of the Taunton River by a receding glacier over ten thousand years ago. "It's relatively soft sandstone," said Kitchen, "so no special tools were needed to carve it."

A decade after Danforth's discovery, the Reverend Cotton Mather, in his book, *The Wonderful Works of God Commemorated*, mentions a partially submerged rock in a New England river covered with strange engraved characters. The details and dimensions Mather recorded accurately describe Dighton Rock.

In addition to Indians, Norsemen, and Phoenicians, Kitchen's list of possible authors of the rock's ancient graffiti include medieval Knights Templar, Portuguese explorers, and even the Chinese. Although dismissive of the medieval knights and Chinese theories, Kitchen gives serious consideration to the Vikings. "The Vikings had the means to get here," said Kitchen. "We know that they came at least as far south as Newfoundland."

According to Kitchen, one of the most popular and plausible theories conceived by Brown University professor Edmund Delabarre in 1912, is that at least some of the engravings were created by Miguel Corte-Real, a Portuguese explorer. Corte-Real sailed from Lisbon in 1502 in search of his brother Gaspar, also an explorer, who had failed to return from his second voyage to North America.

Examining the engravings, Delabarre asserted that the rock bore the Portuguese V-shaped coat of arms, the name Miguel Corte-Real, and the date 1511. Like his brother Gaspar, Miguel never returned to Portugal.

In 1960, Bristol, Rhode Island, physician Manuel Luciano da Silva discovered the fourth Order of Christ engraved on the rock. Comparing the rock's engravings with verified Portuguese exploration markings in Africa and Asia, da Silva declared them similar, strengthening Delabarre's theory.

"The similarity of these land markers so many thousands of miles away from each other, is indeed striking," said da Silva in a 1960 presentation in Lisbon. "They have engraved on them the same Portuguese coat of arms, the same Cross of the Order of Christ and the same style of numerals. They were made by Portuguese navigators who received the same training and education at the Nautical School of Prince Henry the Navigator, in Sagres, Portugal," he concluded.

Saying "sometimes people see what they want to see on the rock," Kitchen still believes that the most likely explanation of the markings lies with the native Wampanoag Indians. "For all we know it's just their version of 'Kilroy was here,'" he said laughing.

Note: The topic for this article was presented by Bob Kitchen at the Fall River Historical Society's annual lecture series, generously sponsored by the Grimshaw-Gudewicz Charitable Foundation.

July 20, 2013
Fall River, Massachusetts

12.1.1 "The earliest known photographic representation of Dighton Rock," 1853; Capt. Seth Eastman (1808-1875), a prominent photographer and artist, is depicted sitting on the rock.

ROLLING ROCK

Since publication of our recent article on Fall River granite and the city's quarries, we've received several inquiries as to why there was no mention of the Rolling Rock. Here is the story of the city's most famous rock.

After Plymouth Rock, Fall River's Rolling Rock is the second most famous boulder in Massachusetts. In 2008, Governor Deval Patrick declared the monolith, at the corner of Eastern Avenue and County Street, the Official Glacial Rock of the Commonwealth of Massachusetts.

The designation came from a Statehouse act sparked by the efforts of Wixon School teacher Rebecca Cusick and twenty-one of her students who participated in an after-school project studying the history of the rock and the legislative process itself.

A common misconception is that the 140-ton Rolling Rock is made of granite. Although it does rest on an outcropping of solid granite bedrock, the boulder's actual geological classification is that of a "conglomerate"—a rock consisting of hundreds of smaller individual rocks cemented together within a finer-grained matrix.

Over ten thousand years ago, during what geologists call the Diluvian Epoch, millions of boulders were left in the wake of the great glaciers as they gradually retreated northward ending the last Ice Age. Thousands would become "perched" on bedrock surfaces. In geologic terms many of these are called "foreigners" because they are composed of a different sedimentary substance than the native bedrock on which they've come to rest.

In 1840, geologist Edmund Hitchcock, referring to the huge quantities of water and ice required to move these mammoth stones, wrote: "Bowlders are by far the most instructive index of diluvial activity in Massachusetts."

Fall River is not alone in hosting one of these so-called foreigners. Cradle Rock, also known as Rocking Stone, in northwest Worcester County, is actually a pair of stacked boulders sitting precariously near to the precipice of a ledge. Balance Rock, located in the northeast corner of Pittsfield State Forest, is a 165-ton limestone boulder also resting unsteadily upon bedrock.

Until the mid-nineteenth century, Rolling Rock could actually roll, or at least rock a bit. It was so delicately balanced that a man with a moderate shove could cause the great boulder to tip a few inches to one side with an ominous grinding sound before rocking back to its original position.

Legend has it that the native Wampanoags used the rock as a ritualistic instrument of punishment, rolling it onto the limbs of captured enemies and the fingers of those found guilty of thievery. Around the time of the Civil War, the rock's career as an enforcer was forever ended when a foreman from one of the city's several granite quarries expertly shimmed the boulder into its current stability.

For a time, Rolling Rock was as unpopular as it was once unstable. During the early years of the twentieth century, some sought to have the boulder moved as a traffic hazard. There was even talk of jack hammering it to smithereens to make way for trolley tracks.

In 1930, preservationists won out. Rolling Rock was recognized as scientifically and historically significant in a public ceremony dedicating the small triangular green where it stands. Over the decades, the Ice Age refugee had gone from being feared to being revered, thereby avoiding the ignominious fate of being reduced to a 140-ton pile of pebbles.

The bronze plaque on the pedestal of the Rolling Rock reads:

> Deposited on this spot during the glacial period ages ago. Unique in its tilting feature. It is recognized as of great historic and scientific interest. Preserved by the public in the year 1930.

August 13, 2011
Fall River, Massachusetts

12.2.1 Rolling Rock, Fall River, "the second most famous boulder in Massachusetts," as it appeared in March, 1893.

12.2.2 "Rolling Rock Park," Fall River, as it appeared in the early 1930s, shortly after its dedication. The bronze plaque on its pedestal reads:

> Deposited on this spot during the glacial period ages ago. Unique in its tilting feature. It is recognized as of great historic and scientific interest. Preserved by the public in the year 1930.

12.2.3 Rolling Rock, Fall River, 2011.

CHAPTER THIRTEEN

PROGRESS

EDISON ELECTRIFIES FALL RIVER

Electricity came to Fall River in 1883, and Thomas Edison himself helped flip the switch.

Electricity itself wasn't "discovered" in the conventional sense. Instead of one transformational eureka moment there were many, spanning centuries of evolutionary development.

As early as 615 B.C., the Greeks described what we now know as static electricity by charging pieces of amber through rubbing. In the early 1600s, Englishman William Gilbert coined the word "electricity" from the Greek word for amber and described the electrification of many objects in his seminal work, *De magnete, magneticisique corporibus.*

As for founding father Ben Franklin, there are myriad patriotic reasons why his likeness graces the one hundred dollar bill, but he may be best known for somehow escaping electrocution while flying a kite in a mid-eighteenth-century thunderstorm; Franklin invented the lightning rod.

There were many other contributors: Alessandro Volta and his battery, André Ampere, and his magnetic coil, Michael Faraday and his electric motor, and Georg Ohm and his laws of current and resistance.

But the person most closely associated with modern electricity is Thomas Edison, who, although he was granted over one thousand patents in his lifetime, *did not* invent the light bulb. Rudimentary light bulbs had been around since at least the 1840s. But with the help of an 1874 patent design bought from Canadian inventors Henry Woodward and Matthew Evans, Edison perfected and patented the first practical light bulb in 1879.

Lewis H. Latimer, one of Edison's researchers and a son of escaped Virginia slaves, is credited with creating an improved carbon fiber filament in 1882, greatly extending the life of Edison's original bulb. Latimer had a local connection; he married Mary W. Lewis, a twenty-six-year-old Fall River seamstress in 1873. The couple died in the 1920s and are buried in Fall River's Oak Grove Cemetery.

In 1882, Thomas Edison and his engineers were having problems perfecting his initial two-wire electrical distribution system employed at his Pearl Street demonstration plant in lower Manhattan, New York. The facility, serving fewer than one hundred customers and powering incandescent lighting only, was considered hazardous, having caused several employee injuries.

By the summer of 1883, while the Edison team continued to struggle with Pearl Street, what was to become known as the "Brockton Breakthrough" was taking shape. The newly-constructed Brockton, Massachusetts, plant introduced Edison's revolutionary three-wire system incorporating a standardized and adjustable transmission grid. This more stable and efficient system proved that electricity could safely be transmitted to the general public from a centralized source. It soon became the prototype for generating systems throughout the country and the world, solidifying Edison's fame and fortune.

In a move that would presage the mid-twentieth-century machinations of Madison Avenue pitchmen, Edison's promoters decided to downplay the Massachusetts achievement. Shamelessly, they instead publicized the newly-outmoded Pearl Street plant to take advantage of the perceived economic benefits arising from a "first" centralized generating facility in more populous New York. To this day, Brockton's unique role in establishing the country's first three-wire generation and distribution system remains largely unrecognized.

In 1958, visiting Brockton on the seventy-fifth anniversary of the installation, Edison's son Charles said, "In spite of the strong sentiment he felt toward the success of his ground-breaking work in New York City, Father always referred to his streamlined Brockton facility as his first complete model and his first showcase system." Fall River was next.

Although several Fall River textile mills had installed stand-alone dynamos for lighting and for powering selective machinery, unlike Brockton, the Spindle City had yet to centralize electrification. That would soon change.

In 1883, two competing electric companies were formed: the Fall River Electric Light Company and the Edison Electric Illuminating Company with offices in the Borden Block. The latter company was associated with wealthy Fall River businessman Spencer Borden (Fall River Bleachery) who was Thomas Edison's general manager for all of New England.

On September 26, 1883, Edison Illuminating Company Treasurer W.H. Dwelly wrote to Thomas Edison's Engineering Secretary Samuel Insull requesting a construction quote. The letter reads in part—"Dear Sir: I learn from Mr. Borden that Mr. Edison is expected in Brockton the last of this week. That being so, I beg to suggest that he will bring the estimate for our Central Station with him and our Executive Committee will meet and consult with him regarding it."

Nevertheless, according to *The Phillips History of Fall River,* The Fall River Electric Light Company was first out of the gate in March, 1883:

> This company immediately leased land on Blossom Avenue, and constructed a generating station there. It did not then install any motive power for driving the generators, but purchased its power from a saw mill which was adjacent to the generating station. From the first this company supplied the City of Fall River with street lighting, and soon it began to serve stores with electric lights which were connected with the street circuits.

In late 1883, Thomas Edison came to Fall River to personally supervise the installation of the competing Edison Electric Illuminating facility. Visiting the city often over a period of six weeks, the Wizard of Menlo Park would stay and work for several days at a time.

During installation of the forerunner Brockton plant, Edison stayed at that city's Hotel Palmer and his activities were widely reported. Unfortunately, little is known of Edison's social activities and lodging arrangements while in Fall River, but it might be safe to speculate that many off hours were spent at Spencer Borden's mansion on Rock Street.

One curious fact about Edison's Fall River stay is known. According to Fall River Historical Society Curator, Michael Martins, Edison, who invented the phonograph in 1877, recorded the voices of several of the city's prominent businessmen on tinfoil-coated cylinders as somewhat of a novelty. Designed to be replayed only once, a single artifact of Edison's efforts remains in the Society's collection: the unplayable, now folded tinfoil voice recording of David A. Brayton.

In 1892, electric power rolled up its sleeves for more than just lighting. On August 28 of that year, only two weeks after the infamous Borden Murders on Second Street, the following item ran in the *Fall River Daily Herald*:

TRIAL TRIP OF THE FIRST CAR ON THE NEW ELECTRIC RAILROAD.

The first trial of the electric street cars in the city was made yesterday afternoon from the Stafford Road barn to Rodman Street. The officials of the road were on the trial car when the power was turned on about 3 o'clock. From start to finish the trial was a complete success. The car was run uphill faster than it came down and it was started and stopped easily. The bell was clanged at every crossing and it attracted no end of attention.

Fall River's formerly horse-drawn Globe Street Railway Company soon sold all of its stock except one. Snowball, the employees' favorite, was lovingly cared for as a pet and mascot until its death in 1894.

By 1894, the two power companies were conveniently located adjacent to each other on Hartwell Street. In 1896, with demand for electricity quickly growing, the competitors decided to merge under the banner of The Fall River Electric Light Company.

By the turn of the century, the capacity of the combined Hartwell Street plants was nearing capacity. In 1906, a new generating plant with a capacity of 2500 kilowatts was completed on Hathaway Street. In 1917, with the new facility's capacity already increased to over 14,000 kilowatts, several of the city's mills decided to completely electrify their plants. The added source of power needed to accomplish this was achieved by connecting to the high voltage line that the New England Power Company had installed between Providence, Rhode Island, and Fall River.

In 1923, despite having installed further generating capability, the Hathaway Street station's capacity was again at maximum. Rejecting further expansion of

Hathaway Street as impractical, 1924 saw the company join with the Blackstone Valley Gas & Electric Company of Pawtucket, Rhode Island, and the Edison Electric Illuminating Company of Brockton, Massachusetts, in constructing the Montaup Electric Company plant on the Somerset shore of the Taunton River.

The Fall River Electric Lighting Company (FRELCO) was reorganized into the New England Electric System (NEES), in the 1940s. In 2000, the company became part of what is now known as National Grid.

Thomas Edison's breakthrough system, improved but fundamentally unchanged for 130 years, has gone from powering Fall River's streetcars, light bulbs, and looms, to our TVs, cell phones, and laptops.

January 3, 2015,
Fall River, Massachusetts

13.1.1 Thomas Alva Edison (1847-1931); when "electricity came to Fall River in 1883 ... Edison himself helped flip the switch."

EDISON ELECTRIC ILLUMINATING CO.

10 Hartwell Street,

FALL RIVER.

J. C. BORDEN, President.   ALBERT F. DOW, Treas. and Manager.

Incandescent Electric Lighting.
Electric Current Supplied to Motors.
1-8 H. P. to 25 H. P. Motors on Hand.

CLEAN, SAFE AND RELIABLE.

13.1.2 The first advertisement for the Edison Electric Illuminating Company that appeared in the *Fall River Directory*, 1895.

FRANK S. STEVENS, President.   ALBERT F. DOW, Treas. and Manager.

Fall River Electric Light Co.

ARC LIGHTING.   INCANDESCENT ELECTRIC LIGHTING.
ELECTRIC CURRENT SUPPLIED TO MOTORS.
1-8 H. P. to 25 H. P. MOTORS ON HAND. . .

34 HARTWELL STREET,   -   -   FALL RIVER.

13.1.3 The first advertisement for the Fall River Electric Light Company that appeared in the *Fall River Directory* in 1897, following the 1896 merger with Edison Electric Illuminating Company.

13.1.4 Col. Spencer Borden (1848-1921), in a photograph taken at the Centennial Exposition, Philadelphia, Pennsylvania, 1876; the "wealthy Fall River businessman … was Thomas Edison's general manager for all of New England."

13.1.5 Residence of Col. Spencer Borden, 87 Rock Street, Fall River, as it appeared in the 1890s; Thomas Alva Edison was, undoubtedly, a guest of the Borden family when visiting the city.

13.1.6 This circa 1892 photograph is captioned: "The last horse car on the North Main Street line. Picture taken the last morning the car ran to [*the*] Steep Brook" section of Fall River.

13.1.7 Fall River Electric Light Company, 85 North Main Street, Fall River, early 1920s; "reorganized into the New England Electric System ... in the 1940s ... the company is now known as National Grid."

THE HORSE PROBLEM

In the nineteenth century, Fall River's trolley horses worked four hours per day while the men who drove them worked eight to ten.

"The horses had better working conditions than the carmen," laughed trolley historian George H. Petrin in his June 27 presentation, *Fall River's Trolley Years 1880-1936*. As part of the Fall River Historical Society's summer lecture series, Petrin chronicled the city's early transportation system from its horse drawn start during the gaslight era, to its electric powered swan song in the throes of the Great Depression.

In the summer of 1880, a syndicate led by George F. Mellen—later to found his namesake hotel—was granted a charter to lay track on Fall River's streets. "They called it the Globe Street Railway," said Petrin, "which was unusual because the new systems in those days were usually named after their host city."

The first series of lines included North Main Street to Pleasant Street continuing south down East Main to Slade, and Pleasant Streets east to Quarry, serving the Flint section. The company began operations with ten new cars and fifteen horses and the new service was welcomed by city residents. "A woman rider from Bowenville remarked that she hadn't been uptown in seven years," said Petrin.

In addition to signage indicating their route, horse cars were color coded. Even if you couldn't read, you could get still get around. The red cars ran on North Main Street, the yellow on Bedford Street, and the green line took you to the Globe. At the height of the pre-electric era in the late 1880s, the company counted 142 horses in its stables.

As they did for brewery and cotton freight wagons, Fall River's hills posed a problem for the horse drawn trolleys. On the city's steepest grades, the normal two-horse hitch was doubled at the start of the uphill leg. The company employed a waiting "Pony Boy" who, after hitching the two additional horses at the foot of the hill, would ride to the top, unhitch his pair, and walk them back down the hill to await the next car.

In 1887, Frank J. Sprague, an employee of Thomas Edison, developed the first practical system for electric powered trolleys in Richmond, Virginia. His spring-loaded trolley pole using a wheel to travel along the electrified overhead wires revolutionized the industry almost overnight. Within two years the Sprague System solved the so-called "horse problem" in most of the country's large cities – It wasn't the horses themselves, of course, it was what they left behind.

In 1891, the Globe Street Railway, faced with raising capital for the inevitable electrification of its system, sold out to a group of upstate New York investors. According to Petrin, local newspapers accused the former owners of being "quick buck artists" for selling to out of state interests. Perhaps with a finger to the local political wind, the New Yorkers decided to retain the entire Globe Street Railway team in place to manage the new entity.

On August 18, 1892, only two weeks after the infamous Borden Murders on Second Street, an electric car made a successful trial run from the Stafford Road barn to Rodman Street.

This signaled the end of the horse-drawn era and the company soon sold all of its stock except for its mascot, Snowball. The employee's favorite horse was retired and pampered until its death in 1894.

Charging only a five-cent fare—an amount which never changed throughout the life of the system—the electric trolleys became an integral part of the Spindle City during its "King Cotton" heyday. There were so many mills operating in the city that the main trolley lines couldn't help but be a short walk from an operative's workplace. But to be sure to maximize ridership, the company extended its lines to sections such as Shove Street (Shove Mills), Slade Street (King Philip Mills), and Weaver Street (Border City Mills).

But riding the trolleys wasn't all about work. "Amusement parks were big trolley destinations," said Petrin, mentioning Sunday outings at long ago attractions such as Sandy Beach, Ocean Grove, and Island Park. "When Lincoln Park opened in 1894," added Petrin, "the Union Street Railway had to use flat cars with wooden boards as seats to accommodate the crowds."

With the advent of the automobile, trolley ridership began a gradual but steady decline that accelerated with the introduction of buses in the 1920s. According to Petrin, in 1934 the Eastern Massachusetts Street Railway successor company began abandoning trolley lines. On September 19, 1936, motorman Al Menard began the city's last trolley trip at Steep Brook turning the car over at City Hall to James H. Murphy who took the trolley to its last stop, the Stafford Road barn.

Although it was the end of an era for Fall River, the cars themselves were given a reprieve when they were sold to a transit company in Brazil. In an amusing footnote, Petrin's research indicates that the Brazilians had limited resources and simply never changed or removed the signage on the Fall River cars. "For years," laughed Petrin, "people in some city in Brazil were riding around in trolleys headed for Steep Brook, the Globe, or Stafford Road."

Note: The topic for this article was presented by George Petrin at the Fall River Historical Society's annual lecture series, generously sponsored by the Grimshaw-Gudewicz Charitable Foundation.

June 30, 2012
Fall River, Massachusetts

13.2.1 George F. Mellen (c.1853-1901); he led a "syndicate [*that was*] granted a charter to lay [*streetcar*] track on Fall River's streets."

13.2.2 An electric streetcar, Globe Street Railway Company, Fall River, 1890s; the successful run of an electric streetcar, on August 18, 1892, signaled the end of the horse-drawn era for the company.

13.2.3 A view looking east up Bedford Street, Fall River, late 1890s; the crisscross of cables that powered the city's streetcar system is clearly evident.

THE MOTORING PRESIDENT

William Howard Taft, the twenty-seventh President of the United States, never really wanted the job.

"Taft's real love was with the law," said Dr. Philip T. Silvia Jr. "He only ran because he was expected to by his friend and mentor Teddy Roosevelt." In 1908, after holding a succession of appointive offices including United States Solicitor General and Secretary of War, Taft ran in an election for the first time. With the support of the popular President Roosevelt, who declined to run at the time, Republican Taft easily defeated William Jennings Bryan for the presidency by a comfortable 159 electoral votes.

Taft was considered a "trust buster," launching almost one hundred antitrust suits during his term of office. One such action targeted the country's biggest corporation, United States Steel Corporation (U.S. Steel), ultimately abrogating an acquisition that had personally been sanctioned by his friend and predecessor, Teddy Roosevelt. Thus embarrassed by his protégé, Roosevelt remained barely on speaking terms with Taft for years, reconciling only just before his death in 1919.

In 1921, eight years after leaving the presidency, Taft finally achieved the office he'd always coveted when President Warren G. Harding appointed him Chief Justice of the Supreme Court. Thus he became the only man ever to serve in both offices, and the only former president to administer the oath of office to subsequent presidents, when he swore in both Calvin Coolidge in 1925, and Herbert Hoover in 1929. Taft viewed becoming Chief Justice as the pinnacle of his career, once remarking, "I do not remember that I was ever President."

Nicknamed "Big Lub" because of his size while an undergraduate at Yale, Taft who tipped the scales at well over three hundred pounds during his presidency, would be the butt of jokes about his weight throughout his life. Once, while Governor-General of the Philippines, Taft telegrammed Washington, D.C. saying, "Went on a water buffalo ride today; feeling good." Secretary of War Elihu Root wired back, "How's the water buffalo?"

While visiting Fall River during the 1911 Cotton Centennial Celebration, President Taft felt right at home touring the city in an open car. Unlike his predecessor Roosevelt who carefully crafted an image as a horseman, Taft was a lover of the horseless carriage. Known as the Motoring President, Taft once referred to the fresh air taken on a motor ride as "atmospheric champagne." As president, he had the White House stables converted to a four-car garage for automobiles.

Taft wasn't the first sitting president to visit Fall River, nor would he be the last. A few stopped only while making the rail/sea connection on the Fall River Line while traveling between Boston and New York. Making these brief stopovers were James K. Polk in 1847, Millard Fillmore in 1851, Ulysses S. Grant in 1869, and Benjamin Harrison in 1889. President Theodore Roosevelt made more than one trip on the Fall River Line.

In 1936, President Franklin D. Roosevelt came to the city for the funeral of his close friend and confidant Louis McHenry Howe. Following the funeral and interment in Oak Grove Cemetery, FDR spoke to a Depression era crowd of about 20,000 in South Park.

1952 saw President Harry S. Truman visit Fall River as he campaigned for the Democrat presidential nominee Adlai Stevenson. Truman was accompanied by Massachusetts Governor Paul Dever and a young congressman by the name of John F. Kennedy. At South Park, the president was given the key to the city by Mayor John F. Kane before delivering a stump speech to a sizeable crowd.

In 1996, President Bill Clinton made a campaign speech at Kennedy Park endorsing local Democrat candidates running for election.

May 27, 2011
Fall River, Massachusetts

13.3.1 President William Howard Taft (1857-1930) arrives at the State Armory, Bank Street, Fall River, during the Cotton Centennial Celebration, June 23, 1911.

13.3.2 President William Howard Taft touring Fall River, during the Cotton Centennial Celebration, June 23, 1911.

13.3.3 President William Howard Taft shakes hands with a local boy during his visit to Fall River, for the Cotton Centennial Celebration, June 23, 1911; seated to his right is prominent Fall Riverite Leontine Lincoln (1846-1923).

13.3.4 President Franklin Delano Roosevelt attends the funeral of his close friend and Chief Advisor, Louis McHenry Howe (1871-1936), at Oak Grove Cemetery, Fall River, April 22. 1936; Howe was lauded as "The Man behind Roosevelt." The photograph, headed "President and Family in Final Tribute to Col. Howe" is captioned:

> Faces marked by sadness, the Chief Executive and his family pay final tribute to their longtime friend and associate Colonel Louis McHenry Howe. At the left is Mrs. Roosevelt with her youngest son, John, at her right, in Oak Grove Cemetery. The President leaned on the arm of Franklin D., Jr.

13.3.5 President Harry S. Truman (1884-1972) photographed at South Park during his visit to Fall River, October 28, 1948; the photograph was taken during the president's re-election campaign tour of New England.

A Century of Caring

In 1910, over 30,000 operatives toiled in Fall River cotton mills, then the nation's premier textile city. Although diminishing, child labor was still a significant component of this workforce and a troublesome reality to reform-minded citizens concerned about the quality of life for working class families. But not all of the city's children were forced to answer the factory whistle. "This was the so-called Progressive Era of our nation's history," noted Fall River historian Dr. Philip T. Silvia Jr. "In 1910, the factory work week was shortened in Massachusetts to fifty-six hours with momentum building toward fifty-four, and political reformers were taking an overdue interest in the well-being of children of hard working but financially disadvantaged parents who by necessity devalued formal education. Children could easily become a commodity," added Professor Silvia, "receiving scant attention along the way and then being pressed to contribute to family economic survival at the earliest opportunity permitted by law."

According to Silvia, the Spindle City at that time had one of the Commonwealth's highest school dropout rates, with as many as seventy per cent of students among at least one of the city's newest ethnic groups leaving the classroom between the fourth and fifth grades. Fortunately, there were those of a mindset who thought that quality devotion to a mill child's upbringing would help to combat this depressing reality. One hundred years ago this March, local chapter members of the American Association of University Women conceived a project to provide quality, affordable day care for children of Fall River's working parents. The Ninth Street Day Nursery was born.

"The textile industry may be gone but parents still go to work," said Ninth Street Board President, Sandra Dennis. "We continue to provide not merely day care, but a high quality pre-school education as well."

As its name implies, the school was originally located at 37 Ninth Street. "Many parents of the early students simply dropped their children off and walked to the nearby Durfee Mills," added Dennis. Reorganized as a charitable corporation in 1956, the nursery remained on Ninth Street until 1974. That year saw it relocate to its current quarters on Highland Avenue in a spacious former residence donated by the family of Dr. Bill Kenney.

Under a volunteer board of directors representing a diverse cross section of the community, the school is one of the oldest continuously operating facilities of its type in the country. Having added an educational curriculum to its original day care mission, Ninth Street provides comprehensive early childhood care for three-to-six-year-olds in Southeastern Massachusetts and nearby Rhode Island. "We operate under license from the Commonwealth of Massachusetts Division of Early Education and Care," said President Dennis. "All of our teachers are certified."

With a low seven-to-one teacher-to-student ratio, Ninth Street is able to effectively employ innovative training techniques. As an example, students are encouraged to take home "activity pouches," each containing books, puzzles, and educational games on different subjects. "Our approach is intensive and fairly advanced for the age group," said Education Director Susan Rowe. "We not only develop the student's cognitive skills, we train and support them in their personal and social relationships as well."

"When students leave us," said President Dennis, "they are definitely ready for the next step. It's a tribute to Susan and her staff that we regularly receive calls from kindergarten teachers complimenting us on how well prepared our graduates are."

According to Dennis, student tuition is calculated on a sliding scale based on the parent's income, with some scholarships subsidized by education vouchers. As a non-profit entity and a United Way agency, the school also relies on financial and in-kind support from a variety of volunteer sources both public and private.

Recently, National Grid refurbished the school's landscaping and erected a new flagpole on the grounds. The Bristol County Sheriff's Department provided inmate labor for exterior renovation including power washing and painting. "Both National Grid and the Sheriff's Department have been of enormous help," said Dennis. "Add the infrastructure maintenance by House Committee Chairperson, John Freeman, and I don't know what we'd do without them."

The cotton looms of 1910 have long since stopped spinning. But a century later the need for first-rate day care and early childhood education persist. "Our mission is the same," said President Dennis, "quality, affordable childcare, in a safe environment."

January 24, 2010
Fall River, Massachusetts

13.4.1 Current location of the Ninth Street Day Nursery at 533 Highland Avenue, Fall River.

CHAPTER FOURTEEN

THE BRAVEST AND THE FINEST

Fall River Fire Museum Steams Ahead

The horses slept on the first floor, the men slept on the second, but when the alarm bell rang, they all knew where to meet.

Anawan No. 6 engine house, like most nineteenth-century fire companies, had the drill down pat. While the men slid down the brass pole leading from their living quarters, the horses were led—often walking by themselves—to their positions in front of the wagons to be harnessed and hitched. "To save time," said Fall River Fire Department Lieutenant Mike Lepage, "the harnesses were suspended from the ceiling and quickly lowered onto the horses."

Amid all this clamor, one of the men would be torching the coal fueled firebox to begin building pressure in the boiler of the station's steam powered pumper. "It must have been a sight to see the horse drawn steamer racing down the cobblestone streets," added Lepage.

Lieutenant Lepage is the President of the Fall River Fire Museum project, a committee of volunteers who, in conjunction with The Preservation Society of Fall River, are dedicated to preserving the history and heritage of the Fall River Fire Department. "According to local fire buffs, Anawan No. 6 was the oldest continually manned fire station in the country until it was closed in 2002," said Lepage. The committee hopes to transform the station, which is on the National Register of Historic Places, into the museum's permanent home.

A tour of the building reveals quintessential Victorian touches and technology. The second floor sleeping quarters of the privates was once heated by two graceful marble fireplaces, one of which remains. The brass firemen's pole is covered at the floor by a wooden disc attached to a counter-weighted chain for easy raising and lowering. "Once the men had slid down to respond to a fire, the cover would again be lowered over the hole to preserve the heat in their quarters," said Lieutenant Lepage.

According to Fall River Fire Department Fire Inspector and Museum Committee Vice Chairman Ken Leger, Anawan's nineteenth-century firefighters had assigned work details for each day of the week. "We know that Friday was 'brass day,'" said Leger. "Everything made of brass including the pole was polished bright."

The original 1873 firehouse included a stately bell tower approximately sixty feet tall, since shortened and capped to preserve the structural integrity of the rest of the building. A primary purpose of the tower was the drying of fire hoses. "The men would wash the cotton hoses in the basement and string them up vertically in the tower to drain," said Vice Chairman Leger.

Although the tower may also have been intended for use in spotting fires, by the time it was built new technology was already taking hold. "Early in 1870 the city had introduced a Gamewell Fire-Alarm Telegraph System," said Lieutenant Lepage. "This station being built in 1873 was right around the change in technology."

Captain Thomas E. Lynch in his 1896, *History of the Fall River Fire Department,* tells us that in 1874 the city purchased a "second-class rotary steam fire-engine Anawan No. 6" from the Silsby Manufacturing Company. "It was stationed at the engine house on North Main Street and was placed in service June 3, 1874." This was the first apparatus to operate from this location. At the time, the station was manned by one officer, a certain Pardon Macomber, and twelve privates.

Not to be overlooked is the fact that Anawan No. 6 also served as a police substation for the city's north end. The south wing of the building contained administrative offices as well as several jail cells for the temporary housing of the city's criminals, drunkards, and assorted ruffians.

Fall River has a long history of major fires dating from the early-nineteenth century. Three of the more recent conflagrations, Notre Dame Church, Kerr Mill, and St. Stanislaus Church are fresh in our memory. In October, 1987, tragedy struck the Fall River Fire Department when Lieutenant Paul Bernard perished in the Roma Color Co. fire on Quequechan Street. Unable to find his way out of the building, Lieutenant Bernard died when he was overcome by smoke and fumes.

From this tragic event, however, came an ingenious invention designed to prevent a recurrence of Lieutenant Bernard's fate. The brainchild of retired FRFD Lieutenant Cliff Clement, the cylindrical devices bearing raised, luminous arrows pointing the way out are placed over the hoses at regular intervals. Called the "Bernard Easy Exit," it is now in use by fire departments throughout the United States.

The Fall River Fire Museum committee has collected an impressive array of vintage and antique firefighting artifacts and memorabilia intended for display. The centerpiece exhibit will be the Department's retired 1936 Maxim Fire Engine.

"More than just a static display," said Committee President Lepage, "we want the museum to have a fire prevention and fire safety educational component, and to serve as a memorial to those who have given their lives to the fire service."

February 20, 2010
Fall River, Massachusetts

14.1.1 Anawan No. 6 Engine House, North Main Street, Fall River, depicted in an early-twentieth century postcard. Until it closed in 2002, it was the oldest continually manned fire station in the United States.

14.1.2 Steamer Anawan No. 6, a second-class rotary steam fire engine manufactured by the Silsby Manufacturing Company and purchased by the city of Fall River, in 1874. The image depicts the thirteen charter members of the company posing on June 3, 1874, the day the engine was placed into service.

THE SILSBY MANUFACTURING COMPANY

Founded in 1845 in Seneca Falls, New York, the Silsby Manufacturing Company began life as a fabricator of agricultural implements and farming tools. In 1856, the company became a pioneer in the field of steam fire engines with the production of the first Silsby Steamer.

Most early fire steamers used piston engines and reciprocating pumps. Silsby introduced a revolutionary rotary-style pump that ultimately was acclaimed by experts as the most reliable and efficient fire pump available during the steam era. The company was to become the largest manufacturer of steam fire engines in the world with over one thousand units buiLieutenant

In 1874, the Fall River Fire Department purchased a Model 1869 rotary pump steamer from the company and dubbed it Anawan No. 6, after the firehouse of the same name. The unit was Silsby's popular "straight frame" design and its brass factory serial plate was stamped No. 459. Silsby stopped production of this model at No. 490 in 1875.

Drawn by a two-horse team, Anawan No. 6, featured a 700 gallon boiler that developed enough pressure to throw a stream of water up to 250 feet. The engine's coal filled firebox would be touched off while the horses were being hitched and continue building steam *en route* to the fire. Because the unit was equipped with a flash-flue boiler (more dangerous but quicker than a smoke-flue type) the engine would typically be up to useful pumping pressure within five to seven minutes.

Anawan No. 6 remained in service until 1879, when according to Lynch's *History of the Fall River Fire Department*, "… the machine was dispensed with, and the company organized as a hose company." In 1891, the Silsby Manufacturing Co. merged with three other firms to form the American Fire Engine Company.

February 21, 2010
Fall River, Massachusetts

14.2.1 Steam fire apparatus outside the Granite Block, South Main Street, Fall River, 1890s.

FIRE ALARMS

If there's an entire generation that's never used a public telephone booth, there's at least two generations who've never even seen a street corner fire alarm. But in the days before Dick Tracy's two-way wrist radio evolved into the cellphone, the ubiquitous little red boxes were the quickest way to report a fire.

A decade after the 1841 invention of the telegraph, the first practical fire alarm system to use the new communications device was developed by Dr. William Channing and Moses G. Farmer. A rudimentary system was installed in Boston, Massachusetts, in 1852, and in 1854 the inventors applied for a patent for an "Electromagnetic Fire Alarm Telegraph for Cities."

In 1859, John Gamewell of South Carolina purchased exclusive rights to the patents and began marketing the system nationally. The patents were seized by the government after the Civil War but a benefactor, John F. Kennard, bought them back and formed a partnership with Gamewell. In 1867, they began manufacturing the alarm systems and The Gamewell Fire Alarm Telegraph Company was officially formed in 1879.

"A Box a Block" was a catchy slogan of Gamewell advertising, and the firm was selected to install Fall River's system in the 1880s. By 1890, alarm boxes bearing the familiar logo of a fist holding lightning bolts had been installed in over five hundred North American cities, necessitating the opening of a new factory in Newton Upper Falls, Massachusetts. By 1910, Gamewell was estimated to have captured over ninety per cent of the municipal fire alarm market.

In 1925, a year in which Fall River still maintained 349 gas lamp street lights, the Municipal Register lists a total of 320 four-digit coded fire alarm boxes citywide. That year, Superintendent of Fire Alarms, James J. McGuine oversaw the functioning of these sentinels at an annual salary of $2,700.

In a piece of Fall River trivia, it was box No. 1352 that guarded the Pocasset Manufacturing Company on Pocasset Street. In 1928, the sprawling Pocasset Mill complex would become the origin of the February firestorm that leveled much of the city's downtown north and east of City Hall, taking with it thirty-six buildings. Ironically, the box that sounded the first, second, third, and general alarms was destroyed in the fire and was never officially re-set, or "rung out."

"The old system was pretty simple," said retired firefighter and Secretary of the Fall River Fire Museum, Ken Leger. "When an alarm box lever was pulled a mechanism would trip a wheel that would tap out that box's number over the telegraph line to the central signal station. The box location would then be verified from a numbered card file that also indicated which station house should respond," said Leger.

According to Leger, each fire station employed a loud gong that sounded whenever an alarm box number was being relayed from central. The neighborhood station's watchman would then quickly check his own card file to see if the location was one of their assignments. "The gong would wake everybody up at night," chuckled Leger. "If it wasn't their call, they could all go back to sleep."

But it was by no means certain that sleep would ensue. "Each numbered box also contained a small telegraph key," added Leger. "When the chief arrived on scene, if he needed help he would manually tap out the code for a second or third alarm."

On January 12, 1987, Fall River alarm boxes 4387 and 4388 were pulled at the Kerr Thread Mills, repeatedly signaling the start of the conflagration that destroyed the three-building Martine Street complex. "It was my first big fire," said Leger, "I still have the numbered file cards for those boxes as souvenirs."

In the late-nineteenth and early-twentieth centuries, Fall River, like many cities, employed a network of "key holders" as an integral part of the telegraph box alarm system. Because of the anonymity of the process—anyone could pull an alarm and simply disappear—false alarms were a constant problem.

"Prominent citizens who lived or had a place of business near alarms were given keys to the otherwise secure boxes," said Leger. Signs near each locked box gave instructions as to where the key could be obtained in an emergency.

The 1925 *Fall River Municipal Register* "Signals" section included these sensible, if obvious, instructions: "Key holders upon changing their locations, will please give word at the Chief's office." According to Leger, the system cut down on false alarms but unfortunately also delayed response times and the locked boxes were eventually replaced by more easily accessible alarms.

As the telephone became widespread, it became easier and quicker for citizens to call in so-called "still alarms" to local fire departments. As early as 1968, New York City implemented a 911 system for its police department only. Throughout the 1970s and 1980s, enhanced 911 systems evolved and were adopted by emergency service agencies in general including fire departments.

Fall River long ago phased out its street-centered Gamewell telegraph alarm system. But even with today's cellphones seemingly glued to everyone's ear, centralized systems operating by radio transmission or telephone lines guard public and private buildings by communicating directly to fire departments.

Nevertheless, in many cities, some as large as Boston, the venerable telegraph systems live on. Fire officials point to the September 11, 2001, attacks which overloaded cellphone networks. The old systems have often been called "emergency security blankets" even operating in a power outage when hand held phones are unable to be recharged.

October 12, 2014
Fall River, Massachusetts

14.3.1 A pedestal fire alarm box in situ at the southwest corner of North Main and Central Streets, Fall River, 1920s.

14.3.2 A vintage 1953 pedestal fire alarm box awaiting restoration at the Fall River Fire Museum headquarters on North Main Street in 2014.

THE BIG RED HOOKER

The Big Red Hooker is coming home.

A 1937 Seagrave tractor aerial fire truck, better known as a "hook and ladder," will shortly return to its original duty station at the Anawan No. 6, fire house on North Main Street. Destined to become the permanent home of the Fall River Fire Museum Inc., the station, built in 1873, will welcome the vintage apparatus to its familiar north bay where it served from the late 1930s through the early 1970s as Ladder No. 3.

The truck was purchased from the city at auction in the mid-1970s by the late Jack Gleason, then manager of the city's landmark Belmont Club and a retired Fall River fire fighter. Dubbed "The Big Red Hooker" and with that nickname painted on its sides, the truck was manned by the club's so-called Belmont Brigade, often appearing in holiday parades in Boston, Fall River, and surrounding towns.

"It's rare to be able to bring a vintage apparatus back to the station where it actually served," said Fall River Fire Museum President Mike Lepage. "We were lucky to find it."

Lucky, indeed, the truck has had a nomadic existence. It is unclear when, but Gleason eventually donated the truck to South Carver's Edaville Railroad Museum where it was displayed along with antique automobiles for several years. Facing financial difficulties in the 1990s, Edaville auctioned off Ladder No. 3 to the Ocean Spray Cranberry Company.

For a time the truck was stored inside an Ocean Spray warehouse before eventually finding a prominent spot in front of the company's building on Cranberry Highway (Route 6), in Wareham, Massachusetts. In 2000, Charles L. Rowley, a retired Wareham fire captain, began taking photographs and measurements of the truck which by then was suffering from vandalism and the theft of some parts and emblems. In 2002, working from scratch and after two years and some 550 man-hours, Captain Rowley completed an exact 1/25 scale model of Ladder No. 3.

It was around this time that the full size Ladder No. 3 was again on the move. "One day Captain Rowley saw the truck on the back of a wrecker going west on Route 28, and then on to Route 58," said LePage. "He had no idea exactly where it was headed."

In 2008, the Fall River Fire Museum received several leads on the whereabouts of Ladder No. 3, all resulting in dead ends. On one occasion, the fire museum committee members Freddie Almeida Jr. and Scott Boyer embarked on a road trip to seek out the location of the truck with no success.

Finally, in November of 2008, the fire museum committee caught a break. Through his sources, Captain Frank O'Regan of the Fall River Fire Department, learned that Ladder No. 3, was hidden away in a metal storage building of the Kingston Sand and Gravel Company in Kingston, Massachusetts.

Apparently not hidden well enough, as vandals and thieves had continued to take a toll on the truck. Nevertheless the owner was in the process of replacing and restoring the truck when thieves struck again stealing his vehicle's prized "sweetheart" grille. "He was devastated by this and gave up on the restoration project," said LePage.

There the venerable truck sat until early 2011, when it was sold yet again and moved to the Atlantic Recycling Company in West Bridgewater, Massachusetts. But this proved to be the move that would ultimately pave the way for Ladder No. 3's return home.

Fall River recruit firefighter Tom "TJ" Gauette, whose stepfather now owned the truck, notified FRFM committee member, Henry "Spud" Santos Jr. that Atlantic Recycling was interested in seeing that the museum acquire Ladder No. 3. On May 14, 2011, with permission from Fall River Line Pier, Inc. manager, Diane Butler, Mr. Gauette delivered the truck to the Line's Water Street warehouse pier.

For a purchase price of $4,500 – over half of which was donated by Fall River Fire Department Chaplain Monsignor Thomas J. Harrington in memory of his firefighter grandfather John S. Harrington—the prodigal truck had finally returned to its home city. "It wasn't a bad price," said museum President LePage. "I understand that the 12-cylinder Seagrave engine is worth that much alone."

The Seagrave Fire Apparatus Company, founded in 1881 in Detroit, Michigan, by Frederic Seagrave, is the oldest continuous manufacturer of fire apparatus in North America. The company continues as a major supplier to both the New York City and Los Angeles fire departments.

With an open cab and carrying narrow wooden ladders, Fall River's 1937 Seagrave is a classic throwback example of mid-twentieth-century fire apparatus. "Only three men actually had seats on the truck," said Clerk/Secretary Ken Leger of the fire museum, "the driver, his assistant, and the tiller operator. The rest of the crew stood on running boards hanging off the sides on the way to a fire."

Last summer, museum committee members retrieved parts removed from the truck during the halting restoration attempts at Kingston Sand and Gravel, temporarily storing them courtesy of committee member Jay Chatterton, at the Old Colony and Fall River Railroad Museum. The committee has also located various authentic missing parts at sources around the country. The Fall River Fire Museum, Inc. intends to restore Ladder No. 3 to its former glory to serve as a centerpiece attraction at its once and future Anawan No. 6 home.

February 13, 2012
Fall River, Massachusetts

14.4.1 "The Big Red Hooker," Ladder No. 3, a 1937 Seagrave tractor aerial fire truck, in service outside the Anawan No. 6 fire station, North Main Street, Fall River, circa 1960.

ONE OF THE NATION'S OLDEST

Nineteen-century Fall River police officer George W. Allen is the answer to a local trivia question. When on August 4, 1892, he was the first policeman to respond to the infamous Borden murders on Second Street, the Fall River Police Department was already thirty-eight years old.

With its origins tracing back to a seventeenth-century Colonial constabulary, the city's law enforcement arm, along with those of Boston and New York City, is one of the oldest in the nation. On September 20, 1680, a Taunton man, John Hathaway, was appointed "Constable of Falls River and places adjacent."

When formally sanctioned by the city charter adopted in 1854, the department consisted of seven day and eight night men, headed by a chief constable. The officers were paid $8.50 a week with William Sisson, the first chief constable receiving the princely sum of $10.50 weekly.

Seeking to preserve the long history of the department, Police Chief Daniel S. Racine has formed the Fall River Police Historical Committee under the direction of co-chairs, Capt. Wayne Furtado, and Lieutenant Joseph Cabral. "The department has a rich heritage," says Lieutenant Cabral. "Our goal is to honor the men and women who have faithfully served the city for over 150 years."

In its early years the department recorded the occupations of those arrested. According to the Fall River Police Department's official history; "In 1877, among those listed were one phrenologist, two physicians, one school master, one music teacher, one druggist, eleven firemen, two undertakers, and one hundred forty four housekeepers. The remainder were laborers, spinners, and weavers. Out of a total of 2,419 arrests, 1,319 were for drunkenness." Given the inordinate number of housekeepers listed, it would seem that many were often either lightheaded or light-fingered.

For the first three years of its existence, the department made its headquarters in a Central Street townhouse and later in the basement of the City Hall. In 1857, the department moved to the so-called Central Station on Court Square where it would remain until 1916. The former Court Square was near the area of what is now the southwest corner of Purchase and Granite Streets.

In 1916, the department moved to a new headquarters on the corner of Bedford and High Streets, a building still standing and familiar to most Fall Riverites. The old court house housing the Central Station was demolished and Court Square itself disappeared when Purchase Street was widened.

Since March of 1997, the department has been operating out of its new, modern Pleasant Street facility, the site of the former Fall River Stadium and more recently, Britland Park.

"Our plans are to establish a rotating showcase of historical department artifacts, photographs, and memorabilia," says Captain Furtado, "the station's spacious outer lobby is a perfect location." Although the department already has an impressive collection of historical materials, the committee is looking for additional Fall River Police memorabilia to add to the comprehensive array.

"We're asking for former Fall River police officers and their families to donate things such as original uniforms or police equipment for display," says Furtado. "If requested, memorabilia will be considered on loan to the department and attributed to the donor in the display," he adds.

Another key aim of the committee is to raise sufficient funds to recover the majestic eagle-topped architectural medallion perched high atop the old Bedford Street police station. "That's a pretty big badge," says Lieutenant Cabral. "It would look great out in front of headquarters."

January 1, 2011
Fall River, Massachusetts

14.5.1 The Central Police Station, Court Square, Fall River, 1915; the department operated from this location from 1857 until the year this photograph was taken.

14.5.2 Detail of the imposing architectural element that surmounts the façade of the "new" police headquarters on the corner of Bedford and High Streets, Fall River; the department operated from this location from 1916 until early 1997.

FALLEN

A windswept rain failed to dampen the moving ceremonies held [*August 24, 2010*] for three Fall River police officers killed in the line of duty.

With members of the fallen officers' families in attendance at Police Headquarters, department and city officials memorialized officers Thomas J. Giunta, Richard G. Magan, and John W. Ruggiero. "As the son of a police officer, it's very special for me to be here today," said Mayor Will Flanagan, "I am proud to recognize and pay tribute to those who have made the ultimate sacrifice for this city and this department."

Police honor guard commander Sergeant James Machado presented a member of each family with a flag that had flown over the Capitol in Washington D.C. City Councilor Raymond Mitchell, who helped obtain the flags from Senator John Kerry's office, said, "I hope we never have to honor another policeman who has fallen."

At the urging of his grandmother Patricia Magan, seventeen-year-old Timmy Magan accepted his father's flag. Officer Ruggiero's flag was accepted by his wife, Vivianne, a police department dispatcher. Giunta's son Tim, himself a police officer, received his father's flag from Sgt. Machado.

Following the presentations, and moving with military-like precision, the six-man department honor guard paid tribute to the fallen officers by raising the American, state, and city flags into the misty skies at the memorial green fronting police headquarters.

Less than an hour later, the entire gathering reassembled at the Bicentennial Park pier for the christening of a new police patrol boat. The twenty-five foot, 400 horsepower, Parker craft was dedicated as the "Patrolman Thomas J. Giunta" in a champagne pouring ceremony presided over by Giunta's wife, Doris, and his former motorcycle unit partner, Harbormaster Roland Proulx.

Janet Lebel, of Senator Kerry's office, read a proclamation the Senator sponsored in tribute to Officer Giunta, praising the twenty-one years he "served the city with pride and distinction."

According to the Fall River Police Department's official memorial page;

> Officer Thomas J. Giunta was fatally shot in the line of duty on August 24, 1994, while distributing parking passes on Middle Street. Fall

River's annual Holy Ghost Feast attracts thousands of people from across the country. In an effort to ease parking congestion, Officer Giunta was issuing parking passes for neighborhood residents.

Officer Giunta was killed when he attempted to issue a parking pass to a man who became unexpectedly aggressively with him. The man shot and killed Officer Giunta during a struggle. Officer Giunta was forty-nine years old when he died. He was appointed on October 23, 1973. He was survived by his wife and three children. Officer Giunta's son, Timothy Giunta, is a Fall River Police Officer assigned to the Uniform Division.

Officer Richard G. Magan was killed in the line of duty on August 11, 2000. Detective Magan died from injuries sustained from a fall while he was responding to another officer's call for help during the city's annual waterfront festival, "Fall RiverCelebrates America."

Detective Magan responded to the intersection of Davol and Central Streets after another officer called out for help while attempting to subdue two men fighting in a mill yard. Detective Magan fell twenty feet down a steep embankment and later died as a result of related injuries. Detective Magan was thirty-nine years old when he died. He was appointed on May 6, 1982. He is survived by three children. Detective Magan's father, George Magan, is a retired Fall River Police Officer.

Officer John W. Ruggiero was fatally shot in the line of duty on July 23, 1973. He had been following a suspicious motor vehicle from Pleasant Street to Boutwell Street. Two suspects exited the motor vehicle and approached Officer Ruggiero's cruiser. One man fired five to six shots at close range at twenty-seven-year-old Officer Ruggiero, who was killed. Both suspects were arrested and convicted.

Officer Ruggiero was appointed on May 8, 1971. He was survived by his wife and two children. Officer Ruggiero's wife, Vivianne Ruggiero, is a dispatcher with the Fall River Police Department. Officer Ruggiero's son, John, is a Detective in the Fall River Police Department's Major Crimes Division.

For more information, see the Fall River Police website at frpd.org/

August 29, 2010
Fall River, Massachusetts

14.6.1 Memorial dedicated to police officer John W. Ruggiero, Fall River, Massachusetts; Officer Ruggiero lost his life in the line of duty on July 23, 1973.

CHAPTER FIFTEEN

GONE BUT NOT FORGOTTEN

THE TWICE BOMBED BRIDGE

Last year, the Brightman Street Bridge marked its one-hundredth birthday in relative quiet, but its life started out with a bang.

Shortly after midnight on April 26, 1908, a dynamite charge exploded under the Fall River side of the unfinished span sending a shockwave through the north end of the city. The blast was felt as far away as the Steep Brook neighborhood and eyewitnesses counted more than 300 broken windows in homes and businesses along nearby Brightman and Davol Streets.

Although perilously close to the blast, night watchman J.T. Redmond was miraculously uninjured and he immediately sent word to the Northern Police Station. According to a newspaper account of the time, "… men were sent to the bridge, but by this time the perpetrators of the job made good their escape."

Heavy rain pelted the construction site that spring night and fog enshrouded the waterfront. Police speculated that the saboteurs had awaited just such dirty weather to carry out their plan, hoping that the explosion would be mistaken for thunder allowing them time to flee unnoticed.

Although no one was ever convicted of the crime, it was widely believed that labor union radicals were responsible. It was no secret that union agitators were incensed that the general contractor, Holbrook, Cabot, & Rollins of Boston, Massachusetts, was employing less costly non-union construction workers.

Less than two months later, on June 15, another blast rocked a stack of structural steel awaiting installation on the Somerset, Massachusetts, side of the bridge. Because the dynamiting method used was similar to the April explosion, police believed that the same parties were responsible for both events.

Half an hour after the explosion, an unemployed iron worker by the name of George O'Donnell was arrested on a street car by Somerset Police Chief Patrick Donahue and accused of setting the charges. He was carrying a loaded Colt revolver and, following a struggle with police, he was placed in custody and charged with drunkenness and assault on an officer. After having his case continued and posting court ordered surety of $2,100, O'Donnell jumped bail, skipped town, and was never brought to trial.

Despite these setbacks, the 922-foot-long, four-lane, two-leaf, bascule drawbridge opened for traffic on October 10, 1908. Completed at a cost of just over $1,000,000, the Brightman Street Bridge was the widest span crossing the Taunton River, easily surpassing the narrow Slade's Ferry Bridge built in 1875. At the time, it was considered by engineers to be one of the finest examples of its kind in the country.

Time has not been kind to the Brightman Street Bridge. In over a century of service, it has been battered by the elements and has absorbed its share of nautical mishaps. With a mere one-hundred-foot-wide draw channel, wind and tidal currents have contributed to many a vessel colliding with the structure. Modern ships and barges often have only ten feet of clearance on either side as they transit the opening. Factoring in wear and tear from the marine environment, mechanical breakdowns, and normal roadway upkeep, the state must budget $300,000 annually in maintenance and repair costs for the bridge.

Approximately 1,000 feet north of this venerable old bridge, its replacement is taking shape. As the largest Massachusetts Highway project in the state, the new bridge will have cost an estimated $300 million upon its scheduled completion in 2012.

Like its predecessor, the new span will be a bascule-type drawbridge, but that's where the similarities end. With the bascule leaves closed, its sixty foot clearance above the water line doubles that of the original. Anyone who's ever had to wait on the old bridge while a medium sized sailboat glided by will appreciate this feature. Rarely will the new bridge have to open for pleasure craft.

At two hundred feet, its channel width is twice that of the old bridge thus doubling the current margin of safety for pilots and tugboat captains guiding ships and barges up and down river. This, coupled with the cylindrical fenders protecting the east and west bascule piers as well as improved state of the art navigation lights, greatly diminishes the probability of dangerous and costly vessel collisions.

The general contractor, Ciambro/Middlesex, and multiple subcontractors employ upwards of one hundred workers on the project. Despite working at great heights over a tidal river in all kinds of weather, the project has maintained a near perfect safety record.

According to Adam Hurtubise, spokesman for MassHighway's Executive Office of Transportation, when complete, the project will boast four miles of roadway, 3,700 feet of ramps and bridges, 23,800 cubic yards of concrete, 14,600 lineal feet of steel piles, 6.4 million pounds of reinforcing steel, and 14.1 million pounds of structural steel.

"Maintaining access and traffic flow while constructing new roadways and bridges over and around Route 79 in Fall River, and over and around Route 138, in Somerset," required careful logistical planning Hurtubise said. "Working within the seasonal restrictions for fish spawning," was also a challenge he added.

In addition to carrying U.S. Route 6 and State Route 138, the new bridge will be more pedestrian friendly and feature bike paths and a dedicated fishing pier. "There are no plans to demolish the existing bridge," Hurtubise said. "We will evaluate potential uses for the old bridge after completion of the new bridge."

Between now and its scheduled completion in November of 2012, there is one more thing the bridge will need: a name. Veterans groups have suggested honoring various individual war heroes or as an alternative naming it simply "Veterans Memorial Bridge." The area's Portuguese community has proposed naming it "Miguel Corte-Real Bridge" after the sixteenth-century Portuguese explorer who first explored the area.

Whatever its ultimate name, the new bridge promises to be a welcome improvement not only to maritime traffic, but to area motorists, cyclists, pedestrians, and fishing enthusiasts as well.

January 18, 2009
Fall River, Massachusetts

15.1.1 View of the Brightman Street Bridge, Fall River, October, 10, 1908; this image was taken the day the 922-foot-long drawbridge was opened for traffic.

ATTEMPT TO BLOW UP NEW BRIDGE

Charge of Dynamite Placed Under Iron Girders on Second Pier from East Embankment at Brightman Street---Structural Damage Not Great---Suspect Union Bridge Workers.

15.1.2 Article that appeared in the *Fall River Daily Herald*, April 27, 1908, detailing the "Attempt To Blow Up New Bridge."

SECOND ATTEMPT TO BLOW UP BRIDGE

Dynamite Exploded Under Pile of Structural Steel at New Railroad Draw at Somerset ---Suspect Arrested After a Hard Fight by Sergt. Donahue and Carmen---Drew Loaded Revolver on Captors.

15.1.3 Article that appeared in the *Fall River Daily Herald*, June 16, 1908, detailing the "Second Attempt" to destroy the Brightman Street Bridge.

DRUGSTORES

While waiting for your prescription, you can buy almost anything in today's big-box drugstore.

The CVSs, Rite-Aids, and Walgreens of the world have evolved into eclectic bazaars selling everything from cosmetics to clothing to groceries. Sadly, one thing has gone missing in the wake of these mega-stores: the soda fountain.

The popularity of the drugstore soda fountain can be traced to the harnessing of carbon dioxide in convenient tanks at the turn of the twentieth century. With the advent of Prohibition in 1919, the newly available carbonated drinks became an occasional sweet substitute for booze.

Treating a date to an ice cream soda or a lime rickey at a pharmacy quickly became a ritual in the art of courting later memorialized in the lyrics to Glenn Miller's "Jukebox Saturday Night";

> Moppin' up soda pop rickeys
> To our heart's delight,
> Dancing to swingeroo quickies
> Jukebox Saturday night.

Soda fountains, with or without jukeboxes, reached their height of popularity during the bobby-sox '40s, and the doo-wop '50s. Although most often a focal point of a pharmacy, soda fountains were also found in five-and-tens, ice cream parlors, and so-called "spas." Fall River had more than its share of all variations.

In the early 1950s, familiar names such as Liggett's, Central Drug, and Cascade Drug served downtown. Walter Nichipor's Main Street Drug, located in the Granite Block, had a busy fountain accessed by a convenient side entrance from the adjacent Eastern Mass bus terminal.

Seemingly, there was a drugstore on every corner of the city with every neighborhood having at least one or two within easy walking distance. There was Touhey's on Rock Street, Fitzgerald's on Locust Street, and Highland Drug on the corner of Robeson and New Boston Road.

Former Mayor Nick Mitchell's pharmacy was on South Main near Bradford Avenue, with Lambert's and Brow's, both on Stafford Road, serving the Maplewood section. The Globe had the Marcoux Pharmacy at South Main and Dwelly, and Raiche's further south at King Philip Street, and of course Corrigan's right at the four corners itself.

Among others, the north end had Sanft's across North Main Street from Morton Junior High School, and Mulvaney's at the foot of President Ave.

Fall River's Flint section was well represented with Duffy's Pharmacy, Pleasant Drug, and Lafayette Drug, all on Pleasant Street, and Bart's, Oak Grove Drug, and the Ventura Pharmacy on Bedford Street.

All of these pharmacy soda fountains served a mouthwatering array of sundaes, splits, and frappes while featuring specialized Fall River drinks such as vanilla cokes and the iconic coffee cabinet.

"Ventura's had the best coffee cabinets in town," said Attorney Natalie Cabral, whose grandfather Antonio T. Cabral was an apprentice pharmacist at Ventura's before buying the Bedford Street business in 1946. "My father Paul worked there and ran the soda fountain for seventy years," added Cabral, "and my mother Dorothy ran the herbal department as well as made cabinets."

"It was a true family business," recalls Cabral. "If you called in an order or a prescription, it was wrapped and waiting for you when you walked in." Cabral remembers her parents frequently celebrating a customer's birthday or rewarding a neighborhood child's good report card with a free ice cream cone. "Needless to say," laughed Cabral, "they were very popular in that closely knit Portuguese neighborhood."

Cabral fondly recalls Ventura's as a social gathering place for the neighborhood comprising St. Anthony of Padua Parish. "After church let out on Sunday mornings, the counter was five or six deep with people wanting a cabinet," she remembers. "My father would often be asked to load film cameras so the little ones could be photographed in their Sunday best."

The last operating pharmacy soda fountain in Fall River, Ventura's closed in 2006. Happily, the fountain itself lives on at the Battleship *Massachusetts*.

Retired Fall River Fire Lieutenant Mickey Piela was a soda jerk at Carl Dubitsky's Highland Drug in the early 1960s. "We served coffee cabs, and lime and raspberry rickeys, it was crazy after a Durfee [*High School*] football game," he remembers. "Carl watched me like a hawk; I had to be doing something every minute."

Ron Berube worked the soda fountain for Jack Reilly at Brow's on Stafford Road from 1960 to 1962. He remembers the rough formula for the pharmacy's famed coffee syrup as nine pounds of coffee to five pounds of sugar per gallon of water. "Bottomley's Ice Cream was on the opposite corner of Peckham Street," said Berube, "and Frank Bottomley would frequently come in for one of our coffee sodas. He was always asking to buy quantities of our coffee syrup, but I was under strict orders from Jack never to sell him any."

The highlight of the young soda jerk's career came during Jack Kennedy's 1960 bid for the presidency. Jack's brother, Bobby, came to Fall River to meet with Berube's father, Edward, who was the candidate's campaign manager for Fall River, Somerset, and Westport. "They decided to meet at Brow's but Bobby showed up first, so to kill time, I made him a coffee frappe and he loved it," remembers Berube. "He was a down-to-earth, regular guy and we just chatted until my father came."

Berube claims there was a secret to the pharmacy's acclaimed coffee sodas. "In addition to the syrup, milk, and soda," he said, "we added a little cream." He even remembers the price: fifteen cents. "Come to think of it," he laughed, "in all the time I worked there I never received a single tip."

One of the oldest continuously owned and operated independent drugstores in Fall River is deVillers' Pharmacy at the corner of Brayton Avenue and Rodman Street. "My grandfather, Romeo deVillers, opened the store in 1931 after buying out Lambert's on Stafford Road," said third generation owner Denise (deVillers) Lopes, who succeeded her late, locally well-known father, Andre "Andy" deVillers. "We're a true neighborhood pharmacy; many of our customers have been coming here for decades."

Paul Rioux worked the counters at deVillers from 1962 to 1967. "I was there when we took the soda fountain out in 1965," said Rioux. "Replaced it with a cosmetic department. Made the store look nice but I sure missed the fountain."

Rioux waxed nostalgic about early 1960s cigarette prices; "Lucky Strikes were twenty-seven cents a pack, but you could buy a pack of Wings for a quarter." Rioux also has another, more mischievous memory of his time at deVillers. "The condoms were always in their special little drawers. I remember making my sarcastic little comments every time I sold them," he laughed.

Denise (deVillers) Lopes' most vivid soda fountain memory didn't even happen in her own family's pharmacy. "I met Annette Funicello at Bshara's Restaurant when I was four," she remembers. "She was on a bus and got off to get a drink and use the phone. Talk about excited!"

The introduction of full self-service chain drugstores in the 1950s signaled the beginning of the end of the soda fountain pharmacy. The rise of suburbia and the ever increasing car culture made a walk to the corner drugstore for an ice cream soda seem quaint by today's standards. Today, although the memories linger on, only a handful of working soda fountains survive nationwide.

Note: Special thanks to the members of Grew Up In Fall River (GUIFR) for their help in researching this article.

January 19, 2014
Fall River, Massachusetts

15.2.1 The elegant soda fountain at an unidentified establishment in Fall River, early 1930s.

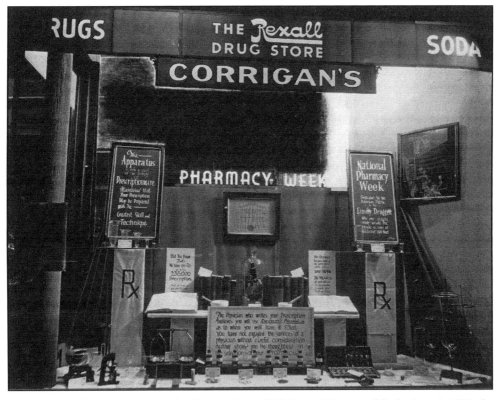

15.2.2 Corrigan's Drug Store, 1412 South Main Street, Fall River, 1934; opened for business in 1898, the pharmacy remained in operation until 1984.

15.2.3 Paul T. Cabral (1928-2013) counts receipts behind his soda fountain at Ventura Pharmacy, Bedford Street, Fall River, circa 1955.

GHOST SIGNS

Fall River's ghost signs are fast disappearing.

Before the internet, television, or even radio, a major staple of advertising was the roadside sign. In rural America, the sides of barns were the sign painter's preferred canvass. But in urban settings such as Fall River, any prominent brick building with blank wall space was a candidate for a colorful product pitch.

Beginning in the last half of the nineteenth century, and lasting through the early 1950s, buildings throughout the country were touting everything from beer to buggy whips. Itinerant painters called "wall dogs" stood on scaffolds or sometimes hung precariously from bosons' chairs to create what was known as "advertising art."

Because of the durable lead-based paint used by the early-twentieth-century wall dogs, many of these signs remain visible, if not entirely readable, decades after their creation. In some cities, vintage signs have even been repainted in an attempt to recapture the quaint nostalgia of a bygone era.

Period post cards of Fall River from the early 1900s, show downtown and Flint business districts festooned with signage of all types including many wall paintings. Sadly, urban renewal, Interstate I-195, and the elements have reduced the city's painted sign population to a handful of faded, ghostly survivors.

Although there may be others that were missed, a quick survey of the city found only two surviving examples of the classic painted building sign. The first, high on an east-facing wall near the corner of Pleasant and Jencks Streets is only partially decipherable. The abbreviated word, "Bros." followed by the word "clothiers" is barely readable. The name of the brothers who owned the clothing store has been lost to the ravages of time.

The second, on a south facing wall of an East Main Street apartment house has fared better, even retaining a hint of color, helped by the later construction of a weather-shielding building only a few feet from the sign. Along with Coca-Cola, and Mail Pouch Tobacco, this wall advertised what was arguably once one of the most famous of American products: Uneeda Biscuit.

A product of the National Biscuit Company (NABISCO), the Uneeda Soda Cracker was developed in 1898 and was the first to "seal in the freshness" with its new inter-folded wax paper box lining. Before then, crackers were sold unbranded from barrels and carried home in paper bags. One of the most successful of advertising campaigns ever, Uneeda Biscuit signs adorned buildings all across America, some freshly repainted over and over.

Presumably, Fall River's ghostly but still legible version of the sign continued to be at least marginally useful to NABISCO up until only a few years ago. In 2007, the Uneeda Biscuit itself became a ghost when it was discontinued by the company.

April 30, 2012
Fall River, Massachusetts

15.3.1 A "Ghost Sign ... on a south facing wall of an East Main Street apartment house," in Fall River, advertising Uneeda Biscuits, 2012.

THE PHONE BOOK

Today there's an entire generation of tweeters and texters who hardly ever use a phone for what it was originally intended—to actually talk to somebody.

Although the telephone has been around since Alexander Graham Bell beat Elisha Gray to the Patent Office by a couple of hours in 1876, it's only been the past twenty years or so that the original's offspring—the ubiquitous mobile phone—has become an essential part of life. Provided you have the latest generation "apps," a phone can be used to access email, shop online, listen to music, play games, and take and store photos. If you have the download, it can also whistle Dixie.

These phones also perform financial wizardry; all you need is money. Not too many years ago, "mobile banking" meant you got in your car and drove to the bank. Today, in our hyper-connected world, we're able to check balances, move funds, and pay bills on Blackberrys, iPhones and Androids.

But some seventy-plus years ago, the telephone was only just coming of age. A recently discovered 1940 local telephone directory provides a time-capsule-like glimpse into what everyday life was like in pre-World War II Fall River.

The Great Depression was drawing to a close and although Nazi jackboots were already marching through Europe, the Japanese attack on Pearl Harbor was still eighteen months away. Emerging from state supervised bankruptcy imposed nine years earlier in 1931, Fall River welcomed the beginnings of a new industry.

According to Fall River historian Dr. Philip T. Silvia Jr., in his book *Victorian Vistas*, in 1940 the garment industry began substituting the needle for the loom, in part replacing the thousands of jobs gone south with the cotton mills. "Although critics might complain about this low-paying 'sweating system' of female oriented labor," he writes, "the needle trade had found a perfect home, for Fall Riverites were used to subsisting on cotton textile wages."

That year's New England Telephone & Telegraph directory, issued in July, was all of 170, six-by-nine-inch inch pages, less than half the size of the current Verizon book. Only a small minority of city families could afford residential telephone service. The vast majority of telephone numbers were a mere four digits, with a smattering of older, three digit numbers thrown in from early adopters. But since the phone was becoming increasingly more important to commerce, the telephone company took pains teaching everybody how to use it.

In a quaint section of the directory entitled "How to use dial telephones," Ma Bell mothers users thusly: "Remove the receiver and listen for dial tone—a steady humming sound. Then place your finger in the space over the first figure of the desired number and turn the dial around until your finger strikes the stop. Lift your finger and without touching the dial allow it to return to its original position."

My guess is that most people caught on fairly quickly. Interestingly, that "steady humming sound," having survived all technological advances, still comforts us on landlines today. Pointedly, the directory admonishes party line users to "Always listen before starting to dial to be sure that the line is not in use." There were no instructions as to when to stop listening if the line was in use.

The same section explains how to use a payphone. Apparently, there were lots of them in 1940.

With 911 service still years away, you were told that in an emergency the operator—now a vanishing species—was your friend. The conference call, common today, was just coming into vogue. The book tells us that "up to six telephones—more by special arrangement) any distance apart can be connected at one time."

The 1940 phone book is unabashedly sprinkled with promotional ads extolling the virtues of—what else—the telephone! "Keep in touch" is a repetitive theme with reminders to "Save up to 50% on long distance calls after 7 P. M. evenings and all day Sundays."

Although the seventy-two-year-old pages of the vintage directory are suitably yellowed, there are no "Yellow Pages" as such. That term had not yet been coined and the seventy- page advertising section is called simply, the Classified Telephone Directory. This is where 1940 Fall River really comes to life.

The R.A. McWhirr Company, Fall River's iconic department store, in a surprisingly small classified ad, urges Tiverton and Little Compton, Rhode Island, customers placing orders to call a special Enterprise four digit number at "no charge." All other callers were advised to dial 112 at "regular charge." McWhirr's not only had its own post office, lending library, and radio studio, it had its own telephone exchange as well.

There are several ads for coal, a still popular heating fuel of the day. The Fall River Gas Works advertised a product called Glo-Coke, "made in Fall River by Fall River people." It was said to contain more heat and less ash.

There were no semi-disposable quartz wristwatches in 1940. They were all mechanical and in need of regular service and repair. The Swiss American Watch Hospital on Central Street advertised cleaning your mainspring for one dollar. While waiting you could grab a bite at the well-known Central Lunch, a couple of doors down the street.

New car ads, including long forgotten marques take up two full pages in the classifieds. You could buy a Nash or a De Soto in the city or even a high-end La Salle at Everett Motors on South Main Street.

There were no laptops, notebooks, or Ipads yet, but you could keep your books with a calculating machine from the Burroughs Adding Machine Company in the Granite Block.

In 1940 television was in its infancy with sets not appearing in Fall River for another decade or so. Radio, on the other hand, was in its golden age with upwards of thirty phone book listings for sales, service, and parts. Radio Jim's Service Engineers on Elm Street advertised service "Days and Nights, 7 days a week." God forbid your set should go on the blink while listening to "Fibber McGee and Molly" on Tuesday night.

With the Depression waning and prosperity seemingly around the corner, 1940 now seems like a nostalgic, tranquil interlude in Fall River history. Along with the rest of the country, the city's tranquility would be shattered on December 7, of the following year.

Note: Many thanks to Michael T. Walsh for his invaluable assistance in researching this article.

November 25, 2012
Fall River, Massachusetts

15.4.1 Advertisements for radio service companies in Fall River, that appeared in the Classified Telephone Directory of the 1940 issue of the *New England Telephone and Telegraph Company*.

TRUESDALE HOSPITAL

A 1940s handbook of The Truesdale Hospital School of Nursing describes its Fall River location as affording, "a variety of social and cultural types of entertainment." It's unclear exactly how students could avail themselves of outside "entertainment" because a few pages later the booklet warns sternly, "Students are not allowed to absent themselves from the school except in extreme cases."

Aspiring nurses were required to live in the Highland Avenue residence adjacent to its namesake hospital for all but nine vacation weeks during their three-year matriculation. "If you were on the honor roll, you could have one overnight pass a month," said Aurore "Ora" Chace, class of 1942. "Otherwise, you were allowed one 'late' per month when you could stay out only until 11:00 p.m."

This year marks the one-hundredth anniversary of the school's 1912 founding by surgical pioneer Dr. Philemon E. Truesdale. The private hospital bearing his name was founded in 1905 on Winter Street and moved to its Highland Avenue location in 1910. Two years later, Dr. Truesdale along with his head nurse, Mary K. Nelson, saw the need for well-trained nurses and decided they would do the training.

Initially concentrating on care of surgical and obstetrical patients, students of the fledgling nursing school spent six months studying at Allied and Bellevue Hospitals in New York City. In 1915, with Nelson as superintendent, Truesdale graduated its first class consisting of four students: Daisy Manchester Gayton, Mary Larter, Ruth Adams Thompson, and Mildred Vanambury.

The life of a Truesdale student was highly regimented; meals were communal and scheduled and students reported to the residence living room each morning before breakfast for inspection. "Everything had to be just so," said Ora Chace. "We had to have our cap on straight, our I.D. pin, our watch with a second hand, and our bandage scissors."

When not in class or working hospital shifts, students were under the watchful eye of the house mother. In the evening, 7 to 9 p.m. was reserved for study, 9 to 10 p.m. was free time, and lights-out at 10 p.m. was enforced by a flashlight bed check.

According to Ruth Hurley, class of 1946, the school actually preferred to enroll girls from out of town. One line of thinking was that out-of-area students were unlikely to be familiar with Fall River families thus better protecting patient privacy. "They were also afraid of 'fire escape dates,'" said Hurley. "They felt that girls from outside of Fall River were less likely to be courted by the local boys."

Truesdale Hospital depended on its next door nursing school even before the students became full-fledged registered nurses. "The hospital was staffed with students," said Ora Chace. "Without us the place couldn't have functioned." According to Chace, during World War II there was often only one graduate RN on every floor.

Chace remembers the long hours put in by the students. "Just because your shift was up didn't mean you could leave," she says. "You had to finish all of your assigned work." She recalls one fellow student who was so exhausted from a shift lasting until the wee hours of the morning that she couldn't make it back to the dorm. "She just curled up and went to sleep in a laundry basket," laughed Chace.

According to Chace there was one rule for dealing with Dr. Philemon Edwards Truesdale, the austere founder of both the hospital and school. "Just stay out of his way," she chuckled. "When the doctors made their rounds, we had to have the answers." From 1927 to 1945, Mrs. Delight S. Jones, a pioneer leader of nursing education in Massachusetts, served as the school's director of nursing. "She presented quite a distinguished figure," said Chace, "in her organdy cap and starched white uniform with every sleeve button fastened all the way up to her elbows."

Life in the nurses' residence, later named Mitchell House in 1961, had its formalities. There was a tea every Tuesday afternoon at 3:00 where students took turns pouring. Once a month there was a formal tea where a member of the school's Women's Board did the honors using a sterling silver service over a lace table cloth.

But the school was far from Dickensian. As a 1949 handbook proudly notes: "A recreation room is equipped for various games—A tennis court and outdoor fireplace offer opportunity for outdoor exercise—School dances, picnics, and class parties contribute to the student's personal growth."

At the outset of World War II, the United States faced a dramatic shortage of nurses. As more and more medical personnel joined the armed forces, it became apparent that something needed to be done to prevent the collapse of nursing care in stateside hospitals, health agencies, and war related industries.

In early 1943, Congresswoman Francis P. Bolton (R-Ohio) introduced a bill establishing a federal program to provide grants to nursing schools to facilitate the training of nurses to serve in the armed forces, government and civilian hospitals. The Bolton Act passed Congress unanimously and in July 1943 one of the most successful yet least known efforts of the war began.

The United States Cadet Nurse Corps became the largest group of uniformed women to serve their country during the Second World War. At its height, the Corps comprised 1,250 nursing schools nationwide graduating the last of its 124,000 wartime-enrolled students in 1948.

In 1945, fully eighty-eight of Truesdale School of Nursing's ninety students were cadets. In return for tuition, expenses, and uniforms, cadet nurses were committed to government service for the duration of the war plus one year. It is estimated that Truesdale graduated over one hundred nurses from the U. S. Cadet Nurse Corps program.

Required to complete their training within thirty months instead of the traditional thirty-six, students spent their final six months "Senior Cadet" service where they were most needed. Truesdale's Hurley was one of only thirty students nationwide selected to serve in New York City and was assigned to the Visiting Nurse Service in Harlem. Although the war ended before Hurley could become commissioned a Lieutenant in the armed forces, she nevertheless applied to become a Navy nurse. "They wouldn't take me in peacetime," she added ruefully, "I was too short."

The Truesdale School of Nursing graduated its last class in 1972. But true to the school's Latin motto—*Non nobis sed allis* [Not for ourselves but for others] – the Truesdale Nurses Alumni Association, through fundraising and donations, provides scholarships to aspiring nurses attending UMass Dartmouth, Bristol Community College and to family of Truesdale's nursing alumni.

Although Truesdale Hospital outlasted its nursing school only to merge with Union Hospital in the late 1970s forming Charlton Memorial Hospital, the Truesdale name continues prominently in Fall River medicine. Along with several other physicians, Dr. Philemon E. Truesdale established the clinic that bears his name in 1914. The President Avenue facility with over seventy practicing physicians is the oldest private clinic in New England.

May 30, 2012
Stowe, Vermont

15.5.1 Dr. Philemon Edwards Truesdale (1874-1945).

15.5.2 Truesdale Hospital, 1820 Highland Avenue, Fall River, early 1930s.

15.5.3 Student nurses at afternoon tea in the parlor of the Nurse's Home, Truesdale Hospital School of Nursing, Highland Avenue, Fall River, circa 1945.

15.5.4 Ruth Elizabeth Hurley, Truesdale Hospital School of Nursing, Class of 1946, in her United States Cadet Nurse Corps uniform, late 1944.

CHAPTER SIXTEEN

THE BIG PARTY

CENTENNIAL

In 1911, as America and the world were hailing recent technological advances, Fall River was marking a century of achievement. The year saw the Titanic launched, the first transcontinental airplane flight wing coast to coast, and New York receive its first overseas Marconi wireless. In the midst of this new engineering wizardry, the Spindle City and its textile industry had already been in business for one hundred years.

1811 saw Revolutionary War hero, Col. Joseph Durfee, establish the Globe Manufactory at the Cook Pond outlet stream near what is now known as Globe Four Corners in the city's south end. What would become Fall River's first cotton mill wasn't in Fall River at all, but in neighboring Rhode Island.

In 1856, the town of Tiverton voted to spin off its northern industrial section creating a separate township called Fall River, Rhode Island. It wasn't until 1861 that the United States Supreme Court enlarged the Massachusetts section of the city by shifting its boundary south from Columbia Street to its present State Avenue location. But, there was compensation. In a straight-up swap, the Commonwealth handed over Pawtucket, Massachusetts to Little Rhody.

Next week, beginning with a Ms. Bicentennial Pageant on June 8, 2011, and culminating in a parade and grand ball on June 11, the city will host a series of events celebrating the 200th anniversary of Col. Durfee's seminal venture. "The 1911 Cotton Centennial was unique," said this year's pageant coordinator James Rogers. "For the first time it brought together all classes of Fall River, rich and poor."

It's impossible to overstate how big the cotton industry in Fall River had become in the century since Col. Durfee's mill began spinning operations. By 1911, with a population approaching 120,000, the city had over one hundred textile firms, operating in over forty mills, employing more than 30,000 wage earners. According to Dr. Philip T. Silvia's *Victorian Vistas Vol. III,* "North Carolina was the only *state* with more cotton textile mill hands than Fall River." In 1911, Pittsburgh, Pennsylvania, was steel, Milwaukee, Wisconsin, was beer, and Fall River was cotton.

No one knew it at the time, but the days of Fall River's textile supremacy were about to run out. Entering World War I, the mills would experience one last surge of business fueled by government orders; it would be the final blip of prosperity on what would become an irreversible downward spiral. But that would come later. In 1911, the city threw itself a party.

Officially called the Cotton Centennial Carnival, the festivities adopted the slogan, "Fall River Looms Up," and ran for six days from Monday, June 19 to Saturday, June 24. Mayor Thomas F. Higgins kicked off the proceedings in ceremonies on the steps of City Hall by crowning Miss Marion Pierce Hills, Queen of the Carnival. By an amazing coincidence, Miss Hills happened to be the daughter of George H. Hills, president of the sponsoring Manufacturers' Association.

In 1911, the State Armory (1897), and the Public Library (1899), were imposing, state of the art buildings, and each was to play a part in the schedule of events. The Armory (later visited by President Taft) housed a display of modern textile manufacturing equipment, and the Library featured an impressive array of paintings by local artists including several by Robert Spear Dunning. Dunning, is acclaimed as the co-founder and leader of a genre of still life painting known to this day as the Fall River School of Art.

The automobile, still in its infancy at the time, took center stage on Tuesday with a Main Street parade of gaily decorated touring cars, roadsters, and limousines. The entries included a 6.6 horsepower Knox roadster driven by F. W. Belcher of Springfield, Massachusetts, that, according to newspaper accounts, "won the prize for highest speed in the Indianapolis races, making 82.6 miles per hour."

On Wednesday, the circus came to town. After the always wondrous show of raising the "big top" witnessed by thousands at the circus grounds, Ringling Brothers' steam calliope accompanied a caravan of elephants, clowns, and bareback riders on the time-honored parade through the city streets. In an observation made before the advent of PETA and other humane organizations, one reporter blithely wrote, "The animals appeared to enjoy the spectacle of so many poor humans, standing packed like sardines, while they rode in comfortable wagons." Apparently, nobody asked the animals.

It was a week full of parades. In addition to the automobiles and the circus, there was the Grand Carnival Parade and the Trades Parade. The latter, consisting of local business floats—including R.A. McWhirr Company department store; North End Wet Wash Laundry; Covel & Osborne Company, mill supplies; and Old Mill Coffee— wound its way from Bedford and Twelfth all the way to the original mill at Globe Corners and back downtown.

North Park, carved out of the hillside less than a decade earlier, was the scene of one of the week's most popular events, Fall River's first ever horse show. Thousands perched on the embankments forming the baseball diamond's natural amphitheater to watch everything from brood mares to polo ponies strut their stuff.

Prominent industrialist Spencer Borden's aristocratic Arabians from his *Interlachen* estate on North Watuppa pond stole the show. But attracting much interest were the muscular draft horses entered in their class by the city's manufacturing concerns and businesses. As one observer wrote, "… it was a source of constant surprise that animals used daily in rough and heavy draft work could make so perfect a representation of their type." Because of the hills, Fall River teamsters needed more horsepower, often employing three draft horses on their wagons rather than the more common two-horse hitch used in other cities.

The highlight of the week was the long anticipated visit by President William Howard Taft on Friday, June 23. As Taft steamed up the bay aboard the presidential yacht *Mayflower,* the revenue cutter *Gresham* rattled Fall River's windows with a booming twenty-one-gun salute. The visit was national news. The *New York Times* ran a first section story with the bold type headline: ***Taft At Fall River For Cotton Jubilee.***

Landing at the Fall River Iron Works dock shortly after 2:30 p.m., the affable President was met by a welcoming committee led by Massachusetts' Governor Eugene Foss and Mayor Higgins. According to a contemporary newspaper account: "Quite a spectacle greeted [*the president*]. The first evidence of Fall River's strength in the cotton world was the sight of the big Iron Works plant, which manufactures enough cloth in a year to circle the globe."—Included in that output, of course, was more than enough cloth to encircle the ample girth of the rotund Taft.

Hustled into an open touring car with a single Secret Service bodyguard conspicuously clinging to the running board, the president was whisked off on a whirlwind tour of the city. The presidential motorcade would make several brief stops along the route. Taft notably lingered at Bishop Daniel F. Feehan's Highland Avenue residence, where he warmly greeted his old friend from their boyhood days in the Massachusetts town of Millbury.

Pausing at the Jesu-Marie Academy, the president received a bouquet of flowers from the children at the next door St. Joseph's orphanage. Later, at St. Anne's Church, Taft stood in his vehicle and saluted the "living flag" formed by more than 500 students from the Christian Brothers' school.

At last the president arrived at the Armory for a tour of the machinery exhibition and then crossed the street to visit Bradford Durfee Textile School. After a tour by college president, Leontine Lincoln, and the school's principal—the delightfully named Fenwick Umpleby—Taft was presented with a specially bound copy of H. M. Fenner's *History of Fall River.*

Finally it was off to South Park where a multitude estimated by the *New York Times* at 50,000—thought to be the largest gathering in the city's history—heard the president's farewell address. In his brief remarks, Taft joked that he hadn't planned to make a speech but, rather, "I came here just to say Howdy-do."

Wishing the city, "Godspeed in making greater steps forward in the next one hundred years," President Taft left the city shortly after 5:00 p.m. for an evening speaking engagement in Providence, Rhode Island. Referring to the mill workers of that time, many of whom would have witnessed the president's momentous appearance, Dr. Silvia has observed, "They must have thought that the lifestyle would last forever."

The President's visit would be a tough act to follow. But on Saturday, the final day of the week-long celebration, in accordance with its motto, the city gave it a try. Glenn Curtiss, the world famous aviator who only a few months earlier had made the first successful hydroplane flight in San Diego, came to Fall River.

Launching his fragile looking fifty horsepower, Type-B aircraft in the water off lower South Park, Curtiss first wowed onlookers with a graceful fifteen minute flight up and down the bay. The daredevil took his plane as far east as Danforth Street, but would not venture further over the city because "The wind was puffy" and he "… found it rather dangerous work over the hills."

Later in the afternoon, under calmer winds, Curtiss again went aloft. This time the spectators got what they came to see, a race between an aeroplane and a fast motorboat.

Landing to begin the brief contest, Curtiss made a wide turn through the water to the starting mark. Despite spotting the twenty-three miles per hour, speedboat *Porpoise* a 200-yard head start, it was no contest. Before the *Porpoise* had traveled another 100 yards Curtiss, with his craft skipping intermittently on the water, had overtaken her reaching speeds estimated at over fifty miles-per-hour.

As the crowd cheered and the cutter *Gresham* whistled a salute, Curtiss beached his plane to the care of his crew. The speed event was hailed as a world record and the first ever race between a fast motorboat and a hydroplane. As for the aviator, he nonchalantly changed his shoes and was off to the Fall River Line pier to catch the night boat to New York.

And so ended what one newspaper called "The greatest carnival New England had ever seen."

Although World War I, and its aftermath, would temporarily bring continued prosperity to Fall River's textile industry, there were ominous signs on the horizon. While the 1920s roared in the rest of the country, the city's mills began facing fierce challenges from southern competitors.

Soon, mill owners began transferring textile machines to Dixie, and along with them went Fall River's jobs. By 1931, the year in which the city was forced to declare bankruptcy, Fall River's textile workforce had shrunk by seventy per cent with only a little over 9,000 jobs remaining.

As Professor Silvia wrote in his introduction to *Victorian Vistas*, "Fall River richly deserved a self-congratulatory Cotton Centennial celebration." But now the party was over. Fall River would more than survive, even regaining a measure of prosperity over the years, but for one magical week in 1911, the Spindle City was on top of the world.

May 27, 2011
Fall River, Massachusetts

1811———MERCHANTS - MANUFACTURERS———1911

Cotton Centennial Carnival

ONE HUNDRETH ANNIVERSARY CELEBRATION

——OF THE——

Building of the First Cotton Mill in Fall River

First Cotton Mill erected 1811 by Colonel Joseph Durfee

WEEK OF JUNE 19 - 24, 1911

OFFICIAL PROGRAM

16.1.1 The Official Program of the Cotton Centennial Carnival, provided a detailed schedule of the events to take place. The six-day celebration had a theme assigned to each day: Manufacturers' Day; Automobile Day; Fall River Day; Merchants' Day; President's Day; and Aviation Day. It was "what one newspaper called 'The greatest carnival New England had ever seen.'"

16.1.2 Advertising postcard for the American Printing Company advertising the Cotton Centennial Carnival. No company was better qualified to celebrate one hundred years of cotton cloth production than the American Printing Company; it was said that they "put out under [*their*] trade mark 6,000,000 yards each of dyed and printed wash fabrics, seven times around the earth each year." They were known as the foremost cotton cloth printing company in the country.

16.1.3 Although "officially called the Cotton Centennial Carnival, the festivities adopted the slogan, 'Fall River Looms Up.'" This promotional postcard urged Fall Riverites to come join in the celebration. Existing photographic evidence shows that they did, in droves.

16.1.4 Thousands gathered in front of City Hall to gain the best vantage point to witness the coronation of the Queen of the Cotton Centennial Carnival; Miss Marion Pierce Hills (1885-1935), daughter of the president of the Manufacturer's Association, George Henry Hills (1851-1917), was selected by the carnival committee to preside over the week's festivities. Following the coronation, the queen and her retinue, seen standing on the platform near the City Hall entrance, proceeded in a cortege throughout the streets of Fall River.

16.1.5 A postcard view of one of the participants in the Automobile Day parade on Tuesday, June 20. Featured that day was a procession of cars all bedecked in flowers, banners and various other decorations. The line-up was comprised of the following categories: touring cars, roadsters, large touring cars, small roadsters, large roadsters, and limousines; a drenching shower occurred during the parade, but did not disrupt the schedule, nor did it mar the beauty of the vehicles.

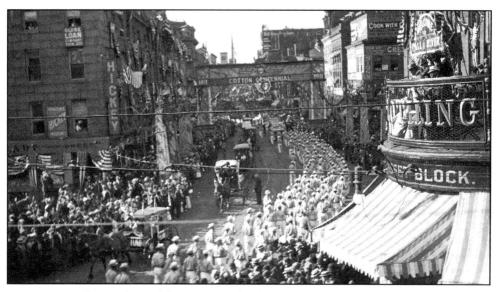

16.1.6 A postcard view of one of the many parades that took place during the six days of the Cotton Centennial. "In addition to the automobiles and the [*Ringling Brothers*] circus, there was the Grand Carnival Parade and the Trades Parade.

16.1.7 View on North Main Street, Fall River, looking south toward the arch built especially for the Cotton Centennial, decorated for the festivities but prior to the arrival of the thousands of spectators. The streets in the vicinity were strung with nearly 9,000 incandescent globes hung by the Fall River Electric Company. Circular frames containing twelve bulbs each, some of which were colored; one can be seen in the sky just above the arch. At night, the square at City Hall was "brighter than a noon-day sun" and was said to have been "stronger than astonishing."

16.1.8 A parade procession moving north down Main Street, Fall River, during the carnival. Note the overflow of spectators standing in the street as a result of the crowds of pedestrians on the sidewalks.

16.1.9 Trade card for George E. Bamford (1855-1933), proprietor of a bookstore and stationer located in Granite Block, Fall River; a Cotton Centennial program appeared on the reverse side. It is interesting to note that Friday, June 23, was not listed as President's Day, but rather as Merchant's Day. Apparently, the card was printed prior to the commitment made by President William Howard Taft (1857-1930) to appear at the carnival. It was described that "on this day there will be band concerts all day and a grand Mardi Gras and genuine confetti carnival."

16.1.10 The presidential yacht *Mayflower* delivered President William Howard Taft to Fall River for the Cotton Centennial Carnival. "The visit was national news."

16.1.11 President William Howard Taft delivered his farewell address at South Park in Fall River at the end of the afternoon he spent in the city. The crowds present were "estimated by the *New York Times* at 50,000—thought to be the largest gathering in the city's history."

16.1.12 The Wilbur hotel was one of several buildings decorated for the Cotton Centennial Carnival. "For one magical week, the Spindle City was on top of the world," blind to the troubles that would befall the textile industry, and the city itself, in the years to come.

BIBLIOGRAPHY

Published Works:

Art Work of Fall River, Massachusetts. Chicago, Illinois: The W. H. Parish Publishing Company, 1897.

Barber, John Warner. *Massachusetts Historical Collections.* Worcester, Massachusetts: Warren Lazell, 1839.

Bradley, James D.D. *A Brief History of the Diocese of Fall River, Mass.* Fall River, Massachusetts: Published by the Diocese, circa 1931.

City Document No. 67: Report of the Superintendent of Parks, 1913. Fall River, Massachusetts: Lawlor Press, Printers, 1914.

Delabarre, Edmund Burke. *Dighton Rock: A Study of the Written Rocks of New England.* New York, New York: Walter Neale, 1928.

Da Silvia, Dr. Manuel Luciano. *Portuguese Pilgrims and Dighton Rock.* Bristol, Rhode Island: 1971.

The Fall River Directory 1893, No. XXIV. Boston, Massachusetts: Sampson, Murdock & Company.

The Fall River Directory 1895, No. XXVI. Boston, Massachusetts: Sampson, Murdock & Company.

The Fall River Directory 1897, No. XXVIII. Boston, Massachusetts: Sampson, Murdock & Company.

The Fall River Directory 1909, No. XXXIX. Boston, Massachusetts: Sampson, Murdock & Company.

The Fall River Directory 1927, No. LVIII. Boston, Massachusetts: Sampson, Murdock & Company.

Polk's Fall River (Bristol County, Mass.) City Directory for 1941. Boston, Massachusetts: R.L. Polk & Co.

Polk's Fall River (Bristol County, Mass.) City Directory for 1942. Boston, Massachusetts: R.L. Polk & Co.

Fall River (Bristol County) City Directory 1972. Boston, Massachusetts: R.L. Polk & Company.

Fall River Illustrated. Chicago, Illinois: H. R. Page & Company, 1891.

Fenner, Henry M. *History of Fall River, Massachusetts.* Fall River, Massachusetts: The Munroe Press, 1911.

Gilbert, William. *De Magnete, Magneticisque Corporibus.* London, England: Peter Short, 1600.

Hitchcock, Edward. *Final Report on the Geology of Massachusetts.* Amherst, Massachusetts: J.S. & C. Adams, 1841.

Hutt, Frank Wolcott, Ed. *A History of Bristol County, Massachusetts.* New York, New York: Lewis Historical Publishing Company, 1924.

Lima, Alfred J. *A River and Its City: The influence of the Quequechan River on the Development of Fall River, Massachusetts.* Fall River, Massachusetts: Green Futures, 2007.

Lynch, Capt. Thomas E. *History of the Fire Department of Fall River, Mass.* Fall River, Massachusetts: Press of Almy & Milne, 1896

Martins, Michael & Dennis A. Binette. *Parallel Lives: A Social History of Lizzie A. Borden and Her Fall River.* Fall River, Massachusetts: Fall River Historical Society Press, 2010.

Binette, Dennis A. and Michael Martins and Joyce B. Rodrigues, Ed. *Women at Work: An Oral History of Working Class Women in Fall River, Massachusetts, 1920 to 1970.* Fall River, Massachusetts: Fall River Historical Society Press, 2017.

Hutchinson, Nelson V. *History of the Seventh Massachusetts Volunteer Infantry in the War of the Rebellion of the Southern States Against Constitutional Authority 1861-1865.* Taunton, Massachusetts: The Regimental Association, 1890.

Mather, Cotton. *The Wonderful Works of God Commemorated.* Boston, Massachusetts: S. Green, 1690.

Peck, F. M. and H. M. Earl. *Fall River And Its Industries.* New York, New York: Atlantic Publishing and Engraving Company, 1877.

Phillips, Arthur S. *The Phillips History of Fall River, Fascicle I.* Fall River, Massachusetts: Dover Press, 1944.

Phillips, Arthur S. *The Phillips History of Fall River, Fascicle II.* Fall River, Massachusetts: Dover Press, 1945.

Phillips, Arthur S. *The Phillips History of Fall River, Fascicle III.* Fall River, Massachusetts: Dover Press, 1946.

Peirce, Palo Alto. *A History of the Town of Freetown, Massachusetts.* Fall River, Massachusetts: J. A. Franklin & Company, 1902.

Peirce, Ebenezer W. I*ndian History, Biography, and Genealogy: Pertaining to the Good Sachem Massasoit of the Wampanoag Tribe, and His Descendants.* North Abington, Massachusetts: Zerviah Gould Mitchell, 1878.

Raven, Rory. *Wicked Conduct.* Charleston, South Carolina: The History Press, 2009.

Silvia Jr., Philip T. PhD., Ed. *Victorian Vistas: Fall River 1865-1885.* Fall River, Massachusetts: R.E. Smith Printing Company, 1987.

Silvia Jr., Philip T. PhD., Ed. *Victorian Vistas: Fall River 1886-1900.* Fall River, Massachusetts: R.E. Smith Printing Company, 1988.

Silvia Jr., Philip T. PhD., Ed. *Victorian Vistas: Fall River 1901-1911.* Fall River, Massachusetts: R.E. Smith Printing Company, 1992.

United States Geological Survey Bulletin 1911. Washington, D.C.: Government Printing Office.

Watson, Bruce. *Bread and Roses: Mills, Migrants, and the Struggle for the American Dream.* New York, New York: Viking-Penguin, 2005.

Williams, Catherine. *Fall River and Authentic Narrative.* Boston, Massachusetts: Lilly, Waite, and Co., Boston, 1833.

Wright, Otis Olney. *History of Swansea, Massachusetts 1667-1917.* Swansea, Massachusetts: Published by the Town, 1917.

Manuscripts (unpublished):

Silvia Jr., Philip T. PhD. *The (John) Golden Rule.*

Newspapers:

Boston Globe
Boston Daily Globe
Fall River Daily Herald
Fall River Herald News
Fall River Weekly News
New York Times
New York World
The Sporting News
The Syracuse New York Herald

Periodicals:

Federal Congressional Record
Harper's Weekly: A Journal of Civilization
Frank Leslie's Illustrated Newspaper

Ephemera and Pamphlets:

"A Brief Sketch of the Occurrences on Board the Brig Crawford." Richmond, Virginia: Samuel Shepard & Company, 1827.

"Catalogue and Circular of the State Normal School at Bridgewater, Mass. for the Spring and Summer Term, 1868." Bridgewater, Massachusetts: State Norman School, 1868.

Durfee, Col. Joseph. "Reminiscences of Colonel Joseph Durfee." Fall River, Massachusetts: Privately published, 1834.

"Fall River and its Points of Interest." New York, New York: Mercantile Illustrating Company, 1896.

"Fall River Municipal Register 1925." Fall River, Massachusetts.

"Fall River: The Spindle City of the Country." R. J. Lawton, 1909.

"History of the Granite Mill Fire." Fall River, Massachusetts: Slade & Franklin, 1874.

"LINES Written on the death of Sarah Maria Cornell," 1833.

Maiocco, Carmen. "The Narrows." Fall River, Massachusetts: Privately printed.

New England Telephone and Telegraph Directory 1940. New England Telephone and Telegraph Company.

"The Correct, Full, and Impartial Report of the Trial of Rev. Ephraim K. Avery." Providence, Rhode Island: Marshall and Brown, 1833.

"The Terrible Haystack Murder." Philadelphia, Pennsylvania: Barclay & Company, 1870.

Silvia Jr., Philip T. "Sarah Anna Lewis." Bridgewater, Massachusetts: Hall of Black Achievement, Bridgewater State University,

ACKNOWLEDGMENTS

Many thanks to my editors at the *New Bedford Standard Times* and the SouthCoast Media Group: Mick Colageo, Phil Devitt, Dave Humphrey, Beth Perdue, and Rick Snizek. They patiently taught me how to write for a newspaper. Thanks also to Fall River Historical Society Curator Michael Martins and Assistant Curator Dennis Binette. They not only encouraged me to compile the book, but professionally managed the process while generously providing access to the Society's extensive archive of historical photographs.

I am extremely grateful to Stefani Koorey PhD, whose design talents helped to bring *Granite, Grit and Grace* to life. I would also like to acknowledge the contribution made by James M. Smith, who readily, with camera in hand, fulfilled many photographic assignments to aid in illustrating this book.

And finally I am indebted to my friend, Dr. Philip T. Silvia Jr., who graciously agreed to edit, proofread, and sequence the book while cheerfully replacing many of my boring commas with his dynamic semi-colons.

W. A. Moniz

INDEX

by Stefani Koorey, PhD

Entries are arranged in word-by-word order, using the *Chicago Manual of Style, 16th Edition.* References to page numbers for illustrations are indicated by numerals in bold type.

All females are listed by their last known surname with cross-references provided from maiden name for ease of location. In places where maiden surnames are unknown, first names are provided.

NOTES

NOTES

NOTES

NOTES

Made in the USA
Middletown, DE
01 February 2018